Contemporary Security Concerns of India

About the Editor

Dr. Herkan Neadan Toppo has been working as an Assistant Professor since 2007 in the Department of International Relations, Jadavpur University, Kolkata. He has done PhD from the Centre for Russian and Central Asian and East European Studies, School of International Studies, Jawaharlal Nehru University, New Delhi. His area of specialization is conventional and non-conventional security issues and interested in the changes concerned with strategic questions not just with the military aspects but with the socio-economic sources and political and moral implications of the use and existence of armed forces, in other words, with the basic problems of peace and has deep interest in the politics and military strategy and an assessment of threat perception, education and politics, human security and area studies as well.

In his initial phase he has worked with Association of Indian Universities as a research fellow-cum-trainee and published report in 2009 on *"Foreign Education Providers in India"*. He has attended many national and international seminars presenting papers on diverse subjects related to international relations, non-conventional security issues and education as well. In addition, he has published several research articles like: *India-Mongolia Relations: Continuance of Endeavour-2011,China - Central Asia in the New Emerging Regional Geopolitics, Russia in Changing Paradigm, Russia's Response: Toward NATO Expansion: A New Challenge.*

E-mail id: hntoppo@rediffmail.com; hntoppo2007@gmail.com

Contemporary Security Concerns of India

Edited by

Herkan Neadan Toppo

CONCEPT PUBLISHING COMPANY PVT. LTD.
NEW DELHI-110059

ISBN-13 : 978-81-8069-938-2

First Published 2013

Published and Printed by

Concept
Since 1974

Concept Publishing Company Pvt. Ltd.
A/15-16, Commercial Block, Mohan Garden
New Delhi-110059 (India)
T: 25351460, 25351794, *F*: 091-11-25357109
E: publishing@conceptpub.com, W: www.conceptpub.com
Editorial Office: H-13, Bali Nagar, New Delhi-110 015, India.

Cataloging in Publication Data--*Courtesy:* D.K. Agencies (P) Ltd. <docinfo@dkagencies.com>

Contemporary security concerns of India / edited by Herkan Neadan Toppo.
p. cm.
Contributed articles.
Includes bibliographical references and index.
ISBN 9788180699382

1. National security—India. 2. India—Foreign relations—Asia. 3. Asia Foreign relations—India. 4. National security—Social aspects—India. 5. India—Politics and government—21st century. I. Toppo, Herkan Neadan.

DDC 355.033054 23

Foreword

Contemporary security concerns of India is a very relevant and appropriate theme in the context of globalization and its far-reaching implications for the political stability, economic growth and cohesive social order of this multi-ethnic, multi-linguistic and multi-religious country. The extant challenges which India faces from its unpredictable and covetous neighbours especially Pakistan and China have generated a sense of urgency to deal with this reality. It is in this larger and meaningful context, this study is a welcome addition to the existing corpus of literature on security issues of India, a country of sub-continental proportions.

Theoretically, the book is divided into three broad sections thematically and twelve well-conceived chapters, foreword, acknowledgements, introduction and index. In section one "Dimensions of Security" chapters one, two, three, four and five successively deal with the general idea and understanding of non-military threats to India's security, *jihad* and its ramifications for India, changing paradigm and the need for demystifying India's security dilemma, the emergence of security dynamics, national security, viz., environmental security with reference to natural disasters, role of geo-informatics. On the other hand, in section two "India's Security and its Neighbours" chapters six, seven, eight and nine deal with different dimensions/factors relevant to India's security such as regional issues. Furthermore, the contributions in section three "Social Dimensions of Security" chapters ten, eleven and twelve constitute an important aspect of this book. The themes discussed relate to religion, immigration/influx of refugees to North-East India and trafficking in women into forced prostitution.

This volume has interesting contributions from a number of academics, scholars, intellectuals and other important personalities of the society. While addressing the relevant issues the contributors have in their own way, enriched the existing literature available on this important issue of security.

Hence, in this sense the articles are diverse in coverage and analysis, though these comments do not undermine the value of the study. The editor has cast his net wide and accordingly contributors deal with a number of security issues and the response of the Indian State to this multi-faceted threat perception.

A close perusal of the articles points out to the need for revisiting/redefining the concept of national security in the context of epoch-making changes in our immediate and distant neighbourhood.

All in all, the study focuses on India's crucial security issues and, therefore, will be of great interest to social scientists, academicians, policy-makers and others in the government and all others interested in a stable, peaceful and growth-oriented India, playing its rightful role in the comity of nations.

Dr. V. T. Patil,
Former Vice-Chancellor of Pondicherry University,
Presently Visiting Professor of Political Science,
Karnatak University, Dharwad,
Karnataka

Preface

Contemporary India is faced with both conventional and non-conventional 'security issues' due to the geographical proximity and changes taking place in its neighbourhood alongside its own programme for the advancement of science and technology and overall human development.

'Security concerns' as a term for India in the changing political and strategic scenario in South Asia draws the attention of intellectuals, academicians, policy makers diplomats civil societies and etc. Moreover, the current trends in the present day international politics is a pointer to the fact that the focus is now more Asian-centric than Euro-centric especially India-centric. Both these phenomena together with the respective domestic challenges of South Asian countries makes it necessary to examine and think over potential problems which one may commonly be termed as 'security issues or concerns'.

The study of 'security concerns' is no longer limited to its conventional form but it depends on as what one views and examines in relation to major change in the referent objects, securitizing actors and functional actors of security. Besides this, the issues pertaining to security have also multiplied eventually. The topics therefore cover nuclear regime, strategic security, security concepts, human dimensions, security dilemmas, migration, gender and environment security etc.

As a result, for ensuring the security of the country political and diplomatic means are supplemented by military capability, and to ensure national security unending sources of both existing and potential to a periodical re-appraisal of security procedures to cope with them is a requisite.

India is considered as an emerging power – rising from the quagmire of Third World politics. This kind of emergence in perception indicates a shift from the status of a troubled entity to a major power poised to play a meaningful role in international affairs. The perception gradually evolves through the experience of behavioural patterns of a state and its economic abilities, political resilience, military strength and a general assessment of how the state secures its interests and steers itself towards better positions. As the shift brings in new responsibilities, it is within the perspective of a changing world. So as to security challenges to India and her responses can be meaningfully positioned and a security strategy is construed. The projection of India as the emerging power and its consequent ramifications also seeks to take a holistic view of security and argues that flexibility as policy choice has been the hallmark of this era of transitional expediency. Indian security strategy in effect consists of successive improvised steps more towards an ambition rather than security per se.

The focus of the chapters is to analyze multifaceted approach to any kind of upcoming security challenges in the region which can inspire academicians to break off customary typical ways of thinking about the security issues and investigate further in their own research to intricate these trends and their consequences. The whole volume has been divided into three important sections depicting 'security issues'.

The first section 'Dimensions of Security' converge discussion on the general ideas of security issues having potential of existing in India and in neighbouring countries which has direct implications in the region. As it is observed by Professor Arun Kumar Banerji, in article "India's Security Concerns in the 21st Century: Non-Military Threats to India's Security" the contemporary meaning of security implies much more than maintenance of territorial integrity of States through acquisition of military power. It means security of territory as well as security of life and property of individuals living within the boundaries of States, their right to live in peace and move around freely. An entirely new dimension has been added to the concept of security in recent years by the UNDP, by linking it to the concept of development. As the UN Secretary General put it, "...humanity cannot enjoy security without development or development without security, and neither without respect for human rights." An attempt will be made here to articulate India's security concerns in the 21st century with particular reference to the non-military dimensions of threats to security. While some of these threats are deeply rooted in India's society and polity, others emerge from outside the boundary – from India's unstable neighbourhood - and it is the close links between these two types of threats that pose the greatest challenge to India's security planners.

While Professor Jyotirmoy Banerjee in his chapter titled "Digging for Jihad: 'Mad Mullahs' Against the British in South Asia: A Glance Behind Today" says if jihadist terror looks formidable today, there is a little-remembered history of several nations across the globe, now the targets, contributing to it. These include Germany, USA and India. Germany and colonial India's freedom fighters separately went about supporting the phenomenon at various times as anti-British measures. USA subsequently meddled in to cause trouble for Moscow's military presence in the Afghanistan in the 1980s.This was Washington's own on-going 'jihad' against communism during the Cold War. While Germany and later USA worked among Afghan and Northwestern Frontier Province tribals, so did Indian revolutionaries in the first half of the 20th century. The names of Raja Mahendra Pratap and subsequently Netaji Subas Chandra Bose spring to mind. In addition, there was Indian support for the Khilafat movement involving even the Mahatma but that took a different hue.

It is indeed refreshing to find that Osama bin Laden had at least one worthy predecessor. Like Osama, who dared to challenge successfully the sole superpower today from the mountain fastnesses of Afghanistan, the Faqir of Iqi took on the almighty and ubiquitous British Empire in its heyday from the same country. Like Osama he managed to remain ever elusive. This paper attempts to dig into the past and bring out half-forgotten episodes which nonetheless remain fascinating. A survey of the past will bring out today's concern about jihad in a different effervescence. The purpose of this paper is to throw light on the security threat from radical Islamic terrorism today by profiling it historically. An in-depth analysis of the issues involved will help understand them better.

In chapter three, Herkan Neadan Toppo in an article 'Demystifying Indian Security Dilemmas in 21st Century" discusses the Indian peninsula, which is incredibly inhabited by different tribes', castes and communities. It is a confluence of language, tradition and culture. The political and security changes that are taking place in the hemisphere gives India predominant strategic position in the South Asian regional hub. The existing conventional and non-conventional security threat dominates the northern Indian Ocean with a coastline that is 7,683 km long and an Exclusive Economic Zone (EEZ) that is over two million square kms in size. India's experience after the nuclear test of 1998 made it obvious that the national security of India was threatened in the field of technology and economy, as in the fields of military capability, political relationship and internal security. The overall security environment of the country has been dealt with under the following heads: global security trends, external security environment, internal security threats.

Therefore, for ensuring the security of the country political and diplomatic means are supplemented by military capability and to ensure national security at three parameters: global, regional and national. The focus of the paper is to analyze multifaceted approach to any kind of upcoming challenges in the region.

In chapter four, Bijaya Kumar Das, "Conceptualization of National Security in changing Paradigm", discusses security as a relative concept of an objective and subjective reality. It is objective in the sense that it denotes a state of affairs in which freedom from threats, fears and wants are assured. It is subjective in the sense that the individual, community or the state can determine the way how and when security can be achieved. National security in an objective sense, measures the absence of threats to acquired values, in a subjective sense, the absence of fear that such value will attach.

The conceptualization of national security merely in terms of external military threats portrays a profoundly wrong image of the concept, as it draws attention away from the non-military threats which would be even more harmful and dangerous to the stability and integrity of nation.

On the contrary, the broader view of National Security policy embraces not only use of armed forces but normal diplomatic, economic and domestic policy. In essence, security of a nation consists of its territorial integrity, stability of the regime and safe guarding the life of its inhabitants from any threat, action or situation and realization of its other national and international interests.

The understanding and nature of security differ from state to state as each one of them is exposed to different types of threats depending upon the conditions of the nation-states. Whether the threats are internal or external, both undermine the security of the state as well as its inhabitants as their security is inter-linked with the security of the states. Security of a state can be pursued either by taking action to reduce vulnerability, or by trying to eliminate or reduce the threat by addressing their causes at source.

The making of National Security policy requires choices about both objective of policy (ends) and the technique, resources, instruments and action which will be taken to implement the means. If National Security strategy is adopted, vulnerabilities can be reduced by increasing self-reliance, and countervailing forces can be built up to deal with specific threats. However, security cannot be achieved by either individuals or states acting solely on their own behalf. Some collective measures are necessary among the members of the system of each to achieve security.

In Chapter five, Parthasarathi Chakrabarti, discusses in his article "Natural Hazards/ Disasters – Environmental Security: Role of Geo-informatics", that the objective of environmental security is to tackle the ever increasing menace of ecological/ natural as well as anthropogenic hazards/ disaster – a global threat to the human being. In this regard, leaving aside the anthropogenic disaster, basic issues reflect on study of bi-directional relationship between human subsystem and physical environment in the context of rising population, rapid urbanization and industrialization, unplanned use of land and water resources with vulnerability and risk due to natural hazards/ disaster. In this respect, the core business is to establish dynamic viewing capabilities for identification of acceptable changes between the Environment (E) and Human Capital and Mobility (HCM) in terms of:

- Conservation and rational utilization of natural resources.
- Agro-ecological characterization and industrial development for ecological stability.
- Setting up of 'Early Warning System' to minimize the adverse effects of natural calamities.

- Prioritization of 'Bio-prospecting zones' for biodiversity conservation.
- Information dissemination for building public awareness to ensure public participation.

Some of the Case History Examples are: 1. Tsunami on 26th, December, 2004; II. Integrated Coastal Zone Management, West Bengal; III. Bank Failure & Flooding in Ganga – Padma River; IV. Arsenic Contamination in Groundwater, West Bengal: Drought Hazard in the Western Upland, West Bengal.

In the present day scenario, the baseline geo-spatial information generated using RS and GIS technologies supported with past history of anthropic-development (- the 'strategic datasets') emerged as a synergistic tool, reflects on human oriented future directives interlinking food and shelter, education and vision/ policy decision – i.e. poverty alleviation and building natural resources assets for environmental security.

In (chapter six) section two 'India's Security and its Neighbours', Binod Kumar Mishra states in his article "India's Nuclear Policy: Regional Ramifications" that India's nuclear programme was guided by an ambivalent policy that neither admitted exercising the nuclear weapons option nor denied its possibility. At the same time India showed its commitment to Global Nuclear Disarmament. The nuclear policy was given a direction after the second nuclear experiment in 1998 and thereby brought India above the nuclear threshold. The rationale for the ambivalence India maintained over her nuclear programme was the regional security environment and the hegemonic attempts of N5 to perpetuate their monopoly over nuclear weapons and nuclear technology. There have been ideological cries of foul over India crossing the nuclear threshold. Apprehensions are expressed that India's nuclear programme has lent the deathblow to global disarmament efforts and thrown the region into instability. Building upon the contributing factors, the paper seeks to look into the regional fallouts of India's nuclear weapons programme. The main argument of the paper is that India's nuclear doctrine is the result of the regional (in) security complex and has added to that complex while giving India a sense of elevation in her global and regional standing.

Whereas in chapter seven, Bhagaban Behera in an article 'China as a Major Security Threat for India in Post-Cold War Era' discusses how the progressive strengthening of India's post-Cold War policy of de'tente towards China led the two nations to commit in 1996 to a constructive cooperation. After the Atal Bihari Vajpayee government took office in 1998, the two nations reached consensus on comprehensive bilateral cooperation in 2003 during Prime Minister Vajpayee's visit to China. Manmohan Singh's government later established a strategic partnership with China geared towards peace and prosperity, but at the same time promoted nuclear agreement and joint military exercises with the United States and strengthened strategic cooperation with both the United States and Japan. Authoritative sources on Indian strategy interpret this as an explicit move to balance China. This article takes India's security concept as a starting point, exploring the influence of India's security concept on its China policy, and interprets the substance of changes in India's post-Cold War China policy and the direction in which it is likely to evolve.

In the eighth chapter, Herkan Neadan Toppo's article "Is Indo-Naga Peace Process Moving towards National Integration?" discusses the conflict in Nagaland between the Government of India and the National Socialist Council of Nagalim (NSCN-IM) that has been one of the oldest in South Asia. Fourteen years into the Ceasefire Agreement and about more than 70 rounds of peace talks has led to nothing but controversies instead of creating an atmosphere of negotiations. As in all ethno-nationalist conflict, the politics of recognition is an underlying theme in the Naga conflict too. The latest development in the Naga peace process has to be understood keeping the role of civil society in mind.

In chapter nine, Homen Thangjam & Konthoujam Indrakumar Singh jointly discuss in an article "Emerging Security Dynamics: India's Security & Southeast Asia" about the relationship and the threat concerns of India and Southeast Asian countries. Emphatically, it invites some kind of threat perception. Also, it discusses how ASEAN countries and India together can overcome security challenges. Some of the common issues and its implications in the south Asia region especially on India have been highlighted.

In the third and the last section of this volume 'Social Dimensions of Security' in chapter ten, Chandreyi Alam, in a paper "Contemporary Security Concerns of India – Religion and

Security", discusses religious practices which find their roots in the Primitive Religions where the consecration of life is involved in (1) Education (2) Government, (3) Food supply, (4) Kinship, (5) Family (6) Sex, (7) Personality. Presently we shall confine ourselves to the question of family and sex since this is a cause of gross violation of social security. Encyclopedia Britannica states that "Women for certain physiological reasons is always for primitive peoples hedged round with sanctity, whilst man does all he can do to inspire awe to his powers in women in keeping religion largely at his own hands (Emphasis added). The result so far as the woman is concerned is that in company with those males who are endowed with sacredness in a more than ordinary degree, she tends to lose in freedom as much as she gains in respect. (Emphasis added). This is also India's experience. She is Mata, Devi, Shakti – worshipped idolized yet a victim of incessant violence, humiliation and discrimination in innumerable forms.

What is most significant is that all religions are democratic, the woman treated with dignity and respect as well as humiliated. Faced with such contradictions, we find that the balance of Indian society tilts Bills heavily in favour of values that are discriminatory to women and society seeks refuge in religious texts to justify its actions. But religious texts must be considered in the context of the prevalent social conditions with the passage of time. Existence of a constitution that enshrines justice, social-economic and political in its preamble and equality before law as a Fundamental Right implies that our society does face situations that disturb its equilibrium and the reactions therefore give rise to security concerns.

Meanwhile, in chapter eleven, Lianboi Vaiphei discusses in article "Migrations in Northeast India and its implications for the Strategic Security of Northeast India" which covers a total area of 255.08 million hectares, which is about 8 per cent of country's land mass and is the sentinel of the Indian continent. It is strategically surrounded by five foreign countries i.e., Bangladesh, Myanmar, Bhutan, China and Nepal and with the rest of the country through a narrow stretch of plains which is known as Siliguri Corridor. This narrow stretch of land is sometimes referred as chicken-necked region since it connects with the rest of the country. In fact, the geographical location of the region gives the region an insularity which is because she is isolated by her natural border which has become a part of the international boundary that India possesses as out of the seven international boundaries, five of them is in the northeast region, namely Bangladesh, Bhutan, Myanmar, China and Nepal, except Pakistan and Sri Lanka.

Migration occurs from the two neighbouring countries of Myanmar and Bangladesh, which has a deep strategical impact and consequences for the security of India. These migrations are Illegal migrations and occur since India is not a signatory to the 1951 Convention to the Status of Refugees and therefore they cannot be called Refugees. The geo strategic location of the North East of India, which shares more than 80% borders with international boundary with countries such as Bangladesh in the south and West with Assam, Meghalaya, Tripura and Mizoram; and Myanmar in the east with the states of Manipur, Mizoram and Nagaland boundary while the States of Assam and Mizoram in the East share 16 percent of the border and Myanmar in the east, sharing 2 international boundary with Manipur and Mizoram has become extremely vulnerable to migrations which occurs across the borders due to conflicts in India's neighbouring.

Both the neighbouring countries of Myanmar and Bangladesh face religious persecutions, against Hindus for Bangladesh and against Christians in Myanmar due to which there is an exodus of population from the two countries into India's northeast. Besides, the two countries are also struggling with democracy and their practices, which make it a breeding ground for militancy that spreads across the geo-political borders. The militancy finds an easy nexus with insurgencies of the northeast which makes it economical for drug smuggling as the region is very close to the Golden Triangle, one of Asia's two main illicit opium-producing areas. It is an area of around 367,000 square miles (950,000 km^2) that overlaps the mountains of four countries of Southeast Asia: Burma, Vietnam, Laos, and Thailand.

The chapter seeks to analyse the implications of the migrations that occurs, especially with regard to Myanmar and Bangladesh and its implications as well as link for the rise of insurgencies movement and the consequences for the security of the Northeast region in particular and the country as a whole.

In chapter twelve, Amrita Banerjee in her paper titled "Trafficking of Women into Forced Prostitution" discusses the trafficking of human beings which has become the third largest source of profit for organized crime after drugs and arms, generating billions of dollars each year. As a result the trafficking of women plays one of the important parts in the trafficking of human beings a business which leaves no country untouched. Driven by poverty, unemployment, and media images of Western lifestyles, women accept risky offers of employment and marriage in hope of finding a better life. Non-governmental organizations (NGOs) report that in many cases, once a woman decides that the solution to her problems is to go abroad, she will try every agency or strategy, regardless of the risk. Although some women may find the jobs, romance, and opportunities they seek, many become victims of violence, sexual exploitation, and sex trafficking. Trafficking violates all known canons of human rights and dignity. In this world of tragic and complex human abuse, women form a particularly vulnerable class. With no freedom of choice and options for a life with dignity, these hapless women are merrily trafficked and exploited forcing them to lead a life crippled with indignity, social stigma, debt bondage and a host of ailments including HIV/AIDS. Trafficking in its widest sense includes not just exploitation of prostitution of others or forms of sexual exploitation, it also includes forced labour or services, slavery or practices similar to slavery or trade in human beings for removal of organs. Trafficking clearly violates the fundamental right to a life with dignity. Unfortunately, there is little awareness of the ramifications of trafficking as a transnational organized crime. The purpose of this paper is to highlight the major reasons behind the origin of this problem with special reference to trafficking of women into forced prostitution. The paper will also discuss how the sex trade has converted itself into a power house and its affect on society. It is unfortunate that the infrastructure for rescue and rehabilitation is grossly inadequate. Both the law as well as administrative policies have not addressed these issues adequately and with imagination. As a result, many rescued victims are re-trafficked.

This book is coming out in a very apt moment because it addresses certain existing issues related to security concerns relevant to the national security interest and some of the contemporary issues which have both direct and indirect security implications. The papers are contributed by eminent scientists, academicians, scholars, and will be of immense use to scholars, policy makers and all those who are interested in these issues. The papers are based on the research exercises of each contributor.

In this regard, invaluable help was provided by people both from within and outside the academic world. I express my heartfelt gratitude to Prof. V. T. Patil, Former Vice –Chancellor of Pondicherry University, presently Visiting Professor of Political Science Karnataka University, Dharwad, Karnataka, who has gone out of his way to painstakingly read the manuscript and wrote the foreword for the book. As is known to everybody, he had always been a constant source of encouragement to me personally.

I would also like to state my earnest gratitude to all the contributors who have all made the effort to submit the articles timely.

Especially, I would like to convey my gratitude to Prof. Sumita Sen to whom I am indebted for her continuous advice and guidance and for helping me in understanding the subject and relevance of the intrinsic values of security. Moreover, I would like to thank all my colleagues in the Department of International Relations, Jadavpur University, for their immense support and encouragement. I thank the research scholars of the Department for their assistance.

Last but not the least, I would like to thank Mr. Ashok Kumar Mittal of Concept Publishing Company (P) Ltd. for processing the book as without their help this book could not have seen the light of the day.

Herkan Neadan Toppo
Editor

Acknowledgements

During the progression of the publication of the edited book/ volume titled "Contemporary Security Concerns of India" I came across people of different walks of life and would like to gratefully acknowledge all those from whom I received invaluable help both from within and outside the academic world.

I take special opportunity to express my heartfelt gratitude of Prof. V.T. Patil, Former Vice-Chancellor of Pondicherry University, presently Visiting Professor of Political Science, Karnataka University, Dharwad, Karnataka, who went out of his way to painstakingly reading the manuscripts and writing the foreword for the book. As is known to everybody, he had always been a constant source of encouragement to all of us here and me personally.

I would also like to state my earnest gratitude to all the contributors who made all efforts to enthusiastically submit the articles on time and also for their kind co-operation and encouragement which helped me in publication of the book.

Especially, I wish to convey my deep gratitude to Prof. Sumita Sen of the Department of International Relations, Jadavpur University, Kolkata, to whom I am indebted for her continuous advice and guidance, and also helping me in understanding the subject and relevance of intrinsic values of security.

Moreover, I would like to thank all my colleagues in the Department of International Relations, Jadavpur University, Kolkata for their immense support and encouragement. My thanks also go to my research scholars of the Department who have lent their assistance.

Last but not the least, I would like to thank Mr. S.P. Singa and all the team of staff of the Concept Publishing Company (P) Ltd., New Delhi, who are involved in the processing of the book for the publication and without whose help this book could not have seen the light of the day.

Needless to say that each author remains responsible for the views expressed in their respective sections of the book.

Herkan Neadan Toppo
(Editor)

Contents

Section I
DIMENSIONS OF SECURITY

Section II
INDIA'S SECURITY AND ITS NEIGHBOURS

Section III
SOCIAL DIMENSIONS OF SECURITY

Contributors

Alam, Chandreyi is an Advocate in Kolkata.

Banerjee, Amrita is teaching in Vivekananda College, Calcutta University, Kolkata-700032 Email: hutomsona@yahoo.com

Banerji, Arun Kumar, Former Professor of International Relations, Jadavpur University, Kolkata-700032.

Banerji, Jyotirmoy, Former Professor of International Relations, Jadavpur University, Kolkata-700032.

Behera, Bhagaban is an Assistant Professor of International Relations, Jadavpur University, Kolkata-700032.

Chakrabarti, Parthasarathi is a Chief Scientist, Department of Science & Technology, Govt. of West Bengal, Bikash Bhavan (4th Floor), Salt Lake, Kolkata-700091.

Das, Bijaya Kumar, Assistant Professor, Department of International Relations, Jadavpur University, Kolkata-700032 Email: bijaydasju@gmail.com.

Mishra, Binod Kumar, Director, Centre for Studies in International Relations and Development, Kolkata.

Singh, Konthoujam Indrakumar teaches at the Department of Political Science, Tamenglong College, Imphal, Manipur.

Thangjam, Homen is an Assistant Professor, Department of Political Science, Maharaja Bodhchandra College, Imphal, Manipur.

Toppo, Herkan Neadan, is an Assistant Professor, Department of International Relations, Jadavpur University, Kolkata-700032.

Vaiphei, Lianboi is an Assistant Professor, Department of Political Science, Indraprastha College for Woman, Delhi University, Delhi-110054.

SECTION 1

Dimensions of Security

1

India's Security Concerns in the 21st Century

Non-Military Threats to India's Security

Arun Kumar Banerji

In traditional 'realist' discourses, the concept of security was developed essentially in 'State-centric' terms, and security of a State as an actor in the international system was measured in terms of its military power. Since the threats to security of a State were perceived to emerge from outside its boundaries, the best way to counter the same would be, it was argued, through acquisition of military capabilities. This mode of thinking influenced not only the works of International Relations (IR) scholars, but also the policies of statesmen, right from the time of Machiavelli to the present day. In international politics, strategic artistry and balance of power became the name of the game.

That this concept of security was seriously flawed was demonstrated by the collapse of the Soviet Union and the break-up of the erstwhile state of Pakistan, resulting in emergence of Bangladesh as an independent state. The Soviet Union collapsed not because of any external threats to its territorial security; the reasons for its collapse had their roots in Soviet polity and economy. The break-up of Pakistan was, no doubt, precipitated by the war with India, but its real cause is to be found in economic deprivation, cultural domination and political marginalization of East Pakistan and, the reign of terror let loose on the people of East Pakistan when they protested against these injustices. Similarly, the break-up of the erstwhile states of Yugoslavia and Czechoslovakia was caused by internal schisms.

These examples are instructive. To say that security of a State cannot be ensured by accretion to its military capabilities alone is not to argue for total disarmament, however idealistic that goal may be, but to point out that over-dependence on military power may not necessarily guarantee a state's survival or territorial integrity. On the contrary, it is likely to lead to an arms race (as happened during the cold war years, between the US and the Soviet Union, or, say, between India and Pakistan during the 1980s and 1990s,) resulting in an increase in expenditure on arms, and reduction in expenditure in the social sector, thereby weakening the socio-economic bases of a polity.

The 'realist' concept of security – whether in its traditional or 'neo-realist' guise – was based on the idea of the 'Westphalian' state, as an actor in the international system, with a distinct territorial base and sovereign authority, interacting with other states. But this concept of national security remains incomplete if one fails to take note of the internal context of the state – the way it operates, and relates to the groups, communities and individuals over whom it claims the exclusive right to obedience. It may not be entirely unreasonable to argue that in the 21st century the threats to security of states emerge, more often than not, from developments within their territorial boundaries although these may be influenced/manipulated by actors from outside the boundaries. Bary Buzan was the first to draw attention to the need for developing a holistic view of national security encompassing the three levels of the security problem – the individual, the state and the international system.[1] He argued quite convincingly that the concept of security binds these three levels together; but he failed to distinguish between the security concerns of the developing states from those of the industrially developed states. Subsequently, however, he took note of some of these in developing the notion of 'security complex' in the context of the study of regional security.[2]

The contemporary meaning of security implies much more than maintenance of territorial integrity of states through acquisition of military power. It means security of territory as well as security of life and property of individuals living within the boundaries of states, their right to live in peace and move around freely. An entirely new dimension has been added to the concept of security in recent years by the UNDP, by linking it to the concept of development. As the UN Secretary General put it, "...humanity cannot enjoy security without development or development without security, and neither without respect for human rights."[3] An attempt will be made here to articulate India's security concerns in the 21st century with particular reference to the non-military dimensions of threats to security. While some of these threats are deeply rooted in India's society and polity, others emerge from outside the boundary – from India's unstable neighbourhood – and it is the close links between these two types of threats that pose the greatest challenge to India's security planners.

Domestic Threats to Security : Violent Secessionist Movements

Religious Extremism and Maoist Radicalism

In the post-colonial States, Mohammed Ayoob wrote in a perceptive essay in 1992, "there are competing foci of authority, usually weaker than the state in terms of coercive capacity, but equal to or stronger than the state in terms of legitimacy (or the right to rule) as far as the perceptions of substantial proportions of the states' population are concerned"[4] This is because the colonial rulers in most cases included within their colonial territories people having diverse ethnic identities., and these political boundaries often cut across ethnic lines, leaving people of the same ethnic group on both sides of the political divide. During the British days, the colonial rulers thought it prudent not to disturb the traditional structure of authority in the outlying areas of the empire in the north-east, or in the north-west (which is now a part of Pakistan), while the areas controlled by the Princely states also enjoyed substantial internal autonomy. The structure of traditional authority and the foci of loyalty continued to exist in these areas even after the British left. The new Indian state that emerged after independence, included within its boundary most of the erstwhile Princely states of various sizes. However, it is the modernising tendencies of the new state – its attempts to bring the outlying areas within the political mainstream, through introduction of uniform constitutional and legal systems throughout the state – that seemed to threaten the traditional structure of authority thereby creating a divergence, if not tension, between what Ayoob calls 'the loci of authority and power'. This has been one of the principal security problems faced by most of the post-colonial states, including India, and the divergence between the loci of authority and power has been accentuated further in the post-Cold war years, especially after the collapse of the Soviet Union and the break-up of a number of states in Eastern Europe on ethnic lines. Added to this has been a feeling of economic deprivation, articulated by the emergent educated elites among these ethnic groups, and a fear of losing cultural identity/ autonomy. The secessionist movements in India's north-east, in Kashmir, or the development of militancy in Punjab during the 1980s are variants of the same problem, although these regions have different historical backgrounds.[5]

Development of militancy in Punjab during the 1980s was the result of an explosive mix of linguistic, religious, political and economic factors that had their roots in the history of the creation of the state and, the Sikh quest for identity spurred, to some extent, by the fear of Hindu domination. Matters were made worse by the short-sighted policies of India's political class – the machinations of the Congress (I) government in New Delhi to weaken the Akali Dal, the party that has long been associated with Sikh aspirations, and the failure of the Akalis to unite to fight the Congress (I) politically. Some of the Akali factions were even prepared to court the militants, who were planning to set up a separate state – Khalistan – to prevail over their adversaries in the intra-Akali struggle for power. Development of militancy in Punjab resulted in unprecedented violence and put a question mark on the future of India's unity and territorial integrity. Militancy in Punjab was ultimately brought under control through the pursuit of a number of measures that included suppression of terrorism through the use of force, initiation of a political dialogue with a section of the Akali leadership (resulting in the Rajiv-Longwal Accord), and slow revival of political activities in the state, especially after the institution of an elected government in 1992. This was followed by a slew of measures for the rejuvenation of the state's economy.

The lessons from Punjab should have made India's political class aware of the threats to India's security – its territorial integrity and the security and welfare of its citizens; but the lessons have not really been learnt, as may be seen from the continuing unrest in Kashmir, and in India's north-east. The militant secessionist movement that began in Kashmir towards the end of the 1980s was the result of a series of political developments that led to the progressive attenuation of Kashmir's autonomy guaranteed under Article 370 of the Constitution of India.[6] The process began in the 1950s, and was carried to its extreme after the outbreak of insurgency in the valley. Political corruption in the State and financial mismanagement also contributed to peoples' disenchantment with the policies pursued by the successive Administrations in Srinagar, in collusion – as they saw it – with New Delhi. Treating Kashmir as a rebellious province and suppression of the normal political process fuelled peoples' anger and played into the hands of secessionists who resorted to indiscriminate violence resulting in loss of lives – of security personnel and ordinary citizens. The activities of terrorist groups and counter-terrorism measures taken by the security forces led to violation of human rights on an unprecedented scale and created a sense of insecurity among people, and their alienation from the government. However, installation of an elected government in 1996, under the leadership of Dr. Farooq Abdullah, the adoption of a number of measures by the government for the amelioration of peoples' grievances and their disenchantment with the activities of the secessionists led to an improvement in the situation in the valley, especially, since 2003, with the development of a thaw in India-Pakistan relations. However, some of the basic issues in the state of Jammu and Kashmir have not yet been resolved. Since the three parts of the State – Jammu, Kashmir and Ladakh – have distinctive demographic identities, the relationship between the different segments of the State and its population, the pattern of allocation of resources and the distribution of electoral seats for elections to the Assembly and the Parliament are issues which need immediate and careful attention. Above all, there is an urgent need to initiate, and properly implement, measures that will bring about an improvement in the economic condition of the people, especially, in the valley, to wean them away from the militants. That the political class failed to look beyond the immediate gains had again been demonstrated by the row over the Amarnath land issue that broke out in June 2008, and pushed Jammu and Kashmir to the edge.

Matters are likely to improve with installation of a new elected government in the State in January 2009 with Omar Abdullah as the Chief Minister. His main priorities would be, he said, delivering good governance, and to work for improvement in economic conditions of the citizenry by creating more employment opportunities and, removal of imbalances between the three regions – Jammu, Kashmir and Ladakh – besides trying to establish a dialogue with the 'separatists'.

It is important to note that although the various secessionist movements had their roots in India's polity, these could not have been sustained without the encouragement and support from across the border. The geographical location of Jammu and Kashmir, Punjab, and the States in India's north-east, compounded the problem of management of security because of the moral, financial and logistical supports the insurgents received from across the border. It is an open secret that the militant secessionist movement in Punjab during the 1980s could be sustained because of the direct and indirect support the militants received from Pakistan, particularly, from the ISI. It is only when the Pakistan government realised that the proposed State of Khalistan would have Lahore as its capital, Pakistan's support started waning, especially after installation of a civilian government in the State. Similarly, the secessionist movement in Kashmir could be sustained with the help from Pakistan. Cross-border terrorism has fuelled militancy in Kashmir as the militants received not only moral support from Pakistan but also substantive material help, in the form of arms and training, especially, from the ISI. Moreover, they were often joined by the *jihadis* trained by Pakistan, for fighting against the Soviet forces in Afghanistan during the 1980s.

India's North-East has also a long history of insurgency, and even more than sixty years after independence at least four States in the region – Assam, Manipur, Nagaland and Tripura – remain plagued by the insurgency problem. The region offers a classic illustration of Ayoob's categorisation of the security concerns of post-colonial societies arising out of the divergence between the 'loci of authority and power'. Problems have been compounded further by the region's poverty, its strategic location, cultural diversity, inter- and intra-ethnic conflicts, unsettled territorial disputes and involvement of external powers. Lack of infrastructure is one of the basic impediments to the region's economic development. The Central Government is aware of this and has set up a separate ministry for the development of the

North-East region, but the mechanism adopted for attracting investment to the region through organisation of summits under the aegis of the Indian Chamber of Commerce (ICC) is hardly propitious. Because, the ICC has not much presence in the region, except in the State of Assam. Consequently, despite the efforts being made by the government(s) to bring investments to the region, funds are not pouring in. Prospective investors will not feel secured unless the people are involved in the development process and this is exactly what is happening, despite the region's high potentials in oil, tea, agro-processing, cement production and tourism. Above all, there is rampant corruption both at the administrative and political levels.[7]

The movements for autonomy/statehood launched or intensified in various parts of India during the last two decades or so – for example by the Nepalese-speaking population in Darjeeling (West Bengal), the tribal population living it mineral – rich districts of south Bihar, and the southern districts of Madhya Pradesh, the Bodos living in Assam, or the hill tribes in northern UP, demanding separate statehood, within the Indian state – have caused enormous damage to life and property. While some of these movements resulted in creation of new States – Jharkhand, comprising the tribal-inhabited southern districts of Bihar, Uttrakhand, comprising the hill districts of Northern UP and, Chhattisgarh, comprising the tribal-inhabited areas of Madhya Pradesh – others have resulted in devolution of considerable financial and administrative power to identifiable regions within the existing States. However, creation of new States, curved out of existing ones, or devolution of financial and administrative power to identifiable regions, with distinct ethnic identities, within existing States – for example setting up of the Darjeeling Gorkhaland Hill Council (DGHC) in West Bengal, or the Bodoland Autonomous Council in Assam – has not necessarily solved the problem of security. Maoist violence continues unabated in Jharkhand and Chhattisgarh, while demands for greater autonomy/Statehood coupled with the demand for redrawing of boundaries, and frequent inter-ethnic conflicts (for example, between the Bodos and the illegal Bengali migrants) have retarded economic development of the regions and resulted in loss of lives and destruction of properties. One of the basic reasons for these may be found in the lack of economic development and the skewed development policies pursued by the political class resulting in corruption and bad governance. The DGHC experiment in Darjeeling is a good example of what bad governance, corruption and lust for power may do to an honest attempt at devolution of financial and administrative power, leading to the revival of the demand for a separate State (i.e., province), since 2008. It was also reported in *The Times of India* on 20 January, 2009 that a section of Gorkhas – particularly the Gorkha Liberation Army which is supposed to be an offshoot of the erstwhile United Gorkha Revolutionary Front – has tied up with insurgent groups in the North-East, the Kamtapur Liberation Army in north Bengal and the Maoists in Nepal. A poster in Kurseong warned the Gorkha Janmukti Morcha (GJM) that is spearheading a political movement for a separate Gorkhaland that it cannot be achieved through Gandhigiri; the GLA even threatened to shoot 'Bengalis in the heart' to get Gorkhaland.

Religious Terrorism : In the Name of Allah and Ram

While violent secessionist movements pose a threat to India's territorial integrity and result in loss of innocent lives and property, besides damaging India's relations with the neighbours, terrorism perpetrated by religious extremists – both Muslims as well as Hindus – has now emerged as a major threat to India's domestic security. According to a Report compiled by the National Counter – Terrorism Centre in Washington, death toll from Islamic terror strikes in India between January 2004 – March 2007 was 3674; and more than 330 persons have been killed and several others injured in terrorist attacks, between May 2007 to November 2008. The Mumbai terrorist attacks (November 2008) alone resulted in the death of 195 people (including 14 foreigners) and injury to nearly 300.[8] These indeed are alarming figures, but very few cases have been satisfactorily resolved and the perpetrators of criminal activities have mostly gone scotfree. It would be naïve to dismiss such incidents of terrorism as the handiwork of some misguided Muslims acting at the behest of an unfriendly neighbour, although Pakistan has played a significant role in stoking the fire of Islamic radicalism, both in India and other countries. Terrorist organizations in Pakistan – particularly, the Laskar-e-Taiyyaba (LeT), and its front organisation, the Jamaat-ul-Dawa (JuD) – the prime suspects in the Mumbai massacre of November 2008 – have sought to undermine the stability of India's economy and democratic polity.

Emergence of Islamic radicalism leading to terrorist activities is not unique to India. Its origin may be traced to the rising influence of the Wahhabi and Salafist interpretations of Islam spreading from Saudi Arabia – with the Al Qaida as its fountainhead – that is different from the more liberal Sufi and other traditions of Islam prevailing in India and the neighbouring countries. Emergence of this radical Islam in South Asia was facilitated by the policies pursued by the late President Zia-ul-Haq in Pakistan during the 1970s to gain support from the clerics to prop up his illegal regime. Zia was a usurper and when he decided to try Bhutto, he lacked any political constituency and to gain political support he started wooing political parties based on religious ideologies which had long faded from mainstream politics. The support he got from these parties gave him political legitimacy, while Zia's action boosted the fortunes of the political parties with radical religious ideologies. These developments in Pakistan coincided with the Soviet invasion of Afghanistan in 1979. It is no secret that there was a mushroom growth of religious seminaries (*madrasas*) in Pakistan – from 868 in 1975 to 3289 in 1988, and the number rose to 6000, by the year 2000 – with the knowledge and support of the government. What was quite alarming was that nearly 8-10 per cent of these *madrasas* in Pakistan were providing military training to their students, in addition to religious training.[9] Subsequently, these *mujahids* were used by Pakistan, with financial and military aid received from the US, to fight the Soviet troops in Afghanistan during the 1980s. According to Shaukat Qadir, between 1979 and 1989, the USA was 'actively involved' in this process (of supporting and training the *mujahids*) and during the next eight years its involvement was slightly less.[10] After the withdrawal of Soviet troops, many of these *mujahids* – Pakistanis, Afghans, Bangladeshis and citizens from Arab and other Muslim countries – moved out to carry on the *jihadi* war in Kashmir, Chechnya and in the Central Asian Republics. Pakistan was also the home of such other terrorist groups as the LeT, Jaish-i-Mohammad (Jaish), Harkat-ul Jehadi Islam (HuJI) and the Hizbul Mujahideen (Hizb). After the withdrawal of Soviet troops, the Talibans came to power in Afghanistan, with Pakistan's support.

Pakistan became the source of *jihadi* terrorism, as the government turned a blind eye to the activities of these organisations operating from Pakistani territory. These organizations, acting in tandem with the Talibans and the Al Qaida, and with support from the ISI, created a reign of terror in the State of Jammu and Kashmir of Indian as terrorist infiltration across the LoC increased. Local Kashmiri youths, who had taken to militancy, were trained in Pakistani soil by these groups, indoctrinated and armed, with encouragement and help from the ISI, thwarting efforts by the Government of India to establish a dialogue with the local Kashmiri militants. The distinction between *jihadi* terrorism and separatist militancy was gradually getting blurred in Kashmir, due to the support, both logistical and material, the *jihadis* and the Kashmiri separatists received from the ISI.

Throughout the 1990s, *jihadi* terrorist activities in Jammu and Kashmir were limited, mostly, to the valley and the districts bordering Pakistan/POK, (except the serial blasts in Bombay, in 1993, which could be seen as an act of revenge against the destruction of the Babri Masjid in Ayodhya, and the subsequent killing of Muslims in the riots in its wake).This had a tremendous impact on the Muslim psyche, created disaffection among the Muslims and a sense of insecurity, although the destruction of the Babri Masjid was widely condemned in India. By the end of the last century, radical Islam struck the Indian heartland, as demonstrated by the attacks on the Parliament of India (2001), the Akshardham temple in Gujarat and the subsequent terrorist attacks in Mumbai (2003, 2006), Delhi (2005 and 2008), Hyderabad (May and August 2007); Ajmer (2007), and, Jaipur, the CRPF camp at Rampur, Bangalore, Ahmedabad, Mumbai, Agartala and other places, all in 2008, killing nearly 900 people and injuring several hundreds, between the Diwali bombings in Delhi in 2005, and the November (2008) terrorist strikes in Mumbai.

Two factors seem to have brought about this. The first was a change in Pakistan's strategy as a sponsor of cross-border terrorism, to bleed India and to destabilize its economy. But to avoid the tag of a rogue State, it now started cultivating a section of the disaffected Muslims in India, who were indoctrinated with *jihadi* ideologies, and supplied with necessary arms and training to carry on the *jihadi* war against India. After the terrorist attacks in Mumbai, on 26 November, 2008, the 'Deccan Mujahideen', an obscure terrorist group, through an e-mail, raised issues like Muslims being 'targeted and harassed' in India, just the way the Indian Mujahideen – a front organisation of the SIMI that was floated after the latter was banned – had referred to the harassment of Muslims, in its e-mail, after the Gujarat blasts in July (2008), for which it had claimed responsibility.[11] This was in line with the propaganda launched in Pakistan by the JuD, and the Al Qaida. However unrealistic this view may appear to the majority of Indians, it is a reflection of the way a segment of the Indian Muslims view the Indian society and polity, where they feel marginalized and harassed due to a variety of reasons, especially, their socio-economic backwardness. The roots of the Muslim community's backwardness may be traced to the causes that ultimately led to the partition of India.[12] In independent India the Muslims are economically worse off than the Hindus and are underrepresented in the defence services, the police forces and in the higher echelons of administration.[13] In contemporary India a sense of alienation had developed among a segment of the Muslim population also because of the steady growth of a militant rightwing Hindu 'nationalism', especially since the 1990s. If the RSS, the Vishwa Hindu Parishad (VHP) and the Bajrang Dal constituted its core, the BJP was its political face. The RSS is by no means new, nor are all the leaders of the BJP necessarily communalists. But the BJP certainly played the Hindutva card to gain political power at the centre, during the 1990s, as was demonstrated by Advani's *rath yatra* and the subsequent destruction of the Babri Masjid. This and the virtual massacre of Muslims in the BJP-ruled State of Gujarat in 2002 had a traumatic effect on the Muslim psyche and provided the background for the growth of indigenous *jihadi* Muslim groups such as the Student's Islamic Movement of India (SIMI) and the Indian Mujahideen (IM), with ideological and material support from the LeT and other fundamentalist Muslim groups in Pakistan.

The process of radicalisation of Islam was also hastened by two other developments: the attack on Afghanistan by the US and its allies, in the wake of the September 11 attacks on the WTC and the Pentagon by the Al Qaida extremists, and especially, the US-led invasion of Iraq (2003). India had nothing to do with these developments, but the anger and resentments which the Muslims felt, all over the world, against the west, the US in particular, had its reverberations in India as well, especially among the radicalised

Muslims. Though they constitute a minor segment of the total Muslim population (130 million), they are well-organized, constituting sleeper cells all over the country and are guided by their mentors in Pakistan. The frequency of terrorist attacks during 2007-08, was made possible because of the operation of these sleeper modules; but the Pakistani connection was always there, as could be seen from their *modus operandi*. The most tell-tale evidence of the involvement of elements based in Pakistan was the terror strike in Mumbai in November, 2008.[14] President Asif Ali Zardari called them non-state actors, but Pakistan as a sovereign state cannot escape responsibility for the activities of terrorist groups based in Pakistan.

The growth of right-wing Hindu fundamentalism in India in recent years might have been helped by the emergence of Islamic radicalism in Pakistan, but its roots may be traced back to the pre-partition years. The Hindutva groups such as the Bajrang Dal, the VHP or the Sri Ram Sena are all affiliated to the RSS which acts as their mentors. There are also other organisations such as the Hindu Jagaran Manch, the Santana Ashram in Panvel, or Bhonsale Military School in Nashik run by the Central Hindu Military Education Society, established in 1935, by a Hindutva zealot and a former president of Hindu Mahasabha, B.S. Moonje. Moonje was close to the founder of the RSS, K.B. Hedgewar.[15] Thus in one way or the other, the different Hindutva groups have been related to each other, and their memberships may also be overlapping, although they maintain their distinct identities.

Maharashtra Police's Anti-Terrorist Squad (ATS) discovered involvement of some of these organizations in terrorist activities while investigating an accidental bomb explosion on 6 April, 2006, in the house of an RSS member, L.G. Rajkondwar in Nanded, resulting in the death of two Bajrang Dal activists who were engaged in fabrication of a bomb, along with other extremists. In its charge sheet filed in August 2006, the Maharashtra ATS established the existence of a Bajrang Dal-centred terrorist network that was responsible for the terrorist bomb attacks on a mosque in Parbhani (in November 2003) and, similar attacks on mosques in Jalna and Purna (in August 2004) – all in the Marathwada region of Maharashtra. The bomb that had accidentally exploded in Nanded was apparently meant for attack on a mosque in Aurangabad.

If the *madrasas* in Pakistan were churning out Mujahids for operation in Afghanistan, India, and in other parts of the world, especially, Central Asia, the Hindutva zealots have not lagged behind in training the religious extremists. The extremists who were operating in the Marathwada region were trained in bomb-making near Pune, in Goa and in the Bhonsala Military School. An RSS camp in the Bhonsala School imparted training to more than 100 participants in the use of firearms and in martial arts.[16] According to the ATS, all these activities were part of a larger game plan of targeting the Muslims and to create the impression that Muslim extremists would even kill other Muslims for provoking the Muslim community, by spreading disaffection among them against the majority community. This would serve to widen the communal divide, and provide the *raison d'etre* for the activities of the Hindu extremist groups.[17] It was with this intention that the Hindutva extremists had planted bombs outside a crowded mosque in Malegaon in September 2006, that killed more than 30 people – all Muslims, observing Shab-e-Barat. After the Nanded bomb explosion, the local police attempted to cover up the Bajrang Dal-VHP involvement in bomb-making, despite enough evidence collected by the Secular Citizens' Forum, the Peoples' Union for Civil Liberties in Nagpur, and the Movement for Peace and Justice in Nanded that showed that a bomb – fabrication operation was being run by the VHP-Bajrang Dal combine. Similarly, the police tried to pass off the Malegaon bombings of September 2006, as an act of the Muslims, ignoring all material evidence and clues, that pointed to the involvement of the Sangh Parivar extremists. Ironically, two years after the Malegaon bomb attacks (2006), the Maharashtra ATS arrested Sadhvi Pragya Thakur, a serving Army Officer Lt. Col. Prasad Purohit, a former Army Officer, Ramesh Upadhyaya and others, including a collector of vintage arms and weapons, Rakesh Dhawade, for their alleged involvement in the Malegaon motorbike explosion (29 September, 2008) outside the outlawed SIMI office that killed 7 people and left over 70 injured In its chargesheet filed in January 2009 in the Maharashtra Control of Organised Crime Act (MCOCA) Court of judge Y.D. Shinde, the Maharashtra ATS contended that the explosion was master-minded by Lt. Col. Prasad Purohit, Sadhvi Pragya Singh Thakur and a select group belonging to the little – known Abhinav Bharat organisation, based in Pune.[18] The Army Officer was a part of the

Army Intelligence Unit stationed in Panchmarhi, Madhya Pradesh; Sadhvi Pragya is a former member of the Akhil Vharatiya Bidyarthi Parishad, the student wing of the BJP. It is not Maharashtra alone where the Sangh Parivar extremists have been involved in terrorist activities. A Bajrang Dal activist, Dara Singh, was responsible for the gruesome killing of the Christian missionary Graham Staines and his two children in Orissa; and in the summer of 2008, the Bajrang Dal was also responsible for attacks on the tribal population in the Kandhamal district of Orissa, who were Christians. Indeed, the Bajrang Dal and the VHP have emerged as major sources of threats to security of the minority communities living in different parts of India, thereby undermining the security of the Indian State as their activities have provoked counter attacks by the Islamic militant groups, with support, both ideological and material, from their mentors across the border.

What is more disturbing, there has not been any let up in the activities of these Sangh Parivar militant groups. Even after the Nanded explosion, Sangh Parivar activists have been implicated in other explosions that took place while making bombs in different parts of India – for example, in Kanpur and *tenkasi*. Bajrang Dal activists have also been accused of distributing Trishuls (tridents) – four millions in Rajasthan alone – and imparting training to its members in using firearms![19] Even the attack on the Samjhota Express might have been planned and executed by the conspirators who were involved in the Malegaon blasts, although no definite proof has yet been found. Growth of majoritarian terrorism perpetrated by the Bajrang Dal, VHP or other affiliates of the Sangh Parivar over the last two decades has certainly contributed to the feeling of distrust and fear among the Muslims and added some credibility to the allegation of the militant Islamists about the repression of Muslims in India, more so because of the partisan role played by a section of the police and the Administration, at the behest of their political masters, as was seen during the anti-Muslim riots in Gujarat in 2003, or, say, in Maharashtra, during the police investigations after the Nanded explosion, and the Malegaon bomb attacks (2006). A new 'Muslim political party' called the Ulema Council, consisting of the Maulanas of Azamgarh *madrasas*, doctors and others was set up in the Azamgarh district of eastern UP, just before the Parliamentary elections of 2009 to take on other political parties that have always 'used Muslims as a convenient vote bank'. (*The Statesman*, 25 March, 2009) One of the spokesman of the newly-formed party explained that the Muslim youths of Azamgarh lived in fear, because whenever there is a terrorist attack, the UP ATS or other anti-terror agencies might pick them up, thus giving Azamgarh the dubious distinction of being an '*Atankgarh*' (a place of terror). Such feelings contribute to the sense of alienation among the Muslim youth. The only silver lining in this dismal scene has been the role of the civil society and the human rights groups who played a commendable role in reopening nearly fifty per cent of the criminal cases in the Gujarat riots, after the acquittal of the accused in those cases by the Gujarat High Court, because of the absence of proper evidence. In a landmark judgment delivered on 21st October, 2008, the Supreme Court virtually forced the Gujarat Government to drop the charges made under POTA against the accused in the Godhra fire case.[20] It is also important to note that a section of the Sangh Parivar has been trying to distance itself from the terrorist activities of the VHP and the Bajrang Dal. In the wake of the arrest of Sadhvi Pragya and her associates, the VHP President Ashok Singhal severely criticised the Maharashtra ATS for its alleged excesses and likened the treatment meted out to Sadhvi Pragya to the disrobing of Draupadi by the Kauravas in the *Mahabharata.* He also brought wild allegations against Sonia Gandhi and accused the Congress of trying to divide the Sangh Parivar, in a bid to divert attention from the terror tactics of the VHP and its associates. But things had gone too far. Even the RSS tried to distance itself from the policies of that section of the Sangh Parivar who were committed to the Malegaon bomb accused. In an unambiguous statement against terror, the RSS chief, K.S. Sudarshan said "Someone who kills innocent people cannot be a religious person. He can neither be a Hindu nor Muslim. Punish them if found guilty. We are not going to support anyone found involved in terrorist activities. Killers have no religion."[21] Indeed, Sudarshan had gone further than Maulana Marghuboor Rehman, a senior cleric of the Deoband Seminary who declared at a meeting in August 2008 that there is no place for terrorism in Islam, since, seasoned observers argued this did not amount to a condemnation of the *jihadis*. A week after the Mumbai carnage of November 2008, the *Idgah* in Lucknow strongly condemned terrorism.

Side by side the development of right wing Hindutva

militancy, there has developed a new brand of parochialism – as revealed, for example, by the activities of the Shiv Sena, and, one of its offshoots, Raj Thackarey's Maharashtra Nav Nirman Samity – who have often targeted non-Mahrashtrians to give vent to their resentment over certain aspects of government's policy. Similar situations were seen in India's North-East when the militant anti-foreigner movement led by the All Assam Students' Union (AASU) and others had reached its peak during 1979-1985, with more than seven thousand people losing their lives and nearly two million rendered homeless. The United Liberation Front of Assam (ULFA) targeted the non-Assamese population living in Assam, particularly the Bengali Muslims who had illegally migrated to Assam from Bangladesh. The Nellie massacre of 1983, resulted in the death of 1800 Muslims, including infants.[22] In recent years, the Hindi-speaking workers in Assam had been the targets of attack. If such things are allowed to happen, that may lead to the balkanization of India, but India's political class, in the interests of vote-bank politics, have often failed to condemn those responsible for such deplorable activities. The response of the two constituents of the UPA Government – the RJD and the NCP – to the MNNS activists' attack on the Hindi-speaking people in Maharashtra in 2008 is illustrative of the attitudes of India's political class. While the RJD leaders – ministers in the UPA government – were vociferous in condemning the attack on the north Indians, and rightly, their NCP counterparts were muted in their criticism.

The Threats to Security posed by the Maoist Extremists

If separatist movements and terrorist activities perpetrated in the name of religion are creating problems for India's internal security, no less significant has been the growth in Maoist violence. The recent surge in Naxalite violence shows that it is more than a mere law and order problem. From 156 districts in 12 States in September 2004, it had spread to 15 States in February 2005, affecting about 40 per cent of the total area of India's territory, and about 35 per cent of its population. As the recent (winter 2008-09) incidence of violence in Lalgarh in the West Medinipur district of West Bengal showed, their *modus operandi* is also undergoing changes with the Maoists trying to recruit teenagers to their rank, like the LTTE in Sri Lanka. Their objective is to set up a Red Corridor, extending from Nepal and North Bihar, to the underdeveloped hinterland of Jharkhand, Orissa, Chhattisgarh, Andhra Pradesh, Maharashtra and West Bengal, taking advantage of the dire poverty of the population living in these areas. The Maoists are trying to transform themselves into a modern guerrilla force, equipped with sophisticated weapons and modern communications system. They are spreading disaffection among the rural poor by arguing that the new economic policies initiated by the government are detrimental to their interest and that the Panchayati Raj institutions have been used by a handful of well-to-do peasants creating a new class of Kulaks. Their arguments become persuasive because of the failure of the government to deliver the goods. If one takes the case of West Bengal, for example, the spurt in Naxalite violence in the State during the last two years may be attributed, among other factors, to the government's lop-sided policy of industrialisation, and, its failure to alleviate rural poverty by providing 100 days' employment per family, among the rural poor, as stipulated under the National Rural Employment Guarantee (NREG) Act. As the Economic Survey (2008-09) presented along with the vote-on-account budget in the West Bengal Legislative Assembly on 20 March, 2009 revealed, during the year the government could provide employment to the rural poor, on an average, for only 25 days, as against the national average of 44 days. (*The Statesman, Kolkata Plus*, 21 March, 2009)[23]

Against this background of increasing Naxalite violence, the merger of the MCCI (the Maoist Communist Centre of India) and the PWG (Peoples' War Group) to form the CPI (Maoists), with its armed wing called the Peoples' Liberation Army, poses a very real threat to India's security and may bring about a change in the course of revolutionary movements not only in India, but also in other parts of South Asia. The CPI (Maoists) have established links with the Maoists in Nepal as well as the Communist revolutionary organisations in Bangladesh, Bhutan and Sri Lanka, under the banner of the Coordination Committee of the Maoist Parties and Organisations in South Asia (CCOMPOSA).[24] The Purba Bangla Communist Party is a member of the CCOMPOSA, and all these communist parties are also members of the Revolutionary International Movement. The CPI (Maoists) are also collaborating with the separatist organizations in India, and the neighbouring countries, particularly, with the LTTE. There are instances of criminals taking shelter in areas controlled by the Maoists; they are also acting in collaboration with the religious extremist groups. One of the prime accused in the serial Bombay blasts case (1993), for example, was the group led by Dawood Ibrahim who has allegedly been living in Pakistan and has not been repatriated to India, despite several requests by the Government of India, with proof of his involvement in several notorious criminal activities. The annual death toll resulting from the activities of the different militant separatist groups, the Maoists and the criminals exceeds the number of deaths due to the attacks by the religious terrorists, making the life of average citizens insecure.

Porous Border and Problems of Security

Most of India's borders with the neighbouring States are porous and this creates problems of security. These problems are mainly of three types: (i) activities of drug traffickers, gun-runners and smugglers, (ii) cross border terrorism, and (ii) illegal immigration.

India's border with Pakistan in the west, and its borders with the States in the east generally pass through areas that do not have any natural barrier; in many cases the border passes through villages with members of the same religious/ethnic community living on either side of the border. Under normal circumstances, this should not create any problem of security. However, since India's relations with the neighbouring States, particularly Pakistan, have not always been friendly, the porous borders have created serious problems of security, especially because of the activities of drug traffickers, smugglers and gun runners, operating along the borders. Very often they develop close links with the militant groups operating in different parts of India. According to *The International Narcotics Control Strategy Report* 2009, published by the US Department of State, heroin smuggling into India from Pakistan and Afghanistan has increased over the last two years. India's strategic location between South-East Asia and South-West Asia, the two principal sources of illegally-produced opium, makes it a transhipment route for smuggling of heroin. Insurgent groups operating in India's North-East, finance their operations through smuggling of drugs from Burma. Most of the drugs smuggled into India from Afghanistan and Pakistan are brought by West Africans; and most of the drugs meant for the international markets are smuggled into India from Nepal. Although India is a manufacturer and supplier of licit opiates, illicit production is carried on by criminal groups for both domestic and international markets. Such illegal production of opium takes place in different parts of India, especially in UP and in the Birbhum district of West Bengal.[25] Even a part of the opium produced legally, is often diverted for illegal sales, and the drug mafia and the insurgent groups often work hand-in-glove, thus compounding the problems of internal security.

As noted earlier, cross border terrorism became a major threat to India's security during the height of militancy in Punjab during the 1980s, and, subsequently, in Jammu and Kashmir during the 1990s as a militant separatist movement developed in the State, with aid and encouragement from Pakistan. By the end of the 1990s, cross-border terrorism became a major issue in India-Pakistan relations. It was no longer limited to the State of Jammu and Kashmir and, it spread to other parts of India, the latest example being the 26/11 terrorist attack on Mumbai in 2008. What is even more alarming, the Pakistani terrorist networks have now roped in the *jehadis* in Bangladesh in their bid to encircle India; and the ISI of Pakistan has also been active in promoting this. The arrest of a top LeT cadre, Abu Taher, in Kolkata, and the subsequent arrest of Sahabaz Ismail – a former member of the Pakistani border security forces, who later joined the dreaded Al Badar group, and was sent to India *via* the Bangladesh route, for operation in Kashmir – in March, 2009, revealed the close links between the ISI, and the terrorist organisations such as the LeT, and the Harkat-ul-Mujahideen in promoting terrorism. Abu Taher was the head of an LeT-sponsored militant organization, Al Mohammadi, with its headquarters in Bangladesh, entrusted with the task of recruiting Muslim youths from the economically weaker sections for carrying on terrorist activities in eastern India.[26] Indeed, Bangladesh has emerged as a home for numerous international terrorist groups, especially, since the BNP government came to power in 2001, with the help of the fundamentalist Jamat-e-Islam. Admiral William Fallon, head of US military's Pacific Command, said during his visit to Dhaka on 20 April, 2005, that there was a 'strong presence' of international terrorist groups in Bangladesh and they were using its territory for launching attacks abroad.[27] The Bangladesh government had also given refuge to Anup Chetia and other top leaders of the ULFA who were responsible for the acts of violence committed by this militant outfit in Assam.

Illegal immigration from Bangladesh has also created problems for India's security. According to official estimates there are some 15-18 million illegal Bangladeshi immigrants in India and they have now fanned out to different parts of India including UP, New Delhi, and even Gujarat and Maharashtra, especially Mumbai. The influx of illegal immigrants from Bangladesh to Assam over the last three decades has been one of the major factors behind militancy in Assam, but the Government of India's response to the problem has been quite tardy as the Illegal Migration Determination by Tribunal (IMDT) Act of 1983 and the IMDT Rules of 1984, which were subsequently struck down by the Supreme Court, could hardly succeed in dealing with the problem of detection of illegal immigrants. It is not Assam alone which has been affected by illegal immigration from Bangladesh; other States in the North-East such as Tripura as well as West Bengal have also been affected. In 1998, Lt. Genl. S.K. Sinha (Retd.), then Governor of Assam, in a report to the President of India had cautioned that the North-East region could slip out of control because of the demographic changes being brought about by massive infiltration from Bangladesh which was also being used by the ISI for carrying on terrorist activities in the North-East.[28] Illegal migration from Bangladesh to West Bengal over the last three decades has brought about important demographic changes in the districts bordering Bangladesh, including the districts of North and South 24-Parganas, and in parts of Kolkata. General (Retd.) Sankar Roy Chowdhury, a former Member of the Rajya Sabha, also referred to this in the Rajya Sabha on 20 April, 2000.[29] One consequence of illegal immigration is that the border districts of West Bengal are fast developing as safe havens for criminals and insurgents, creating serious problems of security. What is interesting, most of the illegal immigrants manage to get Indian citizenship through procurement of voter ID cards and ration cards because of the patronage of a section of political leaders, for vote-bank politics.

Conclusions

One of the arguments developed in this article is that the domestic threats to India's security now are at least as important as – if not more important than – the external threats to security, and in many instances these two types of threats are linked. Besides, there are also other long term non-military threats to security resulting from, say, climate change, energy crisis or food crisis that may form the subject for another discourse. However, if one takes note of the lapses on the part of India's security establishment that resulted in the attack on Mumbai on 26 November, 2008, one thing becomes clear – the lack of proper assessment of threats. The Committee that was constituted after the Kargil War (1999) pointed out in its report that the main reason for the failure of India to prevent the war was not so much the lack of intelligence inputs, as the lack of coordination among the various intelligence agencies which resulted in their failure to make a proper assessment of the available information and its implications for India's security. It also suggested certain measures for the prevention of recurrence of similar situations in future. The Mumbai terror strikes came almost a decade after that. But those who are responsible for maintenance of India's security, do not seem to have learnt their lessons. There are clear indications of lack of coordination among the various security agencies, and absence of political direction in matters of vital importance to the nation. It is now known that as early as February, 2008 the UP Police had arrested two terrorists—Fahim Ansari and Sabauddin – suspected to be LeT operatives, with maps that highlighted a number of landmarks in Mumbai, such as the Taj Hotel, the CST, etc. Ansari had visited Mumbai several times and also stayed there with a false name and even succeeded in procuring a driving licence. The Maharashtra Police was informed of their arrest by their UP counterpart. But how much credence was given to these bits of information by the Maharashtra Police, is not known; nor is it known whether the information gathered by the IB in September about a possible terrorist attack on the Tajmahal Hotel in Mumbai, and conveyed to the Maharashtra government in the form of an advisory by the NSC, was taken seriously. Finally, on 18 November, the RAW had intercepted a satellite phone communication which clearly indicated that terrorists based in Pakistan were planning to strike Mumbai, India's financial capital, by using the sea route, which they had in fact used. Had these 'actionable' information been acted upon, the Mumbai terror attacks might have been prevented.

The structure of India's intelligence machinery was designed to deal with conventional external threats and is not conducive to the development of an integrated decision-making system in matters of national security, especially, in dealing with terrorism, as it is viewed as a law and order problem which is in the domain of the provinces. But terrorism, whether perpetrated by religious fanatics, or ideological extremists, is a threat to national security and should be dealt with accordingly. The move by the central government to institute a federal investigating agency is, therefore, a step in the right direction. Simultaneously, those who fail to act on the basis of 'actionable' information should be held accountable. Equally important in the fight against terror is the strict enforcement of existing laws. It has been reported, for example, that of the ten pre-activated SIM cards sold in Kolkata, two reached the terrorists involved in the Mumbai attack *via* Kashmir. Had the rules been followed, this could not have happened. But if policemen themselves get involved in the racket, as some Kolkata Police personnel reportedly are, who is going to bell the cat?

It has been argued earlier that the growth of *jihadi* terrorism in India and its links with elements outside the country has been spurred by the emergence of a right-wing Hindu terrorism as perpetrated by the VHP, or the Bajrang Dal, and, the use of religion in electoral politics, for gaining political mileage. Religious leaders have an important role to play in condemning terrorism. As noted earlier, the senior cleric of the Deobandi seminary in India, Maulana Marghoobur Rehman, declared in a meeting in August 2008, that there is no place for terrorism in Islam. Although seasoned observers argued that this did not amount to a condemnation of the *jihadis* this was, nonetheless, an important step; equally important was the unequivocal condemnation of terrorism by Sudarsan, the former head of the RSS. A week after the Mumbai carnage, the idgah in Lucknow also strongly condemned terrorism in a statement.

If the growth of religious terrorism is to be checked, stringent laws should also be enacted to deal with acts of terrorism swiftly, and these should be applied on a non-discriminatory basis. Terrorists are often funded by outside agencies – mafia dons like Dawood Ibrahim, terrorist organisations like the LeT or the JuD, or even by foreign government agencies, out to destroy India's society and polity. Since most of the money is routed through *hawala* channels and fake bank accounts, appropriate steps should be taken to prevent it. This may be difficult, if the example of the Jain Diaries be considered, as beneficiaries of such transactions, apart from the terrorists, cut across party lines.

Socio economic backwardness of the Muslims and of the Dalits has been one of the major causes of growth of terrorism in India whether of the *jihadi* or the Maoist variety. The long term solution for meeting the threat is to bring about a change in their condition through economic upliftment and spread of modern secular education. Finally, so far as Pakistan's role as an exporter of *jihadi* terrorism is concerned, particularly in the context of the Mumbai terror strike, India's response should be cautious. The Pakistan Government should be kept under international pressure to rein in the terrorists operating from Pakistani territory, and ultimately, to abolish the terrorist camps. The future of the India-Pakistan peace process – the composite dialogue and the people-to-people contacts built over the last few years-hinges on Pakistan's willingness and ability to do that. Political instabilities in India's neighbourhood will be a grave cause for concern for India's security-planners.

REFERENCES

1. Bary Buzan; *People, States and Fear: The National Security Problem in International Relations* (The University of North Carolina Press, 1983).
2. Bary Buzan; "A Framework for Regional Security Analysis" in B. Buzan, Gowher Rizvi *et al.* (ed.) *South Asian Security and the Great Powers* (Macmillan, London, 1986); Bary Buzan; "South-East Asian Security Complex" in *Contemporary Southeast Asia;* Vol. 10, No. 1 (1988); and Bary Buzan; "Third World Regional Security in Structural and Regional Perspective" in Brian L. Job (ed.) *The Insecurity Dilemma: National Security of Third World States* (Lynne Reiner, Boulder, Colorado, and London 1992).
3. Cited in *Human Development Report 2005: Aid, Trade and Security in an Unequal World* (Oxford University Press, New Delhi, 2005, p. 151.).
4. Mohammed Ayoob; "The Security Predicament of Third World States: Reflections on State Making on a Comparative Perspective" in Brian L. Job (ed.); *op. cit.*, p. 66.

5. For a discussion on the causes behind the separatist movements in the Punjab, Jammu and Kashmir and the North-East see, Nancy Jetly; "India: The Domestic Dimensions of Security" in Bary Buzan, Gowher Rizvi *et al.* (ed.). *op. cit.*; M.J. Akbar; *The Siege Within* (UBS Publishers Distributors, New Delhi, 1996), Arun Kumar Banerji; "Rethinking National Security", and Samir Das; "National Security and Ethnic Conflicts in India", in Arun Kumar Banerji (ed.). *Security Issues in South Asia: Domestic and External Sources of Threats to Security* (Minerva, Calcutta, 1998).
6. M.J. Akbar; *Kashmir Behind the Veil* (Viking, New Delhi, 1991) and M.J. Akbar; *The Siege Within.*
7. An illustrative example may be found in the report that an amount of Rs. 300,000 was being demanded from each recruit for recruitment to a new unit of the India Reserve Battalion, an armed State police constabulary. At this rate even the recruitment of a new battalion would involve a bribe booty of anything between Rs. 20-30 crores. See, Pradip Phanjoubam; "Who is feeding violence", *The Statesman* (Kolkata) the Northeast Page, 15 Sept., 2008.
8. See, Bibhuti Bhusan Nandy; "National Insecurity", *The Sunday Statesman,* 10 August, 2008, *The Sunday Statesman,* 27 July, 2008, and, 14 September, 2008; and *The Statesman* 30 November, 2008.
9. Shaukat Qadir; "The concept of International Terrorism: an Interim Study for South Asia ", *The Round Table* (London, Vol. 360, July 2001), p. 335.
10. *Ibid.* The point has also been discussed in Arun Kumar Banerji; "Radical Islam", *The Sunday Statesman* 4 January and *The Statesman* 5 January, 2009.
11. See, Saikat Datta and Smruti Koppikar; "The Marks on the Water", *The Outlook,* (New Delhi, 8 December, 2008), p. 43.
12. For further discussion on this, see, Arun Kumar Banerji; "Images and Obsessions: India and Pakistan" in Surjit Mansingh (ed.); *Indian and Chinese Foreign Policies in a Comparative Perspective* (Radiant Publishers in collaboration with the Nehru Memorial Museum and Library, New Delhi, 1998), especially pp. 300-303.
13. The point has been discussed in Sandy Gordon; *Muslims, Terrorism and Rise of The Hindu Rights in India* (Australian National University, Strategic and Defence Studies Centre, Canberra, 2004) http: // rspas.anv.edu.au/paper/sdsc/wp/wp-sdsc-389.pdf. p. 6.
14. Datta and Koppikar; *op. cit.*
15. Praful Bidwai; "Saffron Terror", *Outlook,* 8 December, 2008, p. 101.
16. *Ibid.*
17. *Ibid.*
18. *The Statesman,* 16 January, 2009.

19. Bidwai; *op. cit.* p. 102.
20. V. Venkatesan;" The Terror bogey", *The Frontline,* 21 November, 2009.
21. Cited in Rajinder Puri; "RSS and Terror", *The Statesman,* 5 December, 2009.
22. See Jayanta Kumar Ray *et al.*; "Informal Challenges to Security and Response" in Jayanta Kumar Ray (ed.); *Aspects of India's International Relations 1700 to 2000: South Asia and the World* (Pearson Longman in association with the Centre for Studies in Civilization, New Delhi, 2007), p. 501.
23. *The Statesman, Kolkata Plus* 21 March, 2009.
24. Sam Rajappa; "Red Corridor", *The Statesman,* 22 April, 2005.
25. *The Statesman, Kolkata Plus,* 4 March, 2009.
26. *The Statesman,* 27 March, 2009 and *The Statesman Kolkata Plus,* 23 March, 2009.
27. See the editorial "Khaleda Please Note" in *The Statesman,* 22 April, 2005.
28. Jayanta Kumar Ray *et al.; op. cit.,* p. 501.
29. Jayanta Kumar Ray *et al.; op. cit.,* p. 504.

2

Digging for Jihad : 'Mad Mullahs' Against the British in South Asia

A Glance Behind Today

Jyotirmoy Banerjee

Jihad in Indian History

India's history had long encountered *jihad* since the first Islamic forces entered Sindh in 712 CE and won its first victories after suffering a number of defeats for 78 years. Lands in Seistan, Khurasan, Transoxiana and Afghanistan where Hindu religion and culture had flourished for long, became subject to *jihad*. Names such as Muhammad bin Kasim (712-15 CE), Subuktigin (977-997 CE), his son Mahmud Ghaznavi (997-1030 CE), Muhammad Ghuri (1173-1206 CE), Alauddin Khilji (1296-1316 CE), Timur (1398-99 CE), and Babur (1519-1530 CE) adorn the path of *jihad* in India[1]. But these *jihadi* conquerors had directed their warlike talent against the native Hindus. The same *jihadi* spirit subsequently turned against the West. In this exposition we shall focus on the latter aspect.

Jihad against British Rule in South Asia

Although the 'Sepoy Mutiny' or 'The First War of Independence' of 1857 seems to be the first striking landmark of *jihad* in India's history of British rule, there were other, less publicized attempts in favour of Islamic revival and *jihad* against the British earlier. Imam Ahmad Ibn Hambal, the classical jurist, had sought to establish 'pure' Islam as practiced by the Prophet, his companions and their immediate followers. This was Salafism, a historical movement also called derisively Wahhabism[2].

In the 18th and 19th centuries several personalities in India sought to revive Salafism. Waliullah, the 18th.century scholar, resented the decline of Muslim rule and warned all sections of the people to mend their ways. Though he failed to arrest the decline, his ideological influence remained.

Sayyid Ahmad Shaheed (1786–1831)[3], a militant alumnus of madrassa-i-Rahamiyya, returned from pilgrimage to Mecca in 1824. He was credited with importing Wahhabism into India. He teamed up with Waliullah's grandson Shah Ismail Shaheed and launched a religio-political movement. Six years after his return from Arabia he went to the North-Western Frontier region of British India, reputed to be a Dar-ul-Islam or "domain of the faith" second only to Mecca and Medina, launched a *jihad* against the Sikhs in an attempt to reconquer Punjab for Islam and sought the help of Central Asian monarchs to fight British rule in India unitedly. His additional solicitations were directed against encroaching Christian influence and the 'un-Islamic' ways of the Mughal court. An Afghan betrayal enabled the Sikhs to put him to the sword the following year. But his *mujahedin* network continued underground, spread along trade routes of Peshawar, Ambala, Delhi, Patna and other *jihadi* centres.

A British raid in 1852 discovered highly seditious and inflammatory correspondence of certain hardline maulvis preaching *jihad* against British rule. It came as a surprise since the Wahhabis in India usually denied being Wahhabis. The central figure turned out to be Shaikh Husain Baksh, a prominent Punjabi trader in Delhi. He had close ties with some of the fanatical imams of the Madrassa-i-Ramaiyya. This was dubbed the 'Wahhabi conspiracy' in Delhi.[4] Fear and suspicion of the spread of Christianity under British tutelage, closure of madrassas[5] and proselytisation by missionaries led to the snowballing of Islamic orthodoxy. As Dalrymple observes:

The histories of Islamic fundamentalism and European imperialism have very often been closely, and dangerously, intertwined....The venom of one provides the lifeblood of the other."

The British-Indian army uprising of 1857 was one of the early landmark instances of *jihad* in modern times. Initially a majority of the rebel Indian troops—between 65-85 per cent of the sepoys in each regiment, according to William Dalrymple—were upper caste Hindus[6]. But as the uprising spread and progressed, the sepoys were joined by large numbers of freelance *jihadis*. According to several estimates, noted Dalrymple, the *jihadis* increased to at least half of the remaining resistance, and it was they who put up the stoutest resistance when the British finally assaulted Delhi on 14 September.

Historians have differed on their assessment of the causes of the uprising, though. Some like Karl Marx, Collier, Majumdar, Chaudhuri, and Malleson argued that the actions of soldiers at Meerut were the "last straw" for South Asians who had been victims of British cultural and class-based oppression and antagonism. They rejected the thesis that the religious factor played an overriding role in fomenting it. Others, however, stressed precisely religion as the key to the revolt. Reverend Alexander Duff even considered it a Muslim conspiracy in which Emperor Bahadur Shah's family, and Nawab of Oudh and his *wazir*, were the key players[7]. Palmer and Kaye in their respective works show the religious factor in a broader sociological perspective. They point to the increasing uncertainty in India about British policy gradually intruding into their socio-religious life.[8]

Dalrymple also stresses that the 20,000 rebel documents in Urdu and Persian which survive and which he had researched, refer time and again to the uprising as a war of religion. "There were no doubt a multitude of private grievances, but it is now unambiguously clear that the rebels saw themselves as fighting a war to preserve their religion, and articulated it as such", said he. Further, "the words *din* and *dharma* [the Urdu and Hindi words for religion] appear constantly in rebel proclamations, and were used as war cries by the combatants. They certainly appear far more regularly than secular declarations of the right to self-government or economic freedom, both of which are occasionally mentioned, but far less frequently than concerns over British intentions to impose Christianity on them."[9] Interestingly, today's frequent suicide bombings for religious cause also have a long history. There are references to suicide *jihadis* among the Ismaeli Assassins of Syria and Persia from the 11th Century onwards. There are clear and specific references among the Mutiny Papers to a regiment of *jihadis* arriving in Delhi from Gwalior who are described as "suicide ghazis" who had vowed never to eat again and to fight until they met death at the hands of the *kafirs* [infidels] "for those who have come to die have no need for food".[10]

To the question by BBC: "You say that the flag of *jihad* was raised in Delhi and the mosque [Jama Masjid] was at the centre of it. What was the reason for this "Islamist" uprising in Delhi?"

Dalrymple replied: "It was much the same as the motivation behind the rising of the sepoys: a distrust of British intention with regard to the imposition of Christian laws, education and religious practices. In addition, there were those who believed they were following the Quoranic injunction to turn the *Dar-ul-harb*, the Abode of War, back into what they believed should again be the *Dar ul-Islam*, the Abode of Islam."[11]

Jihad, paradoxically, might have conflagrated to an unexpected Hindu-Muslim civil war.

Emperor Zafar disapproved of flying the *jihadi* flag since that might offend the Hindus fighting against the British. To this Maulvi Muhammad Sayyid, a radical who had put it up, replied that the Hindus supported the British. Hindus present angrily denied the allegation. Zafar, like a true father figure, managed to keep the peace by observing that both Hindus and Muslims were equal in his eyes.

It would seem that Dalrymple's view that takes into consideration a multiplicity of causes but assigns religion as the most fundamental as well as immediate one is the best explanation for the outbreak of the uprising. After all, loading the new .303 Lee-Enfield rifle involved biting the end of the cartridge, which was greased in pig fat and beef tallow. Pig fat is a *haraam*, or forbidden substance to Muslims as both of these are for Hindus. This religious taboo acted as the trigger that set off a conflagration, the ground for which had been prepared by other factors of resentment against the British.

It may be noted here that the catholicity of outlook of the last Mughal emperor, in the true tradition of his famous forebear, Akbar, annoyed hard-core Sunni mullahs. They considered him practically a heretic. Zafar used to enjoy Sufi mysticism, celebrations of the Shia festival of Muharram and Hindu festivals of Ram Lila and Diwali as much as any Muslim occasions. The

Delhi ulama threatened to drop his name from their Friday prayers, thus delegitimising his claim to rule, if rumours that he had converted to Shiism proved true[12].

Also noteworthy is the fact that it was rich Punjabi Muslim traders who financed Delhi's radical *madrasas*, especially those who wanted to wage *jihad* against *kafirs* and to create an Islamic society "pruned of all its non-Islamic accretions."[13] Underground *jihadi* networks were activated from mid-May 1857 as the uprising progressed. The *mujahedin* were bound by their *bayat* (oath) to an *amir* (leader), a system which continues to this day[14].

The **Khilafat Movement** in India was another landmark event of *jihad* on and from Indian soil. Following the First World War the Ottoman Empire lay defeated along with Germany. Constantinople slipped under Allied occupation. While promising to preserve the status of the Ottoman emperor as the caliph, the Allies wrested huge chunks of territory from the empire under the Treaties of Versailles in 1919 and Sevres in 1920. The caliphate seemed endangered. The Muslim world was filled with outrage. As part of this emotion Indian Muslims launched the Khilafat Movement to protect the latter. Maulana Mohammad Ali Jouhar spent four years in prison for preaching resistance to the British and support for the caliphate. Muslim leaders such as Ali and his brother Maulana Shaukat Ali, Dr. Mukhtar Ahmed Ansari, Hasrat Mohani, Maulana Abul Kalam Azad and Dr. Hakim Ajmal Khan got together to form the All India Khilafat Committee. Their aim was to build political unity amongst Muslims and use their influence to protect the caliphate. In 1920, they published the *Khilafat Manifesto,* which called upon the British to protect the caliphate and Indian Muslims to unite and hold the British accountable for this purpose. In 1920 the Frontier *hijrat* took place, which was an exodus of Muslim peasants from the North-West Frontier Province (NWFP) on religious grounds. During the 1920's the NWFP saw Islamic mass activism when Islamic militant movements were at their peak.[15] The Congress Party, India's largest political party, joined with the Khilafat leaders. Gandhi grew personally close to Khilafat leaders like Dr. Ansari, Maulana Azad and Hakim Ajmal Khan. For some time the Khilafat-Congress Party alliance worked well. It spawned widespread but largely peaceful non-cooperation with the British and civil disobedience. Khilafat reinforced the non-cooperation movement of the Congress and its demand for *swaraj*. The British arrested the top leaders of both the movements.

However, Jinnah's Muslim League and the Hindu Mahasabha stayed aloof. The alliance weakened. Gandhi withdrew civil disobedience in 1922 over violence in Chauri Chaura; the Khilafat struggle lost its momentum as Muslims were divided between working for the Congress, the Khilafat cause and the Muslim League. In 1924 Kemal Ataturk sounded the death-knell. He abolished the caliphate altogether in Turkey and cleared the way for it to advance to the modern secular path.[16]

Generally, however, leaders of the Muslim community preferred to accept British rule since the 19th.century, barring a few sporadic flareups. A chief reason for this willing subordination to the British was probably their forebodings of a future 'independent' India dominated by the Hindus. Earlier, Sayyid Ahmad Barelvi and his followers in the early nineteenth century were prepared to wage a *jihadi* war against non-Muslim rule (specifically, the Sikh rule of the North-West). But by the mid-1860s Muslim religious leaders had started to reject such *jihad* against the British rule of India. After 1871, Sayyid Ahmad Barelvi's version of *jihad* petered out. Indian Muslim leaders opted for reconciliation and co-operation with the British government.[17]

The ulama issued various *fatwas* declaring it unlawful to fight a *jihad* against the British government of India. One *fatwa* was given by the *ulama* of northern India, and another by muftis of Makka. Mawlawi Karamat Ali of the Muhammadan Literary Society of Bengal announced:

> Now if any misguided wretch, owing to his perverse fortune, were to wage war against the ruling power of the country, British India, such war would be rightly pronounced rebellion, and rebellion is strongly forbidden by the Muhammadan law.... in case anyone would wage such war, the Muhammadan subjects would be bound to assist their ruler, and in conjunction with their rulers, to fight such rebels.[18]

This suited the British in India just fine.

As an Indian observer writes, "They manipulated the Islamist genie to retain control of the Indian sub-continent. From Sir Syed

Ahmed Khan to Salimullah Khan, the Nawab of Dhaka who gave a command performance in 1906 at Lord Minto's behest as one of the founders of the Muslim League, the object was to rètain India as a house divided, which the Countess Minto related with considerable relish in her diary."[19] In keeping up, even encouraging, the Hindu-Muslim divide the British succeeded famously. The very first resolution of the Inaugural Session of the Muslim League, held at Dhaka on December 30, 1906, declared the following:

> Resolved that this meeting, composed of Musalmans from all parts of India, assembled at Dacca, decide that a Political Association be formed, styled All-India Muslim League, for the furtherance of the following objects: (a) To promote, among the Musalmans of India, feelings of loyalty to the British Government, and to remove any misconception that may arise as to the intention of Government with regard to any of its measures[20].

This resolution was moved by Nawab Salimullah Bahadur of Dhaka, who made a speech explaining these objectives. The British worried over retaining control over Afghanistan's foreign policy and especially securing the North-Western frontier region, inhabited by the unruly wild tribes, from any influence of either Kabul or Moscow. A strongly felt related perception continuing from mid-19th century was that of threat of Russia's irredentism in the region[21]. Against that background the nawab went on to reassure his masters:

> The Government has been convinced of our steadfast loyalty under the most trying situations. In 1897, Lord Elgin bore testimony to the unflinching fidelity of the Mohammedan troops that opposed their own co-religionists on the battle-fields of Chitral and the borderland....[W]e have risen so much in the estimation of our rulers, that leading statesmen of England call us the forces of loyalty in India and one of the greatest assets of the Empire, some portion of which has been won with our own support, and the whole of which we are guarding today. It is no more necessary to waste whole regiments

> in the interior in order to guard against an imaginary danger of rebellion, and the Commander-in-Chief can set free with a light heart the major portion of our army for guarding the frontier of the Empire.[22]

In 1872, W. W. Hunter, a British scholar and civil servant in India published a historic book entitled *The Indian Musalmans*[23]. The book summed up the views of various sects of Islam on the question of whether Muslims were duty-bound by their religion to wage a war-like *jihad* against the British Government of India.

On the Shiah sect, Hunter wrote:

> Their present declaration of the non-obligation to rebel is spontaneous, and it is well that such a declaration has been put on record. It comes to us stamped with the highest authority which the Shias can give to any document, and will be permanently binding on the whole sect. (p. 121)

Regarding the Sunni Hanafis, the majority sect, he observed:

> I now pass to the Formal Decisions of the greater sect. The Sunnis, as they are the most numerous class of Indian Musalmans, so they have of late been the most conspicuous in proclaiming that they are under no religious obligation to wage war against the Queen. To that end they have procured two distinct sets of Legal Decisions, and the Muhammadan Literary Society of Calcutta has summed up the whole Sunni view of the question in a forcibly written pamphlet...
>
> The Law Doctors of Northern Hindustan set out by tacitly assuming that India is a Country of the Enemy (Dar-ul-Harb), and deduce therefrom that religious rebellion is uncalled for. The Calcutta Doctors declare India to be a Country of Islam (Dar-ul-Islam), and conclude that religious rebellion is therefore unlawful. (p. 122)

Jihad in the North-Western Frontier Region

However, the British were fully aware of the potential for volatility of their Islamic troops, be they recruited from Egypt or from India.

The risk at times made its presence felt when these troops were deployed against fellow Muslims, e.g., against the Ottoman Turks during the First World War or in the three wars against Afghanistan (1839-1842, 1878-1881 and 1919)[24]. Fortunately for the British, ethnic, regional and other differences also played a role which prevented unity on the basis of religion alone. Arab nationalism and Ottoman decay prevented the Turks and the Arabs from presenting a common cause based on religion alone. In the Afghan case, there was more of traditional Afghan resentment of foreign interference, territorial dispute and other factors that led to the wars rather than purely Islamic considerations. British sensitivity was seen on 11 December, 1917 when their Egypt expeditionary force overcame the beleaguered Turkish defenders of Jerusalem. General Sir Edmund Allenby, the British commander, took care to approach the Jaffa Gate on the West Wall on foot as a mark of respect for the holy city[25]. The British and Imperial forces included Indian Muslim sepoys who shared the faith of the Ottoman army. The British had conducted operations against dervish rebels in British Somaliland in 1913[26]. After a failed mutiny in the Far East in 1915, the Muslim troops were deemed highly susceptible to the pan-Islamic propaganda of the Central Powers. Allenby, therefore, took care not to offend their sentiments by invoking a Christian victory and the capture of the holy city which had been under Muslim rule for nearly a millennium.[27]

It should be noted that since 1857 the British had tried to forestall disaffection in the North-Western Frontier by recruiting units from a variety of tribes but seldom from the immediate locality. In the Afghan border region, particularly Waziristan, the local tribes,[28] the truculent Wazirs and Mahsuds, were more dangerous than the Afridis. We shall see more of them presently. There were intermittent uprisings against the British in the frontier region, apart from the three regular wars fought between the armies of British India and Afghanistan, which resulted from Afghanistan's precarious status of a buffer state sandwiched between the two expanding empires of the 19th century, the British and the Russian, not counting Persian territorial designs[29]. The Ahkund of Swat, a cowherd-turned-saint from the Indus region, became both the temporal as well as the spiritual authority of Swat when its king died. In 1863 he preached *jihad* against the British, and headed the Swatis and Bunerwals in the Ambeyla campaign. Defeat led to his subsequent befriending of the British, however.[30]

Mullahs and Jihad

Waziristan[31]

> When you're wounded and left on Afghanistan's plains,
> And the women come out to cut up what remains,
> Jest roll to your rifle and blow out your brains
> An' go to your Gawd like a soldier. (Rudyard Kipling, "THE YOUNG BRITISH SOLDIER"}

Hamid Hussein gives a vivid and insightful description of Waziristan, its topography, tribes and culture. Perhaps the most dangerous area within the North-Western Frontier region, it continues to challenge US/NATO forces across the border in Afghanistan as it had done to the British and then the Soviets in the past. Baitullah Mehsud, Pakistan's dreaded Taliban leader, the head of a coalition of smaller pro-Taliban groups who reportedly commands several thousand followers and is said to have been behind Benazir Bhutto's assassination, hails from Waziristan. He openly celebrated his second marriage in his mountain fastness in October 2008.[32]

The land is totally barren and only small tracts are suitable for subsistence agriculture. For centuries the survival of the tribes of the area depended on raids on caravans passing through their area (the nomad tribes of Afghanistan used two passes; Tochi and Gomal in Waziristan territory) and looting raids of villages and towns of the plains. This was their main source of income and there was no stigma attached to this activity. In fact a successful raid on a caravan or robbing adventure was the desirable trait and much praised. In the past, such harsh conditions had not allowed any significant increase in the population. The Pathan hill tribes complained that the British, by pushing their control closer and closer to their areas, cut them off from their traditional recourse to raiding in the fertile valleys running down to the river Indus in the administered districts, which were populated mostly by the people who spoke the same language—Pashto (Pukhtu). Because of poverty in the hills their only choice was to carry out raids or to starve. Following the established practices of the Mughal and Afghan governments, the British first satisfied themselves by paying allowances in cash to the tribal *maliks*. Theoretically, these were paid for services rendered, such as road and camp protection by the local tribal levies called *khassadars*.

Among all the Pushtun tribes on frontier region, the inhabitants of Waziristan are fiercely independent to the verge of anarchy, to the extent that sometimes their own tribal chiefs have limited influence over them. The main tribes inhabiting the region are Wazir (also called Darwesh Khel Wazir), Mahsud, Bhittani and Dawar.

The strength of tribes in Waziristan lies in the inaccessibility of their area. The tribesmen used this to their full advantage. The Pathan tribes also actively relied on their cult of *pakhtunwali*, i.e., traditional values including full protection of guest and seeking revenge (*badal*) by killing if injustice was done.

The People

Wazirs

Like other Pushtun tribes, Wazirs are subdivided in clans and sub-clans. The two major clans of Wazirs are Ahmadzai (living around Wana and Shakai) and Utmanzai (living in Tochi valley and Shawal). Both clans are further subdivided into sub-clans.

Mahsuds

Mahsuds are divided into three main clans; Bahlolzai, Alizai and Shaman Khel. The two main centres of Mahsud concentration during British time were Kaniguram and Makin. The Mahsuds controlled two main passes of the area; Gomal Pass and Tank Zam which was the main route used by nomadic powindahs. Raiding of these caravans provided Mahsuds a lucrative source of income. Regular raiding and plunder attacks of Mahsuds on settled villages irritated British administrators since the 1850s following the acquisition of Punjab in 1849.

The area remained no man's land until the 1893 treaty with Afghanistan negotiated by Sir Mortimer Durand. Waziristan with the exception of Birmal came under British sphere of influence.

The demarcation of boundary was resisted by Wazirs resulting in armed conflicts.

The wild, unruly tribal regions straddling the British-Indian and Afghan border posed a special problem to British India's 'Forward Policy' [33] that was pursued especially since 1876.[34] Part of that policy was building and consolidation of a strategic road that led through the tribal areas, to control the state of Chitral for the sake of that road and also to control key mountain passes of the Hindukush. Overall, the objective was to hold the frontier along Gilgit, Chitral, Jelalabad and Kandahar. Its other objective was to shift from a purely reactive, defensive policy of resisting periodic raids on the plains of India by the mountain tribes to a policy of punitive expeditions, also known as 'butcher and bolt' policy. It seems US/NATO-led ISAF forces have been repeating the same after over a century in Pakistan's west and especially in 2008, though operating from the 'other' side (Afghanistan). Incidentally, though there had been some talk of a 'full steam ahead' policy favoured by the military then, the problem, a "crushing" one (Churchill), was that there simply was not enough manpower, money and material available.[35] Current US/Western debates also complain of the lack of these resources, especially with the US fighting its 'war on terror' simultaneously in Iraq and Afghanistan.

But the tribes did not like the idea of a road. As British intelligence agent Achmed Abdullah so graphically analyzed in a report[36]:

> *For [road] meant British patrols clattering up and down. It meant an end to old days, the free, lusty, rowdy days...It meant the King-Emperor's law running its sharp, pitiless way—and not, as heretofore, the law running the other way, running like a startled rabbit, with the laughing, yelling tribesmen at its heels. So the latter offered resistance to our survey parties and armed forces. ... We tried to parley. We offered them work; offered them financial subsidies. But an Afghan would sooner make five dollars by robbery and by other strong-thewed, lawless violent methods than fifty by legitimate toil. The reason! I have an idea he likes the exciting, dramatic uncertainty of the former way.*

Abdullah adds that the tribes had such a reputation it was

said that even "Satan himself never goes there, for fear that someone might steal his horns and red-hot pitchfork."[37]

The 'punitive expeditions' were a time-honoured custom in this region. Babur's memoirs mention his retaliatory sally against the Khizr-khaili Afghans in October 1519 for sniping at his troops[38].

The 'punitive expeditions' sometimes rebounded. The British misery faced at the Battle of Maiwand in July 1880 was one such case. The horror of fighting in conditions where both men and nature were mercilessly hostile emerges from the following narration:

"Advance to Contact Narrative of Captain Mosley Mayne, commanding a squadron of the 3rd Bombay Cavalry:

"Even by nine in the morning the heat had become intense. It was to become hotter still, with the temperature reaching over 120 degrees in the shade, had there been any. ..."

These punitive expeditions infuriated the tribes and provided religio-ideological fuel for the mullahs.

As Churchill astutely summed up the results of British intrusions:

> But a single class had viewed with quick intelligence and intense hostility the approach of the British power. The priesthood of the Afghan border instantly recognised the full meaning of the Chitral road. The cause of their antagonism is not hard to discern. Contact with *civilisation assails the ignorance, and credulity, on which the wealth* and influence of the Mullah depend. A general combination of the religious forces of India against that civilising, educating rule, which unconsciously saps the strength of superstition, is one of the dangers of the future. Here Mahommedanism was threatened and resisted. A vast, but silent agitation was begun. Messengers passed to and fro among the tribes. Whispers of war, a holy war, were breathed to a race intensely passionate and fanatical. Vast and mysterious agencies, the force of which is incomprehensible to rational minds, were employed. More astute brains than the wild valleys of the North produce conducted the preparations. Secret encouragement came from the South—from India *itself. Actual support and assistance was given from Cabul.*[39]

> The tribes' motivation also stemmed from their fundamental moral codes of Pukhtunwali, and Badal in settling old disputes. And retaliate they did. The Pathan hill tribes simply wanted to retain their age-old custom of plundering periodically the fertile plains. The British, by pushing their control closer and closer to their areas, cut them off from their traditional recourse to raiding the Indus river basin in the administered districts, which were populated mostly by the people who spoke the same language, i.e., Pashto.

Added fuel to fire was the artificially drawn Durand Line (1,519 miles or 2,445 km long) in 1893 which marked the British-India-Afghanistan border but split the resenting Pashtun tribes into Afghan and British Indian halves. This demarcation later gave rise to the North-Western Frontier Province of British India in 1901, which hitherto was a part of Punjab[40].

A contemporary news report on the tribal behaviour also offers highly interesting insights into the functioning of the mullahs, the credulity of the tribesmen and religious fanaticism[41]:

> "Latest Intelligence Rising in the Swat Valley
> (From our correspondents)
> Simla, July 27 [1897]

"Yet another proof has been given of the wave of fanaticism which is sweeping along the North-West Frontier of India. Malakand was the scene last night of some sharp fighting, a sudden tribal rising in the Swat Valley taking place during the day. The story is a curious one, as showing how quickly tribesmen can gather and how readily they respond to an appeal to their fanaticism.

Since the Chitral campaign came to an end the Swat Valley has been perfectly peaceful. The trade with Bajaur and the neighbouring countries has developed considerably, and the Swatis generally have been contented. The Chitral road has been kept open by tribal levies, and no signs of disaffection have ever been apparent. The sons of the late Akhund of Swat have, it is true, tried to excite fanaticism, but hitherto unsuccessfully.

Yesterday, without the least warning, the attitude of the population in the Lower Swat Valley underwent a sudden change.

"The first news which reached Malakand was that a disturbance had taken place at Thana, near Chakdara bridge. A few hours later further news was received that the 'mad Mullah,' a priest who is apparently well known locally, had gathered about him a number of armed men with the view of raising a *jehad*. In the evening it was reported that he was advancing down the valley towards Malakand. Preparations were made to send out a column early the next morning and disperse the gathering. The tribal levies, who fled as the Mullah advanced, reported that Malakand itself would be attacked at 3 a.m. The camp was, consequently, on the alert, but the attack was delivered at half-past 10 that night—a very unusual hour for Pathans to attempt a surprise."

After suffering casualties the British at daybreak sent out a column to reconnoitre towards Chakdara and pursue the enemy. "It was then discovered that the whole valley was up in arms, and it was impossible to open communication with the Chakdara post. The tribesmen were plainly not disheartened by the failure of their night attack, but were prepared to renew hostilities."

It should be noted here that the Chakdara post was held to be impregnable against any force not armed with artillery. It was well provisioned, and the small body of troops had plenty of ammunition. It was nine miles from Malakand, on the further bank of the Swat river, and commanded the vulnerable suspension bridge. Malakand, had a well-fortified position. It was key to keeping the Swat Valley clear relieve Chakdara."

The insight part comes next:

"The Events of 1897 and Their Explanation

"The frontier disturbances that Churchill took such pains to witness began where local political authorities least expected trouble and were initiated by an unlikely antagonist. For some months, British officials had been reporting improved relations with the local people of the Swat valley, and after several years of intermittent hostility, it finally appeared that calm had settled on the region. The postal service now delivered mail to and from the valley, and a medical dispensary located alongside the Chakdara fort was treating patients from the neighbouring communities. Most telling of all perhaps, British officers found that they could ride about freely among the fierce hill men" and were even being "invited to settle many disputes, which would formerly have been left to armed force".

In early July, however, the first hints of disaffection began to appear. The native markets were abuzz with rumours that "great events were impending." At the centre of these reports was an obscure *faqir* and sometime malcontent named Saidullah, whom the British authorities henceforth referred to as the "Mad Faqir of Swat". A native of the region who long before had abandoned his family and home to become a religious mendicant, Saidullah had begun making declarations of an impending holy war in which he would be aided by supernatural forces. A crowd had gathered to hear him, and as it swelled his rhetoric became more inflamed until finally, on the afternoon of July 26, he had set off to attack the British garrisons at Chakdara and Malakand.

Followed at first by only a few of his fellow mendicants and a handful of teenage boys, Saidullah attracted new adherents in each village he passed, gathering some five thousand by the time he reached the fort at Chakdara, located at the confluence of the Panjkora and Swat Rivers, just north of the Malakand Pass that linked the tribal territories with the Peshawar plains to the south. Although their weaponry consisted mostly of primitive flintlocks, swords, and staves, the followers of the Faqir mounted an assault that lasted four days and might have led to the capture of the Chakdara garrison had it not been for the arrival of General Blood's relief column on the first day of August.

Saidullah was variously known as "Mullah Mastun", lewanai faqir or lewanai [God-intoxicated] in Pashto, and by the British as "The Great Faqir" or "Mad Faqir", "Mad Faqir of Swat" or the "Mad Mullah". He declared a *jihad* against the occupying British Empire and led from 10,000 to 100,000 Pashtun tribesmen in the uprising.

The siege of the British garrison in the Malakand region began on 26 July, 1897 and lasted till 2 August. Fighting continued even after that date, though. The British faced a force of Pashtun tribesmen whose tribal lands had been bisected by the Durand Line. What is remarkable is that again this was a mullah-instigated *jihad*. Although the tribal revolt was put down after tough battles, the *esprit* of these tribesmen drew the awe of Western observers, including Churchill:

The strange treachery at Maizar in June was a flash in the pan. Still no one saw the danger. It was not until the early days of July that it was noticed that there was a fanatical movement in Upper Swat. Even then its significance was disregarded and its importance underrated. That a Mad Faqir had arrived was known. His power was still a secret. It did not long remain so.

Churchill, who was an eyewitness and war correspondent, comments on jihadists[42]:

It is, thank heaven, difficult if not impossible for the modern European to fully appreciate the force which fanaticism exercises among an ignorant, warlike and Oriental population. Several generations have elapsed since the nations of the West have drawn the sword in religious controversy... But the Mahommedan religion increases, instead of lessening, the fury of intolerance. It was originally propagated by the sword, and ever since, its votaries have been subject, above the people of all other creeds, to this form of madness. In a moment the fruits of patient toil, the prospects of material prosperity, the fear of death itself, are flung aside. The more emotional Pathans are powerless to resist. All rational considerations are forgotten. Seizing their weapons, they become Ghazis—as dangerous and as sensible as mad dogs: fit only to be treated as such. While the more generous spirits among the tribesmen become convulsed in an ecstasy of religious bloodthirstiness, poorer and more material souls derive additional impulses from the influence of others, the hopes of plunder and the joy of fighting. Thus whole nations are roused to arms.... In each case civilisation is confronted with militant Mahommedanism. The forces of progress clash with those of reaction. The religion of blood and war is face to face with that of peace. Luckily the religion of peace is usually the better armed.

The extraordinary credulity of the people is hardly conceivable. The Mad Mullah worked miracles. ...

British-Indian soldiers at Malakand were confronted by "wave after wave of close-packed tribesmen, flooding out of the darkness and screaming while their war drums thundered". Reports at the time said that the "disciplined musketry" of the Indian sepoys caused heavy casualties. But "even after the fighting—when the tribesmen reeled back from the terrible army they had assailed, leaving a quarter of their number on the field—the faith of the survivors was unshaken. Only those who had doubted had perished, said the Mullah, and displayed a bruise which was, he informed them, the sole effect of a twelve-pound shrapnel shell on his sacred person."

Perusal of Afghan narratives, however, affords a different view. One is strongly impressed with the respect shown to scholar-turned-soldier leaders, so deprecatingly dismissed in Western reportage as 'mad mullahs' or 'faqirs' and the ardent striving for independence.

Experience had shown that while the tribes were tough on their home ground, they were unable to make common cause among themselves or to coordinate their actions with others outside their home territory. Such was the received wisdom. But in 1897, these notoriously fractious tribes acted differently. They mounted coordinated assaults on well-fortified garrisons and demonstrated a degree of organization unprecedented in the history of British rule in India. And it also appeared that the decision to initiate the attacks had been influenced by external factors of the sort to which the frontier tribes had previously been oblivious. These factors included Afghan amir, Abdur Rahman, actively getting involved in frontier affairs—inviting delegations of tribal elders to meetings in Kabul, keeping large numbers of troops near the border and distributing pamphlets in the tribal areas on the proper conduct of *jihad*. A recent victory by the Ottoman Turks over a Greek army had raised hopes of an impending Islamic revival. Further, news of the seizure of Aden and the Suez Canal had likewise encouraged the belief that Great Britain would soon lose its ability to secure troop reinforcements from Europe.

In explaining the sudden spread of such rumours, Churchill assigned blame to one group in particular—the mullahs. It was their vitriolic preaching that had made the tribes aware of distant worlds, their slanders that had magnified British problems in other lands, and their incitement that had produced "a 'boom' in Mohammedanism" in the remote villages up and down the frontier."

No sooner had this uprising subsided than other, equally serious tribal risings broke out in nearby areas along the frontier from the Kohat district in the southwest (where the Orakzais and neighbouring tribes attacked a British base on the Samana Ridge) to the Tirah and Khyber districts, directly west of Peshawar (where Afridi and Shinwari tribes attacked British posts protecting the strategically vital Khyber Pass), to the Mohmand territory (where a force of Mohmand, Mahmund, and other cross-border tribes attacked the British fort at Shabqader and the neighbouring market at Shankargar, just nineteen miles from Peshawar itself). Although none of these attacks ultimately succeeded in dislodging any of the British garrisons in the region, the simultaneous appearance of so many attacks was worrisome to the British administration."

Since the Mutiny of 1857, India had been free of widespread insurrection, but the passage of time and the relative peace had failed to assuage the fear inspired by that episode. During the uprising a mitigating factor for the British had been that the frontier tribes had failed to join the general rebellion. But they were a constant source of headache for the Raj alright, especially when the latter switched to the more aggressive Forward Policy during the reign of Prime Minister Disraeli in England and his Viceroy Lord Lytton in India in the 1870s. During the second Afghan War of 1878-80 Mullah Adkar in Kadam in Khost tried to encourage the Wazirs to attack British convoys. But the British had already made an arrangement with the Wazirs. So there was no major unrest. Then in 1894 Mullah Powindah of the Shabi Khel sub-clan of Alizai clan of Mahsud emerged on the scene of the Waziristan. He took refuge in the village of Idak in Lower Dawar. Powindah became disciple of Mullah Gulab Din. Following the latter's death he became prominent and took the title of 'Badshah-e-Taliban' (King of the religious students). He then settled in Mahsud country near Makin. He made his own zone of influence independent of traditional *maliks*. This brought him into conflict with them. In addition, he got financial support from Kabul (his patron was Amir's brother Nasrullah Khan). The Mullah was a source of irritation for the British authorities until his death in 1913.[43]

Saidullah was surrounded by "crafty politicians", anxious to "seize the opportunity and fan the flame". According to Churchill, these were the masterminds behind the plot of insurrection, and foremost among their number was none other than the Mullah of Hadda.

"In the heart of the wild and dismal mountain region in which these fierce tribesmen dwell, are the temple and village of Jarobi, the one a consecrated hovel, the other a fortified slum. This obscure and undisturbed retreat was the residence of a priest of great age and of peculiar holiness, known to fame as the Hadda Mullah. His name is Najim-ud-Din."[44] Hadda Sahib was connected to an extensive network of support and identification through the *tariqat*[45] system, which provided him with an organizational structure that was unique in the area.

The British report indicates that the Mad Faqir's attack was a classic example of a charismatic leader mobilizing people toward millenarian objectives. Thus religious frenzy was unleashed with the appearance of a leader promising to reclaim a lost glory by defeating a foreign power that is perceived to be responsible for contemporary corruption. There were also promises of supernatural support, including immunity from the effects of the enemy's weapons for all those who support the leader, and a general lack of concern for the practical needs of the movement. Strong and pervasive belief in the imminent victory to the neglect of logistical concerns prevailed. There was also the belief that a mythical plan is about to be realized in the domain of real events and that those who would participate in the fulfilment of that plan would themselves attain an appropriate reward.

The British time and again had to encounter serious uprisings in Waziristan, for instance, in 1915, 1917, 1919, 1937 and even after the end of World War II, in 1946. Despatches of the Commander-in-Chief, Army Headquarters to the Secretary to the Government of India, Army Department are full of reports of mullahs working up tribal frenzy and attacking British positions[46]. For example, "On 15 August 1915 information was received that a certain mullah, known as the Haji Sahib of Turangzai, was in the Ambela Pass with several thousand men, preparing to invade British territory. His gathering included a number of the Hindustani Fanatics, a sect inhabiting the Buner border country...."

Again, "information was received that on August 20th, a tribal gathering of some fifteen to twenty thousand men under the Sandaki Mullah was advancing down the left bank of the Swat River to invade Lower Swat."

"Meanwhile, during August [1915] there had been, some talk of *jihad* on the Mohmand border[47], where various religious leaders had been active, and large tribal gatherings led by these fanatical mullahs were reported to have collected on August 28th." When hostilities started on the morrow, "the enemy resisted stoutly, and displayed great bravery, tenaciously holding on to their sangars, but were defeated with heavy loss and driven from their position."

"Between September 20th and 24th further hostile gatherings were reported on this border, and the Mullahs made great efforts to stir up their followers to invade British territory....Early in October *lashkars*, numbering some 9,000 men, again collected in the neighbourhood of Hafiz Kor."

As reports continued:[48]

"The British authorities knew better than to underestimate the menace of a tribal *jihad*."[49] In 1896, in this very region the 'Mad Bareheaded Mullah', a faqir from Kabul, had stirred up the countryside to revolt. He assured the tribes that he was sent from Heaven to oust the infidel out of the hills and hurl him and his armies back into the plains of the Punjab. He claimed to command a large army concealed in the hills, men fed with food from Heaven. He did not want other men to assist him, he declared. That was not necessary. He himself could go single-handed, if need be, against the Infidel, for even though he went alone there would be armies of angels of Heaven on either side of him, making him invulnerable and invincible. "In scores of hillside villages he preached his message, and soon crowds of tribesmen rallied around him. He promised them plunder such as they had never dreamed of, loot in abundance and undying bliss after. He worked the people up to such a state that he brought about a great rising, in which the Mohmands fought against British forces with almost incredible fanaticism. Peasant boys with stones rushed against our fine Indian infantry; men with sticks tried to fight troops with modern rifles, confident that Heaven was with them. The whole country-side was ablaze..."

The fighting zeal of the nujaheedins is revealed in the following depiction[50]:

Maulvi Muhammad Ali Kasoori narrates that when fighters would start their attack, the Mujahideen would take the cover of mountains, caves and large rocks and as soon as they would pass by, they would immediately proceed further and attack the ground troops.

At Shabqadar fort, the English had installed better canyons [*sic*] that would fire simultaneously. The Barrack in which Haji Sahib Turangzai had taken refuge was struck by cannon fire at least 72 times and the blast would shake the whole ground and walls on each impact. But thanks to the Blessings of Allah, no one suffered major injuries.

Qasoori Sahib narrates in his own words:

"We couldn't find anything to eat in those 72 hours apart from drinking water. Neither would anything go down our throats due to intensity of battle. Despite this, such was the valour of *Jehad* that neither of us felt sleep taking over neither us nor tiredness. After 3 days and 3 nights of continuous assaults, we succeeded in evicting the British out of the fort. As soon as they backed out, our Mujahideen scaled the walls of the fort to lay their hands on the war booty. Like this, hundreds of rifles and thousands of ammunition and their sophisticated cannons came into our possession.

As soon as the fighting was over, local women came out singing pashto battle songs with their daf and dhols. I still can't forget that sight and the sight of such brave women kept me thinking that no matter how much this nation prides itself in its bright future, it will not be enough. They deserve a lot more than just pride.

The women came into the battlefield and turned over the bodies of their martyred sons of Islam and started to inspect their bodies. ...The reason why they inspected the bodies was to make sure that none of the fighters caught a bullet in his back. As this would mean that they were shot while running away. The women then praised Allah that all of them caught their martyrdom from Bullets that struck them on their chests.

A mother would kiss the forehead of her *shaheed* son, [a] sister would cry out of happiness over her *shaheed* brother and the wives would hug their *shaheed* husbands.

They would sing in pashto to their beloved that goes, "we have handed you over to Allah. Because you are a *shaheed,* go and enjoy Jannah. But do not forget us for Allah's sake. Ask Allah that we are also of help in Allah's cause and also ask Allah that he give the ability to your brothers as well that they follow in your footsteps."

It may be added that these ladies were also experts in mutilating the bodies of the dead or dying enemy in a "rather unpleasant way".[51] Hence, surrender for a British (Indian) soldier was no option.

A young British army officer, Francis Stockdale, who was deployed to the Waziristan area of British India in 1919, describes Tank, one of the main towns close by, as being "the worst station in British India". It was known as 'Hell's door knocker' because of both its scorching summer heat as well as an area "where hostile tribesman waited, watched and pounced." The title of his book, *Walk Warily in Waziristan*[52] seems no less appropriate now than it did nearly a century ago, because today the autonomous Pakistani tribal region of North and South Waziristan is the centre of militancy orchestrated by pro-Taleban and al-Qaeda militants.

All this was an unwelcome distraction while World War I was raging in Europe and the Middle East. Indeed, as a dispatch from the Indian Army Commander-in-Chief in 1918, General Sir Charles Carmichael Monro, noted under point 5: "The necessity for the dispatch of large drafts of officers and men overseas to replace wastage in the units fighting in France, Gallipoli, Egypt, Mesopotamia, East Africa, and the Gameroons [*sic*], caused a very heavy strain on the Indian Army."[53] This refrain is repeated under the next two points.

On 3rd May, 1919 an Afghan army appeared in the Khyber Pass and occupied the spring that supplied water to the British frontier post at Bagh, near Landi Kotal. That was bad news for the British who were caught in the midst of post-war demobilization. The British had only two companies of the Khyber Rifles; the famed Scouts (militia recruited from the Afridi tribe) deployed there, which they evacuated. While the British managed to defeat the invading Afghan army shortly, the ensuing tribal rising again in Waziristan "was a far more difficult proposition."[54] The major Pathan tribes in the Khyber were the Afridis and the Orakzais who were on the offensive. The revolt by their kin induced the Khyber Rifles to desert the British *en masse*; some joined their Afghan brethren[55]. Probably an element of religious unity was also present in this apparently ethnic empathy. The Afghan army was ill-equipped and numerically inferior, but the tribes on both sides of the border posed a greater challenge with their zeal for fighting foreigners and their intimate knowledge of the terrain. Pashtun members of the Khyber Rifles were reluctant to fight their ethnic brothers. Six hundred of the 700-man forces chose to be discharged! So the entire unit had to be disbanded![56]

The British Indian troops, whose standards of mountain warfare had reportedly fallen compared to earlier times, now faced many of the deserters who had joined their revolting tribal brethren and were experienced in British ways of tactics. The militant tribes were also far better armed with latest rifles—'arms of precision'.[57] Quite like the picture today in militant attacks taking place in Iraq and Afghanistan against intruding Western forces, the then latest weapons, especially rifles, found *en masse* their way to the hands of the tribes by a variety of means.[58]They gave the British army a harrowing time and inflicted severe casualties upon the Derajat Column. In mid-December 1919 "Imperial troops were nearly defeated at Palosina by well-armed and trained Mahsud and Wazir *lashkar* [army], whose ranks included a significant number of ex-servicemen."[59]

As David B. Edwards concluded: "Despite their superiority in weapons and organization, the British found permanent occupation of the tribal territories to be impractical and, in the final analysis, impossible."[60]

Faqir of IPI

Just before the outbreak of World War II yet another figure appeared on the North-Western horizon of the British Indian Empire. This was Mirza Ali Khan (1897—April 16, 1960) of the family of Mada Khel Wazirs. A labour at Public Works Department, he was pupil of Mullah Alam Khan of the village of Ipi. He was also fiercely hostile towards the British.[61]

What triggered his appearance was a little incident in February 1937. A Hindu girl of 15 from Bannu district eloped with a Pathan tribal youth, a school teacher. They fled to Waziristan. The girl embraced Islam, took the name of Islam Bibi. They then married. The occasion had the blessing of the local *jirga* or assembly. But British authorities intervened. They wanted to undo the marriage, especially in view of the girl' being a minor. Islam Bibi and her parents were whisked away into the interiors of Punjab before a final hearing of both sides could be heard by the local *jirga*. This was taken as an unforgivable insult to the tribal elders. The tribesmen, enraged with the British authorities, mustered two large lashkars 10,000 strong and battled the Bannu brigade, with heavy casualties on both sides. Widespread lawlessness erupted as tribesmen blocked roads, overran outposts and ambushed convoys. The Faqir of Ipi sent out impassioned calls for an all-out *jihad* against the British. "Islam Bibi had set the whole tribal territory on fire."[62] With his call for *jihad* over the Islam Bibi case the Faqir started a campaign to foment insurrection throughout north and south Waziristan, already notorious for defying British 'law and order'.

"By March 1937 many tribes from across the border had drifted into Waziristan in response to the Faqir's call to wreak vengeance upon the British. The situation became critical when the lashkars surrounded the government forces at Miranshah and Mir Ali forts, threatening the very presence of the British in the NWFP. The army was brought to a regular war footing. Two Royal Air Force (RAF) squadrons from Risalpur and Kohat were ordered to bomb and strafe the lashkars in order to break the siege of these forts."[63]

To the British, the Faqir remained elusive, somewhat of a precursor of Osama bin Laden reportedly based in the same rugged region. He was constantly on the move over the rugged but familiar terrain, in which a modern army with its cumbersome equipment and long supply lines proved all too slow and inefficient. The elusive Faqir earned himself the nickname "*The Scarlet Pimpernel of Waziristan*". Although his tactical moves still remained entirely unpredictable, he pursued his major political aim with single-minded determination: stirring up the maximum trouble for British authorities, forcing them thereby to withdraw beyond the administered border. Soon, a number of Waziri mullahs were to demand a complete British evacuation of Waziristan. As Hauner observes, "India's Northern Command, despite substantial numbers of troops at their disposal, must have felt frustrated by their inability to design any coherent pattern of operation against the Faqir."[64] The 1937 campaign was soon bogged down and fragmented into numerous separate operations. The Faqir remained intact.

There is also appearance of another holy man, this time from Syria called Muhammad Saadi al Keilani or the Shami Pir. In January 1938 he entered NWFP and moved further to Southern Waziristan in March. He did his best to unite the Wazirs and Mahsuds. He gained a very large following and was deeply revered as a saintly person like his counterpart the Faqir of Ipi in the northern half of Waziristan. The Pir then openly preached revolt at a *jirga* in June against the ruling king Zahir Shah in favour of Amanullah in Kabul. South Waziristan was electrified. The tribesmen, predominantly Mahsuds, rallied around him. Within days he was on his way leading an army of tribals to Kabul. "It was only with the most determined use of force combined with cajolery", wrote Sir Olaf Caroe, "that the Government of India were able to secure the Pir's surrender and removal, and the break-up of lashkars already on their way to Kabul".[65]

While the British managed to solve the problem posed by the Pir, they singularly ran out of luck with the Faqir. The fame of the Ipi's miraculous powers spread quickly. He attracted a large number of followers. British intelligence sources tried to track down the Faqir himself. They found him hiding in a Mahsud village in the Shaktu river valley. Reminiscent of recent US Drone attacks on alleged Taliban/al Qaeda mountain fastnesses in the same region[66], air attacks were initiated to bomb his hideout, but in vain. The Faqir had moved into the safety of a cave nearby. He was to hide for the rest of his life among the Madda Khel Wazirs. They continued to shelter him despite British reprisals. He occupied inaccessible caves in the mountain cliff at Gorwekht, barely a mile from the Afghan territory into which he could easily slip should the British ever attempt to dislodge him from his eagle's nest. During World War II the Germans and even India's Netaji Subhas Chandra Bose took up contact with him with a view to encouraging a *jihad* against the British in India. But that is another story.

REFERENCES

1. http://www.voi.org/books/tcqp/chi6.htm#38a; http://www.geocities.com/maakhan/my.html
2. Wahhabism: the reformist theology first expounded by Muhammad ibn Abd al-Wahhab (1702/3–91) in Nejd in the 1740s, espoused by the local chieftan Muhammad ibn Saud, and subsequently applied by these two houses—the al-Saud and the aal as-Sheikh (as the descendants of Sheikh Abd-al-Wahhab are known) in interdependent alliance until Wahhabism became the established form of Islam in the state bearing the name of Emir ibn Saud since the 1920s. Charles Allen, The Hidden Roots of Wahhabism in British India, WORLD POLICY JOURNAL, RECONSIDERATIONS: Volume XXII, No 2, Summer 2005; Danish.
3. "Syed Ahmad of Rai Bareilly (b.1786 d.1831) also called Syed Ahmed Shaheed. Syed Ahmed Barelvi though by the name is a barelvi (a sufi sect) BUT HE WAS STRONGLY AGAINST SUFISM AND BIDAH EXISTING IN INDIAN SOCIETY. HIS LINEAGE COULD BE TRACED BACK TO PROPHET MUHAMMAD (S.A). He was also responsible for making the Pushtun's follow right Islam and taking them away from BIDAAS.

A warrior from India who under the influence of Shah Abdul Aziz, son of Shah Waliullah, toured Afghanistan and the areas occupied by the Sikhs raising the banner of *Jihad* and rallying the Pashtun tribes to his banner. His movement posed a serious threat to Ranjit Singh's Sikh Kingdom after it inflicted several defeats on Sikh troops as well as recapturing Peshawar, Mardan and surrounding towns and villages. He was betrayed by some locals and was killed by the Sikhs along with hundreds of his troops and followers including Swatis and Syeds of Kaghan in Balakot, Mansehra in 1831. "http://www.turntoislam.com/forum/showthread.php?t=11151

4. *Mughal*, pp. 83-84.
5. *Mughal*, p. 22.
6. William Dalrymple speaking to the BBC News website's Soutik Biswas on September 7, 2006, on his then new book, *The Last Mughal: The Fall of a Dynasty. Delhi, 1857* (Penguin, N. Delhi, 2006, henceforth *Mughal*), http://www.utopia-politics.com/forums/index.php?showtopic=32758, electronically accessed 26 Sept. 08, 01.10 p.m. IST.
7. Nizam Nasir-ud-Dawlah and Hyderabad's military contingent remained loyal to the British during the Indian Mutiny (1857-58). http://www.onwar.com/aced/chrono/c1800s/yr55/findia1857.htm
8. Cited in The Sepoy War of 1857. Mutiny or First Indian War of Independence? http://www.english.emory.edu/Bahri/Mutiny.html Palmer, J.A.B. The Mutiny Outbreak at Meerut In 1857. Cambridge: University Press, 1966; Kaye, John William. A History of the Sepoy War In India (3 vols). London: W.H. Allen & Co., 1878.
9. Dalrymple, *op. cit*. Present author's parentheses.
10. Dalrymple, *op. cit*. Parentheses in the original. See also *Mughal*, p. 228.
11. Dalrymple, *op. cit*. Parentheses added.
12. *Mughal*, pp. 81-82.
13. *Mughal*, p. 83.
14. *Mughal*, p. 259.
15. Dietrich Reetz , Muslim Concepts of Local Power and Resistance. Islamic Militants in the Indian Frontier Province between 1900 and Independence, http://www.zmo.de/, . pdf.
16. The Khilafat Movement, http://www.indiafirstfoundation.org/Glimpses%20of%20Indian%20History/Articles/Leaves%20From%20The%20Past/ThekhilafatMovement_m.htm; http://en.wikipedia.org/wiki/Khilafat_Movement. _m.htm; http://en.wikipedia.org/wiki/Khilafat_Movement. Atatuerk chased Sheik-ul-Islam the High priest of Islam, out of his office and even threw the *Quran* after him. He had no time for religious 'nonsense' and declared, "The Caliph has no power or position except as a nominal figurehead." H.C. Armstrong, "Grey

Wolf. An Intimate Study of a Dictator", Arthur Barker Ltd., London, 1939, p. 243.

17. Article [unnamed] cited from *Hamdard Islamicus* (Karachi, autumn 1992, pp. 93-100), http://www.muslim.org/light/93-2.htm#arch [a US-based Ahmadiya web site].
18. *Ibid.*
19. Premen Addy, "Squaring the imperial circle", http://www.dailypioneer.com/columnist1.asp?main_variable=Columnist&file_name=Premen%2FPremen2.txt&writer=Premen. Abu al-A'la Mawdudi (1903-79), the Indian and later Pakistani thinker, on the other hand, presented *jihad* not merely as warfare to expand Islamic political dominance, but also to establish a just rule, one that includes freedom of religion. Mawdudi' was active in the post-World War I Khilafat movement which Indian Muslims had launched in favour of retaining the Ottoman caliphate. In line with this *jihad* for Mawdudi was akin to war of liberation; Islamic rule meant freedom and justice, even for non-Muslims. Mawdudi's outlook significantly changed the perception of *jihad*. It picked up association with anti-colonialism that seek not to expand Islamic rule but to establish independent states and even enable non-Muslims to become politically independent. Mawdudi's approach eased the way for Arab resistance against Zionism and Israel to be called *jihad*. However, he and his followers like Hasan al-Banna (1906-49) and Sayyid Qutb (1906-56) did not take up the more secular streak. They preferred to emphasize the establishment of a truly Islamic government.
20. Founders of Pakistan pledged loyalty to British rule of India. Muslim League declared loyalty to British government its first objective. Extracts from reports of League's public meetings. (From *The Light & Islamic Review:* Vol. 69; No. 6; Nov-Dec 1992; pp. 5-7)
21. *Archibald Forbes, The Afghan Wars 1839-42 and 1878-80*, http://gutenberg.org. Henceforth Forbes.
22. *Ibid.*
23. *The Indian Musalmans*, Trubner Co., London , 2nd. edition, 1872, cited in http://www.muslim.org/cont-islam.htm
24. Forbes, *op. cit.*
25. Umej Bhatia, "The Sea Speaks Arabic", History Today May 2005, Volume: 55 Issue: 5, pp.12-14. http://www.historytoday.com/
26. See, Maj Gen Sir Thompson CAPPER 's (1863-1915) papers indexed, Reference code: GB99 KCLMA Capper T, http://www.kcl.ac.uk/lhcma/parsefile.php?file=/lhcma/summary/ca40001.shtml&query=india%20army%20intelligence%20branch%201908.
27. *Ibid.* European media coverage was far less circumspect. Allenby's

victory was presented as the 'consummation of Europe's last crusade'.

28. Churchill writes with great perspicacity: "Except at the times of sowing and of harvest, a continual state of feud and strife prevails throughout the land. Tribe wars with tribe. The people of one valley fight with those of the next. To the quarrels of communities are added the combats of individuals. Khan assails Khan, each supported by his retainers. Every tribesman has a blood feud with his neighbour. Every man's hand is against the other, and all against the stranger. Nor are these struggles conducted with the weapons which usually belong to the races of such development. To the ferocity of the Zulu are added the craft of the Redskin and the marksmanship of the Boer. The world is presented with that grim spectacle, "the strength of civilisation without its mercy." At a thousand yards the traveller falls wounded by the well-aimed bullet of a breech-loading rifle. His assailant, approaching, hacks him to death with the ferocity of a South-Sea Islander. The weapons of the nineteenth century are in the hands of the savages of the Stone Age. Every influence, every motive, that provokes the spirit of murder among men, impels these mountaineers to deeds of treachery and violence. The strong aboriginal propensity to kill, inherit in all human beings, has in these valleys been preserved in unexampled strength and vigour. That religion, which above all others was founded and propagated by the sword—the tenets and principles of which are instinct with incentives to slaughter and which in three continents has produced fighting breeds of men—stimulates a wild and merciless fanaticism. The love of plunder, always a characteristic of hill tribes, is fostered by the spectacle of opulence and luxury which, to their eyes, the cities and plains of the south display. A code of honour not less punctilious than that of old Spain, is supported by vendettas as implacable as those of Corsica. In such a state of society, all property is held directly by man force. *Every Man is a Soldier*. The Project Gutenberg Book of Sir Winston S. Churchill, The Story of the Malakand Field Force, Chapter II, http://www.gutenberg.org. (Henceforth Churchill).
29. The first two wars in the 19th century ensued from British attempt to establish influence over Afghanistan. Battlefield victories did not prevent them from being disastrous for the British Indian army. The Afghans initiated the third war immediately after the conclusion of the First World War owing to their grievances. They lost on the battlefield but managed to regain independence from British political influence.
30. Churchill, *op. cit.*
31. Much of this backgrounder is drawn from the excellent presentation

of Hamid Hussain, Waziristan—The Past Overview of Pakistan's (and by extension the world's) newest trouble spot, *Defence Journal*, November 2004, orbat.com/site/analysis/waziristanthe_past_overview_of.htm

32. The reason for his second marriage is reported to be his wish for a son. Hitherto he begot only daughters. *The Times of India*, Kolkata, 16 Oct. 2008.
33. Govt. of India letter No. 407 dt. 28 Feb. 1879 asserts as its policy "to extend and, by degrees, to consolidate their influence" in the whole drainage system of the Indus. Cited in Churchill. The reasons which dictated Lord Lytton's Forward Policy were as follows: Britain wished to play out the 'great game' by forestalling expansion of Russian influence over Afghanistan and the latter's over the North-West Frontier so as to protect its prized colonial empire of India, and to command the passes of the Hindu Kush mountains.
34. Disraeli had defeated Gladstone in the general elections and was in power during 1874-80. In contrast to Gladstone's liberalism, Disraeli was more assertive in policy matters and so were the protagonists of the 'Forward Policy', the chief of the India Office, Lord Salisbury and the Viceroy of India, Lord Lytton, serving under him.
35. "The "Full steam ahead" method would be undoubtedly the most desirable. This is the military view. Mobilise, it is urged, a nice field force, and operate at leisure in the frontier valleys, until they are as safe and civilised as Hyde Park. Nor need this course necessarily involve the extermination of the inhabitants. Military rule is the rule best suited to the character and comprehension of the tribesmen. They will soon recognise the futility of resistance, and will gradually welcome the increase of wealth and comfort that will follow a stable government. Besides this, we shall obtain a definite frontier almost immediately.Only one real objection has been advanced against this plan. But it is a crushing one, and it constitutes the most serious argument against the whole "Forward Policy." It is this: we have neither the troops nor the money to carry it out. Churchill, *op. cit* Chapter XVIII, and last : *The Riddle of the Frontier.*
36. Achmed Abdullah, An Afghan Raid, in *Fifty Amazing Hairbreadth Escapes*, Bombay, no editor, no date, pp. 213-214.
37. Abdullah, p. 213.
38. "Owing to this punitive raid, the Waziri Afghans who never had given in their tribute well, brought 300 sheep." *Babur-Nama*, Low Price Publications, N. Delhi, 2006, (2 vols bound in one), p. 413.
39. Churchill, Ch. 3.

40. Dr.Ali Jan, Pashto Under the British Empire, http://british empire.co.uk/
41. Edwards, David B. Heroes of the Age: Moral Fault Lines on the Afghan Frontier. Berkeley: University of California Press, 1996. Chapter 5. Mad Mullahs and Englishmen. North-West Frontier Province, *circa* 1897., http://ark.cdlib.org/ark:/13030/ft458006bg/. (Henceforth Edwards); MedLibrary.org, Wikipedia Supplement on Siege of Malakand.
42. Churchill, *op. cit.*
43. Hamid Hussain, Waziristan-The Past.Overview of Pakistan's (and by extension the world's) newest trouble spot. *Defence Journal*, November 2004. orbat.com/site/analysis/waziristanthe _past_overview_of.htm
44. Churchill, *op. cit.*
45. Way or path. One starts with Islamic law, the exoteric or mundane practice of Islam and then is initiated onto the mystical path of a Tarîqah.http://www.wordwebonline.com/search. pl?ww=5&w= tariqat
46. Beauchamp Duff's India Despatches. Printed in the Supplement to the London Gazette of 4 July 1916. http://www.1914-1918.net/
47. The Mohmands are a powerful Pathan tribe, living partly in Afghanistan and partly in the districts around Peshawar. They are turbulent, fanatical, and quarrelsome; ready subjects for fiery Mullahs to stir up to revolt. Long before the outbreak of the war [WWI] they had been in repeated conflicts with the British. Between 1872 and 1908 there had been several expeditions against them. In summer 1915 an attempt was made to raise a *jihad* among the Black Mountain tribes. There was no prolonged respite for the British. F. A. McKenzie, Shadows in the East, from *The Great War*, edited by H.W. Wilson, Volume 7, chapter 128 'The Defence of India'. http:/ /www.khyber.org/people
48. F. A. McKenzie, Shadows in the East, from *The Great War*, edited by H.W. Wilson, volume 7, chapter 128, The Defence of India'. http:/ /www.greatwardifferent.com/Great_War/Brits_in_Caucasus/ India_01.htm
49. F. A. McKenzie, Shadows in the East, from *The Great War*, edited by H.W. Wilson, Volume 7, Chapter 128, The Defence of India'. http://www.greatwardifferent.com/Great_War/Brits_in_Caucasus/ India_01.htm
50. *Ibid.*
51. Abdullah, p.214.
52. Why Britons walked warily in Waziristan, by Alastair Lawson, BBC News / Monday, 21 April, 2008. Capt Stockdale goes on to describe just how dangerous the "hostile tribesmen" were in the Wana, the main town of South Waziristan, when a sniper hit a British camp.

"Like all tribesmen in this area, he was a marvellous shot," Capt Stockdale wrote, "and he killed the commanding officer with his first shot.
"He killed or wounded 11 other men before his hiding place was discovered."

53. [Despatch] No. 17445-1. ARMY HEADQUARTERS, INDIA. Simla, the 20th August, 1918.
From His Excellency General Sir Charles Carmichael Monro, G.C.M.G., K.C.B., Commander-in-Chief in India. To The Secretary to the Government of India, Army Department. "3. In order to meet the urgent demand for trained soldiers which arose during the winter of 1914-15, the British forces in India were further depleted by the despatch to England of a number of Regular units, so that, by the beginning of 1915, the British garrison was largely composed of Territorial troops sent to replace the Regulars withdrawn." http://www.1914-1918.net/despatch_index.htm
[Despatch] No. 17445-1.
ARMY HEADQUARTERS, INDIA.
Simla, the 20th August, 1918.
From His Excellency General Sir Charles Carmichael Monro, G.C.M.G., K.C.B., Commander-in-Chief in India. To The Secretary to the Government of India, Army Department.
54. Tim Moreman, Army In India and Frontier Warfare, http://www.King-emperor.com. Henceforth Moreman I.
55. Of the 1,800 South Waziristan Scouts, there were only 66 Wazirs: compared with 820 Afridis or Orakzais and some 914 other tribesmen. Among the latter were 230 Khattaks, tribesmen recruited from within British administered territory across the Indus River. They would remain loyal because their families and homes were squarely under the British thumb. Trans-border Scouts recruited from beyond British-administered territory were another story. http://www.khyber.org
56. Conflict in Afghanistan. A Historical Encyclopedia p.2 47.http://books.google.co.in/books?i=bv4hz xpo424C&pg=PA247&lpg=PA247&dq=jihad+AND+anglo-afghan +wars&source=web&ots=bCYVrDiu7H&sig=nwmB1SaG-QK0OyOMeqTi_AqhFJI&hl=en&sa= X&oi=book_result&resnum =3&ct=result
57. Dr. Tim Moreman, The Arms Trade on the N.W. Frontier of India 1890-1914, http://www. King-emperor.com. Henceforth Moreman II. The British had discarded the sniper rifle in favour of the Martini-Henry in 1871, and introduced the Lee Enfield .303 calibre from 1902. Machineguns like the Maxims, Vickers and the Lewis gun entered service from the late 19th to early 20th centuries. http://www.britishempire.co.uk/forces/armyarmaments/rifles/armleeenfield.htm

58. The North-West Frontier Arms Trade Committee, led by Major-General L.H.E. Tucker (the Tucker Committee), instituted an enquiry in 1898 that unearthed shocking facts. The most tantalizing fact discovered was that a significant portion of the weapons came from within British India—right under the govt.'s nose! The clandestine supply involved cliques of govt. officials, British Other Ranks and "sepoys". Other sources included pet Maliks (tribal chieftains) who passed on British govt. gift of weapons, sometimes meant for defence of a loyal tribe against onslaughts by rival tribes. To cap it all, weapons supply acquired an international dimension with the Persian Gulf entering the picture. An increasingly lucrative and flourishing international smuggling trade connected Muscat, a major arms sales depot *via* Karachi or other intermediate routes to Kabul or Kandahar, whence to the border with India. Powerful commercial firms, both British and other European, were involved in supplying the highly profitable market of British India's North-Western Frontier Province region. Such better quality rifles, in highly capable hands of the Pathan mountain tribes, was turning out to be deadly and an increasing source of worry for the stability of Britain's prized possession, 'the jewel in the Crown', India. In Moreman's words: "...improving tribal fighting capability helped convince the Committee of Imperial Defence that some form of rapprochement was necessary with Russia... [T]he tribes were able to impose such significant costs in blood and expense on the Indian Army so as to preclude the complete occupation of tribal territory up to Afghan frontier." Moreman II. Further, in 1939 the Marquess of Linlithgow, the Viceroy, admitted that as yet no way had been found to eliminate the gun factories in Waziristan. Hauner, *op. cit.*
59. Moreman I, *op. cit.* In mid-May 1919 the North and South Waziristan Militia mutinied. 1919-24: Waziristan. The Third Afghan War was followed by five years of unrest and intermittent fighting in Waziristan. http://freepages.genealogy.rootsweb.ancestry.com/~finney/cwgc/1465591.htm
60. Edwards, *op. cit.*
61. Hamid Hussain, Waziristan—The Past. Overview of Pakistan's (and by extension the world's) newest trouble spot. *Defence Journal,* November 2004. *orbat.com/site/analysis/waziristanthe_past_overview_of.htm.* The Faqir of Ipi was born in Kirta—a small village situated near Kajhori Fort. He was a quadrilingual mystic who had studied theology extensively. More on the Faqir of Ipi *see* http://www.khyber.org/people; Milan Hauner, One Man against the Empire. The Faqir of Ipi and the British in Central Asia on the Eve of and during the Second World War, *Journal of Contemporary History,* Vol. 16, No. 1, The Second World War: Part 1 (Jan., 1981),

pp.183-212, reproduced in http://www. Khyber.org. Also in Hauner's book-length study, *India in Axis Strategy, Germany, Japan, and Indian Nationalists in the Second World War* (Stuttgart 1980).

62. http://www.khyber.org/people
63. http://www.khyber.org/people. When the British bombed the settlements of a tribe as a punitive measure, it had little effect on the mud houses as the splinters would easily pass through the soft walls and roofs, which could be quickly patched up. This led to combined air force-army operations, in which the aerial attacks were immediately followed up with army action to raze the structures down to the ground. But moving armed columns uphill in rugged terrain and constantly in fear of sudden attack and sniping was easier said than done. Sir Kerr Fraser-Tytler, who served during this period as a young subaltern in a Frontier Cavalry Regiment, and later during the crucial years of 1935-1941 as British Minister in Kabul, recalls his frustrating experience in fighting the tribes: "And always there were the raids, the sudden alarm, the long dust-choked ride through the stifling heat of a July night, clattering out on to the stony glacis of the frontier hills, and away forty miles before dawn only to find as often as not that the birds had flown, leaving a trail of death and destruction behind them". Here is a close-up narrative of the difficulties of fighting the warlike mountain tribes of NWFP:

"The Faqir claimed to be the Champion of Islam and in possession of divine powers, and soon set forth stirring up anti-Government ferment amongst the various tribes of Waziristan. To help settle the Frontier, the Government asked that the Tori Khels who were harbouring the Faqir expel him, but when it appeared that this would not happen, it was decided to send two columns, 'Razcol' and 'Tocol', through Tori Khel territory as a demonstration of Government strength. Both faced unexpected hostile opposition. ...Later on, the bodies of the fallen were found to be well mutilated by tribesmen.

Because of a shortage of rations, casualties suffered and the swelling of tribal opposition up to 2,000 strong, it was decided to pull both columns out of the Khaisora Valley for Mir Ali."... "Waziristan would not really settle down again during the inter-war years. ...[it] had erupted, as in every few years throughout its stormy history." The Faqir of Ipi was rampant and the young militants were coming from all directions to support him in a *jihad*. In a well-planned ambush near Damdil he inflicted heavy casualties on the Gurkhas. ...The Gurkhas' assailants were reported to have withdrawn into the hills to the south, where the Faqir of Ipi was currently touring the Shaktu Valley, this being Bhitanni country. Too far off, therefore, for RAZCOL (the Brigade at Razmak), which anyway had problems of its own; so here was TOCOL (the Brigade from Bannu) with instructions to climb the two thousand feet to the Sham Plain, catch the Faqir and end the war. Rumour had it, afterwards, that the Brigadier was shocked to find what this feat involved, and said he never would have embarked on it had he known."..."Now, still shuffling slowly forward, we began to climb. The way became very rough as well as steep; there was no signs of a path. The mules with the heavier loads were labouring, but there could be no off loading for a rest. We could not be sure of a long enough halt, and the order was KEEP CLOSED UP." [It was evening but] we could do any map reading by moonlight, and another strict order had been NO LIGHTS. The spur went up and up, and was dominated by higher spurs on both sides, on which we could imagine a hundred pairs of eyes watching our progress." http://www.king-emperor.com/officers-indian.htm

64. Hauner, *op. cit.*
65. Olaf Caroe cited in Hauner, *op. cit.* 'Use of force' meant RAF bombing of the lashkar before they could reach the Afghan border, and cajolery translated to a handsome £25,000 bribe to the Pir to get lost and return to Syria at once.
66. Is the U.S.-Pakistan Alliance Against Terrorism Coming to an End? http://www.thejamestownfoundation.org

3

Demystifying Indian Security Dilemma in 21st Century

Herkan Neadan Toppo

Introduction

India is evolving with strategic implications of major international issues, events and trends so as to the geographical and demographical definition of India-centric South Asia region varies. It is due to the lack of clear physical geographical borders in the northern part of the region. According to historical criteria and definitions, India is a large country with horizontal and vertical dimensions, and overstretched landmass nearly 3.3 million square kilometres (70 percent) of sub-continental proportions occupying a predominant strategic position having inhabitations to over a billion people with multitudes of divisions, based on religious, ethnic and other identities.[1]

The Indian topographical diversity with land frontiers extending more than 15,500 kilometres sharing with seven countries (viz., Afghanistan, Bangladesh, Bhutan, China, Myanmar, Nepal and Pakistan) including a small segment with Afghanistan (106 km) in Northern Jammu and Kashmir (J&K), now part of the Northern Areas of Pakistan Occupied Kashmir.[2] The length of India's land borders with its neighbours varies considerably which poses unique challenges to Indian Armed Forces.[3] It dominates the Northern Indian Ocean with a coastline that is 7,683 km long and maritime boundaries overlooking three major shipping lanes.[4] India's peninsular dimension places it adjacent to one of the most vital sea-lanes of the world stretching from the Suez Canal and the Persian Gulf to the Straits of Malacca through which 55,000 ships and much of the oil from the Gulf region transit each year.[5]

Moreover, due to geographical proximity it is not only the region that has changed but also recognizes the seriousness of the potential problem that creates doubt and strong feeling of mistrust and sources of insecurity which creates security dilemma. The phenomenon of Security dilemma is revisiting, and still it is being applied to some of the new referent objects of the security. The newly emerging nation-states in the South Asia region with neo-liberal democratic values are hyper-sensitive about their sovereignty, and the critical contiguous areas such as the Himalayan frontier, Myanmar, North-Western frontiers (Baluchistan/Afghanistan/Pakistan) and Sri Lanka fall in a different category as being essential for India's security. More than that, India has yet to become overwhelmingly preponderant in security and economic arenas and it is argued that this kind of development may take place in a few decades given the rapid economic growth of India. But in recent years, the normative dispositions of most of the states are not quite congruent with the Indian ethos of democracy or secularism but subsequently lessening its power over the smaller neighbours.[6] In many respects, these small states seem to want to create a national identity dissimilar to India's.[7] Therefore, conflict and cooperation patterns in the regional subsystem are a reflection of the particular interdependencies and externalities of the interconnected states as well as societal groups.[8] This region has some sub-systemic characteristics as well as different clusters of relationships. Most of the states emerged in the decolonization era and the two principal actors—India and Pakistan—underwent a bloody partition during that process, although variations can be seen in the levels of state capacity (India with the highest and Afghanistan the lowest), almost all of the eight countries of South Asia are weak states, with strong societies and societal values.[9] Also, they all have experienced difficulties in the midst of the state formation and consolidation, and the congruence between state and nation is not fully developed in these countries.[10]

The security dilemma in the South Asian sub-continent is operating as a chain reaction that includes regional and extra-regional powers with competing interests.[11] These concerns are raising pertinent question to Indian security apparatus. Along with this, political dialogue concerning Indian security profile intensifies the deep understanding of international relations as central to the study of the subject. The changing patterns and the great diversification of global powers are not only reflected in the emergence of new security challenges but also appear to be in a delicate position.

The view from the Indian side about what exactly constitutes the security dilemma reveals the multifarious nature of the security threats and threat apprehensions. For instance, the situation along borders with China and Pakistan has witnessed periods of calm interspersed with hostilities. While, there are other areas of concern that may pose a threat to Indian security. Also, the existing reality of border issues and unresolved disputes continue to remain an important factor in consideration.[12] India has major concerns about the Sino-Pak and Pak-North Korea defence cooperation and sees serious security implications in China's strategic partnership with Pakistan. Moreover, China's efforts to build strategic relations with India's neighbours providing military aid and weapons at friendship prices.[13] It means Indian security dilemma arises out of the anarchic nature of state system.

Meanwhile, in the changing global security environment with specific reference to the region India has strategic engagement with its neighbours and identifies security imperatives. Its impact on the nation and the gradual but distinctly discernible shift towards multi-polarity in power equations and the shift in global centre of gravity to Asia are the most distinct features of this change as the past experience shows that major shifts in power equations create volatility in the international order.[14] So, the power shifts towards Asia can be linked to its phenomenal economic rise especially the rise of China, as also India, in the global economic arena that is the most visible manifestation of the forces of globalisation. These are also resulting in a numerous related socio-economic and security challenges within the region which form offshoots of global and regional elements of terrorism.[15] Despite India being in the region's pivotal geostrategic location, the major powers' presences have a crucial role in South Asia and the presence of weak states in conflict also contribute to this activism by outside powers as in the cases of Afghanistan and Pakistan in the immediate neighbourhood. Thus, security challenges in the region have been serious, including deep involvement in the international sphere of Islamic fundamentalism through the vehicles of terrorism and separatism.

What is Security Dilemma?

Although security dilemma originated out of realist thinking, it is by no means wedded to realism. It has found favour in critical studies literature where it has been used as a tool for expanding the parameter of security studies. The theory of Security Dilemma can be understood under certain conditions of international anarchic environment in which nation-states or region are fearful of each other because of mutual misunderstandings or obliged to assume control over confused or hostile border areas which are incapable of withstanding the mobilized powers. Also the emerging plural society, with divergent ethnic groups interrelated only on the economic plane is an unintended result to the policy of artificially stimulated economic development under an alien kind of government.[16] Security thus becomes the first priority. All countries try to gain security, obtain military superiority and improve one's own security status by increasing military expenditure.[17] Since arms are a perpetual concern, one's military superiority quickly surpassed by other military building up efforts, absolute security is, therefore, impossible, so all countries are trapped in a dilemma. This kind of phenomenon is called 'Security Dilemma'.[18] There is a "vicious circle of security dilemma and power accumulation", and it means that in a self-help system one cannot simultaneously improve one's own security without reducing that of others. That's because the extent of one's security is always the extent of the insecurity of one's opponent. This dilemma characterizes the tension between deterrence and reassurance. It is important to emphasize some of the factors fuelling the Security Dilemma: anarchy, lack of trust, misperception and offence/defence ambiguity. Some writers argue that the security dilemma is an inherent feature of the anarchical international system. Hence Bradly Klein's comment that "the international security dilemma is poised by international anarchy" and according to Burry Buzan "under anarchy, states have to look after themselves to assume both their political and societal values. This structural imperative lies at the core of the power security dilemma which is itself the key statement of the security problematic under anarchy."[19] For that reason anarchy landscapes insecurity as a concept and proves it to be in the delicate position.

Some of the features of international relations in times of high global politics and tensions has in turn is being seen as a threat by the first state, which thinks its defensive intentions are obvious For instance, during the early cold war period the Soviet Union and United States routinely assumed aggressive motivations on the part of each other and are arming without cause or attack. But, the Americans' arms build-up during the cold war did not lead to counter arming by its neighbours (Canada, Mexico, Britain, or France) because those states saw no intended threat to themselves. But it did contribute to arms procurement in countries such as Cuba, which perceived a definite threat. In contrast the simultaneous build-up by the Soviet Union led most of its neighbours to counter arm. It is because they feared Soviet aggressive intentions and the concept is, therefore, subject to gross misapplication to real world events and may utterly misconceive subject matter in a strained search for a rational choice model of human behaviour. According to Kenneth Waltz "in the 'security dilemma' measures taken by one country to increase its own security meant measures decreasing others security", whereas Adolf Worlfers states that "National Security can be a dangerously ambiguous concept if used without specifications".

The multifarious nature of the security threats facing the populace in third world states complicates the application of the security dilemma. It arises out of the anarchic nature of state system. According to John H. Herz "without a superior power to protect itself, each state bears ultimate responsibility for its own security, for its own survival as a member of the state system. So having such pretension with this overwhelming accountability states attempt to expand their power – economically, strategically, and militarily so as to better defend themselves should the need arise. But by augmenting their own power in this fashion, states make neighbouring states less secure. This compels those neighbours to prepare for the worst by taking counter measures to enhance their own power. A common search for security thus results in a situation in which both powers are less secure." [20] Jack Snyder defines the security dilemma as a situation in which each state believed that its security required the insecurity of others.[21]

Barry Posen was the first to utilise the security dilemma concept when examining ethnic conflicts. Posen makes an accurate reference to the security dilemma that arises when states have no expansionists tendencies' (benign intent), but their actions cause reactions that, in the end, can make one less secure' (paradoxical policies).[22] However, even applying the concept although he notes that the participants have reasons to be mistrustful of each other, he highlights the pursuit of policies that cause concern in the other group without linking this specifically to the security dilemma.[23]

Thus, in international relations the concept of 'security dilemma' is used to explain the 'anarchic nature of global politics', especially the degree to which the security dilemma originated operates in the strategic environment receives coverage and indeed has found favour in the critical security studies literature where it has been used as a tool for expanding the parameters of security studies.

Development of Theory of Security Dilemma

Even though the term 'security dilemma' is relatively new and John H. Herz is credited with its first use in *Political Realism and Political Idealism*, written in 1951. Security dilemma describes a situation in which war can occur between two or more participants where none of those involved desired such an outcome. Thus war can occur without the participation of a revisionist or revolutionary state seeking to alter the status quo.[24] At the same time, Herbert Butterfield, a British historian and the grandfather of the theory of security dilemma, highlights key understanding of the theory of security dilemma in his writing "History and Human Relations" and claimed that, the greatest war in history could be produced without the intervention of any great criminals who might be out to do deliberate harm in the world. It could be between two powers both of which were desperately anxious to avoid conflict of any sort. He notes the uncertainty that statesmen have determining others' intentions and focuses upon the fear and suspicion such uncertainty causes.[25]

Only in the 1970s and 1980s the theory of security dilemma underwent a detailed examination by the American political scientist, Robert Jervis and his first substantial contribution is found in his highly regarded monograph, *Perception and*

Misperception in International Politics, in which he highlights the value of perceptions in explaining why the security dilemma can be difficult for statesmen to recognize and ultimately why their prudent policies are contradictory.[26] Robert Jervis also identified a number of factors associated with a security dilemma that impede states ability to work cooperatively towards a mutually desired goal of general security.[27] In 1978 in his article *"Cooperation under the Security Dilemma"* he describes a mechanism by which interstate conflict can arise or worsen.[28] On this basis, the proposition is that actions taken by states to increase their own security can result in a decrease in the security of their rivals. Arms race can be a result of the security dilemma, as can widen security spirals.[29] So the security theorizing does both – it reconstructs the problematic of war on the one hand and it deals with the underlying fault lines of history on the other.[30]

By the early 1980s the security dilemma was still a tragedy in which status quo powers that had not intended each other harm could, because of their uncertainty of each other, pursue paradoxical policies that would bring about exactly that which had been hoped to avoid.[31] The security dilemma was found to contain three characteristics: benign intent, uncertainty, and paradoxical policies and the 1980s were to witness an apparent challenge to the first of these characteristics.[32] According to most security dilemma theorists' writings in the 1990s Nicholas Wheeler and Ken Booth were to label this the deliberate or state-reduced security dilemma as "permanent insecurity between nations and states is the inescapable lot of living in a condition of anarchy."[33] In addition, the 1990s has witnessed the security dilemma, hitherto the preserve of the international system which is applied to explain past shifts and indicate fault lines for possible political seismic activity in the geographical propinquity and ethnic tensions in erstwhile Soviet Union. Thus, the extension of geo-political boundary determining the dilemma's applicability to the international security issues in the particular region needs understanding of the tensions or apprehension that exists within the region due to rivalries and the evolving international order.

Neighbours and Indian Security Dilemma

Although India has a very strong traditional tie with all

neighbouring countries, practically all its neighbours have been strained over a whole range of issues be they of trade, water sharing, migration or ethnic sensitivities. At the same time, there have been no even patterns of relationships in the region. In this immediate neighbourhood almost all the other countries are undergoing varying forms of instability.[34] Some of these are afflicted by internal security problems, which owing to trans-border ethnic affinities which have the potential to spill over into India. India's relations with Bangladesh, Nepal and Sri Lanka have witnessed significant ups and downs over the years but have never been allowed to dip to an unmanageable low. Therefore, illegal immigration from these countries also remains a serious cause of concern.[35] Indo-Bangladesh relations that had become extremely strained over the Farakka issue and the Tin Bigha controversy have witnessed a dramatic improvement with the signing of the historic agreement on sharing of Ganga waters. The signing of the Mahakali Treaty and grant of overland transit route for its trade with Bangladesh by India underlines the positive shift. The radicalisation of the domestic environment in Bangladesh, continues despite inflow of illegal immigrants to North-East.

For instances, Nepal has transited into a Republic, ending the 240 years old monarchy and the future portents for peace and stability in Nepal depend on the approach of the new dispensation to governance.[36] India and Nepal have also been able to put the unfortunate events of the eighties behind them. They are set for a qualitatively improved relationship with closer economic ties and better political understanding. The Indo-Sri Lankan relationship today is a far cry from the palpable antagonism of the eighties and escalation of violence in Sri Lanka are not the issue to India but recent political developments in the international arena is of a deep concern.[37] Also it is important for India to keep Myanmar engaged, due to security and economic reasons, and the emergent humanitarian effort undertaken during the recent cyclone is reflective of our relationship.[38] India's relations with Bhutan and Maldives have been generally smooth and rancour-free. Maldives is stable, however, recent incidents indicate a potential for instability. In addition Bhutan is also transiting peacefully from hereditary monarchy to democratic governance, however, the unresolved Bhupalese problem could destabilise the region.[39] All this calls for keeping a continuous watch on happenings around immediate neighbourhood because they carry considerable conflicts internally and adverse spill over effects externally.

The China Factor

The Sino-Indian security dilemma is also a function of China's desire to establish close relationships with other countries in the Indian Ocean region (most notably Myanmar), a policy that is seen as a potential threat by India and termed as "strategic containment."[40] For India and China, the security dilemma also arises from threat perceptions based on consequences of future historical nationalistic tendencies. Both sides fear that a rise in nationalism in the other could lead to more hostile attitudes.[41] For instance, China harbours deep suspicions about possible future Indian policies toward Tibet. Beijing has been chronically concerned about the stability of its control over that vast, mineral rich, and strategically located region. India's maintenance of substantially ethnic Tibetan paramilitary forces, such as the Indo-Tibetan Border Police (ITBP), which is part of India's Central Paramilitary Forces, and the Special Frontier Force (SFF), which is under India's external intelligence agency, the Research and Analysis Wing of the Intelligence Bureau, touches Chinese vulnerabilities associated with the huge civilizational cleavage between Beijing and the Tibetan population.[42]

India holds similar fears about possible Chinese intervention in a future India-Pakistan war. China has consistently striven to maintain a balance of power in South Asia, a region far beyond its major industrial and population centres. Since about 1998, India has launched a similar project in East Asia. India struggles to maintain control over, and China to neutralize Indian control over, strategic frontier zones in the Himalayan lands of Nepal, Bhutan and Sikkim. The military instruments of each state pose inadvertent threats to the other. China's increasingly powerful and long range naval forces pose challenges, intended or unintended, to Indian security in the Indian Ocean. And both India and China believe their international stature is at stake in interaction with the other. Each state sees small issues to make up larger balance and ultimately to their status as a major power.

Over the past several years, Chinese activities falling into this category include:[43]

- Covert and overt assistance to Pakistan's nuclear and missile efforts, plus assistance to the development of Pakistan's military and military-industrial capabilities.
- Initiation of military relations, including an arms supply and intelligence exchange relations with Nepal.
- Initiation of dense relations with Myanmar including military cooperation and deep involvement in the development of Myanmar's over land transport and maritime sectors.
- Growing People's Liberation Army (PLA) activity in the Indian Ocean, including ship visits and establishment of electronic intelligence facilities.
- Cultivation of military relations with Bangladesh.
- Efforts to entice Bhutan into "normal diplomatic relations".

These points are attributed to Beijing's, strategy of creeping "strategic encirclement" of India, with Beijing deliberately engineering incrementally but cumulatively important advances in correlation of forces between China and India.[44] Amidst such military build-ups and forward deployments on land and at sea, tensions are inherent and the potential for such incidents turning serious in the future remains high.[45] Hence, India always regarded China as the biggest challenge in the region and threat to its security in the 21st century.

India-Pakistan Rivalry

India-Pakistan rivalry, mistrust and violence for more than 60 years now has marked the South Asian security structure by escalating into fear and enmity leading to huge number of minor military skirmishes and three major wars, i.e., 1947-48, 1965, and 1971, and several interstate crises. The disputed status of the Kashmir region, "the root of all evil in Indo-Pakistani affairs", fuelled the conflict repeatedly and tensions often escalated at the ceasefire line/Line of Control (LOC) between the Indian-administered part (Jammu and Kashmir) and Pakistan.[46] As Pakistan acquired nuclear weapons, Beijing began helping Pakistan acquire ballistic missiles capable of delivering those nuclear weapons. In 1988 the two countries apparently signed a secret treaty providing for Chinese supply of M-11 missiles and missile technology.[47] Later China agreed to build a factory in Pakistan to produce these missiles. Beijing resisted sharp US pressure throughout the 1990s over its assistance to Pakistan's ballistic missile programmes and refused to capitulate to US and Indian pressure to end such assistance. Chinese assistance to Pakistan's missile development programmes continued in 2001-02. It is especially in the aftermath of Pakistan's nuclear tests on 28 May, 1998, has created a sort of deterrent relationship, marred by a stability-instability paradox, i.e., some stability at the strategic level, but instability at the sub-strategic level. In 1999, during the Kargil-crisis, the tensions between both states reached a critical level.[48] The international community and especially the United States, while fearing a nuclear war in South Asia, insisted strongly and pressured both states to end the violence. Just a few years later in 2001, right after the 09/11-attacks, the situation deteriorated again and brought India and Pakistan on the brink of war again. Recently after the horrible terrorist attacks in Mumbai and in context to Indian officials pointing their fingers to Pakistan, a further escalation seems to be possible.

The nuclear-armed neighbours have engaged in peace talks, but chances look dim for a final termination of the rivalry or the settlement of the key issues dividing them in the near-term[49] and the tensions between them reached a new and much more threatening dimension and the arms race between both states increased to dangerous strategic competition, which is dominating the security paradigm of South Asia.

A root cause of the security problems of India and Pakistan lies in the condition of uncertainty about the others intentions – a 'dilemma of interpretation' – as a result of anarchy in international politics.[50] In context to hostile relations and a violent history – a 'shadow of the past' – like between India and Pakistan, such uncertainty may result into fear and worst-case planning, what Butterfield named the 'irreducible dilemma' fuelled by 'Hobbesian fear'.[51] Anarchy fuels the dilemma of interpretation and, therefore, the security problems between Pakistan and India. The condition of uncertainty, together with the ambiguous symbolism of weapons – the problem of how to 'distinguish between offensive and defensive weapons' – creates mutual fear. Following the nuclearization of the Indo-Pakistani relationship the fear has been exacerbated extensively due to the possible impact of a preemptive nuclear attack.[52]

Therefore, the anarchy's feature of uncertainty, mutual fear and the nuclear sword of Damocles in South Asia exacerbate the dilemma of interpretation between both states.[53]

India-Bangladesh

Bangladesh exhibits several internal conflicts, with the army and political parties waging frequent battles for control of the state. After its emergence in 1971 following a bloody civil war which saw India's military intervention, Bangladesh has struggled to develop a democracy while restraining its military. The alliance between Allah and the army began taking shape, like Pakistan, Bangladesh was now well set on the path to transform itself into a Islamo-fascist military dictatorship.[54] Even when Bangladesh has had successful elections and representative governments, but the peculiar aspects of its democracy has been the unwillingness of the opposition parties to give the winner a chance to govern. Agitations start the day after an election, causing military rule or anarchic order to re-emerge. As a partly low-lying country that is afflicted by the vagaries of the Bay of Bengal and its storms and floods, Bangladesh's immense poverty pushes a large body of its population to migrate to India for economic reasons. This mass infiltration from Bangladesh into India with a view to radically alter demographics is a form of *jihad*, which has been unleashed on India.[55] This has produced intense opposition in Assam, Tripura and West Bengal, and considerable violence in Assam especially. In order to stem the tide, India's fragile borderlands have been fenced with Bangladesh, but this has created much ill-will among Bangladeshis, who seem to consider borders irrelevant in South Asia, especially *vis-à-vis* West Bengal.

Changing Contours of India-Himalayan States

The Himalayan kingdom's of Nepal and Bhutan occupies an important place in India's foreign policy because of three main reasons:

(a) The strategic importance (location) of these Himalayan actors for India's national security
(b) The place of these Himalayan actors in India's own role perception in international politics.

(c) The have become the southern border of the People's Republic of China.

As such, these three units are right in the middle of India's whole 'Himalayan frontiers', its northern 'borderland' flanks as much as an 821 km stretch of the 1,664 km Indo-Nepalese border adjoins Uttar Pradesh. While India considers Nepal a part of its sphere of influence, it is increasingly being challenged by China's inroads into Nepal. In fact, the growing Nepal-China nexus should be seen in the context of India-China power competition in Asia. Essentially Nepal facilitates China's security interests in the South Asian region. This can be clearly glimpsed from Chinese ambassador, Zheng Xianglin's statement delivered at the Council of World Affairs in August 2008 that "Nepal is situated in a favourable geographical position in South Asia, and a passage linking China and South Asia."[56]

Nepal also has had a violent internal conflict which has recently made a crucial turn for a settlement. A landlocked country, Nepal had monarchic rule until it was abolished in May 2008. The monarchy had little concern for either offering security or prosperity to the Nepalese. The resulting abject poverty has generated intense violence in the form of a Maoist insurgency that lasted from 1996 to 2006. The internal conflict is also accentuated by the inability of the politically dominant group, high-caste Hindus from the hill regions (especially the ruling monarchy), to offer political and economic opportunities to lower-caste groups that include *dalits* (untouchables), and people from the Terai region, or Madhesis.[57] The Maoists exploited the deprived groups' grievances in gaining support for their militant struggle. In April 2008 the Maoists won national elections for a new Constituent Assembly and one of the first decisions they took was to abolish the monarchy. The process of developing a new constitution is likely to be drawn out, with no guarantees of an amicable democratic political system emerging for all groups. Nepal generates considerable internal security challenges for its neighbours, especially for India. The Maoists have links with fellow insurgents in several Indian States. Refugees from Nepal and trafficking in women are two other human security issues in the India-Nepal context.

Part of Nepal's problems is the absence of a healthy relationship with India. The Nepalese do not often view India in a sympathetic light despite the massive economic aid that India has provided to the beleaguered country. India's support for the monarchy, its frequent meddling in Nepalese politics and its inability to restrain border-area groups such as the Madhesis, have caused divisions in this relationship. Nepal borders two of India's weakest States, Bihar and Uttar Pradesh, which also generate security challenges for the country. The larger issue may be Nepal's perennial under-development. Nepal wants to act like a sovereign entity with a distinct national identity without being controlled by New Delhi, but has fragile political and economic structures and divided political elite, making it much more difficult to accomplish those goals.

India-Bhutan

India-Sri Lanka

Sri Lanka carries one of the most violent internal conflicts in the region, a conflict that has lasted nearly three decades. The violent phase of the conflict began in the early 1980s when the Tamil minority began to make stronger power-sharing demands in response to attempts by the Sinhalese political elite to marginalize them and deny equal citizenship rights. The hardening of positions on both sides led to the formation of the Liberation Tigers of Tamil Eelam (LTTE), which began a violent insurgency in the North-East in 1983, where it wanted to create a separate homeland. The Sinhalese government's response was military repression, which further alienated the Tamils. In response, Tamils have employed extremely violent methods, such as suicide bombings and other forms of terrorist activities. In 2002 a peace agreement under the sponsorship of Norway was signed, but after four years of relative calm, it broke down in 2006 when violence resumed once again. The fundamental cause of this conflict lies in the inability of both sides to fulfil national aspirations and the unwillingness of the Sri Lankan state to allow secession by a largely disgruntled minority group.[58]

Role of Major Powers in the Region

The rivalries of geo-strategies represent a peril to the regional security. The USA and China started a quest and the US presence in Iraq, the US and NATO's presence in Afghanistan, US military bases, Russian presence and military bases, China's rising influence, Iran's and Turkey's proximity to the region, and military and economic alliances, show that this region is an arena of great power rivalry. The balance of power, instability and struggle for control over oil and gas reserves mean that the new emerging global activities and regional complexities enjoin upon India to develop matching military capabilities in keeping with its growing economic and technological status, so as to ensure a continued stable and peaceful environment.

The US has a major base in the Indian Ocean at Diego Garcia, which is always operationally active. The evolving situation in US-Pakistan relations provides salience to India-Pakistan relations. If one pillar of Pakistan's anti-India strategy (the other being alliance with China) is becoming shaky, expect Pakistan to avoid confrontation with India.[59] US forces are also well established in the Gulf Region and now in Afghanistan and Pakistan too. Their presence is likely to increase manifold, following the successful completion of the war in Iraq. The US would like to see the Indian Navy safeguarding the sea-lanes of the Indian Ocean, so that its own comments in this regard, are reduced.[60]

Indian Ocean Region (IOR)

The Indian Ocean is a vast geographical entity and it has assumed greater importance in view of the increased maritime activity and the Northern Indian Ocean Region is an important area in the security calculus of India. It is noteworthy that India has approximately 1200 island territories off its Western and Eastern seaboards. Some of these are upto 1300 km from the mainland and an Exclusive Economic Zone (EEZ) that is over two million square kilometres in size. So interests in the Indian Ocean are diverse in every way. Besides this, India's naval establishment and its tri service command in Andaman & Nicobar Islands since 2001 has been a reflection of security concerns in the Indian Ocean. Also India's overseas trade is considerable and is poised for more growth. Almost all of India's oil imports come from the Gulf, the fact that in the northern Indian Ocean exists the Persian Gulf and Central Asia where the most abundant estimated resources of oil and gas are located, is sufficient to create 'vital interests" for the great powers in the Indian Ocean. It is also considered the fact the sea lines of communication are densely concentrated in the Indian Ocean and geo-political significance of the Strait of Malacca and the Andaman Straits. It is inevitable that the Indian Ocean and its littoral will be a major scene of great power activity and involvement.[61] And if they are cut off or otherwise hindered, the country's interests will be very seriously affected. Major sea lane's of the world pass through this area and India uses them extensively. The exploitation of the resources, both within the respective Exclusive Economic Zones (EEZs) of littoral countries and beyond, is also steadily increasing.[62] It is amazing to know that 70 per cent of the world's oil, 33 per cent of global trade and 50 per cent of world's container traffic passes through the IOR. The region, therefore, has importance not only for India but also for the other major economies of the world. In this regard, security of the Sea Lanes of Communication (SLsOC) assumes importance, because of our geo-strategic location. Protection of island territories located far away from the main land, and offshore assets, also assumes added significance.

Conflicts in IOR

Meanwhile, the primary activities that constitute the Sino-Indian security dilemma are Chinese efforts to establish and expand political and security relations with the South Asia-Indian Ocean region (SA-IOR), and Indian efforts to thwart the establishment of such links, on the other. Each side sees the efforts of the other as threatening, as tending to create a situation adverse to its own national security. There is also a powerful tendency on both sides to attribute hostile motives to the actions of the other. In this process of pulling and tugging over China's security ties to Indian Ocean region countries, both Beijing and New Delhi perceive themselves as acting defensively neither of the powers sees itself as aggressive. Yet each views many of activities of the other as gravely threatening actions. These defensively motivate counteractions are, in turn, seen as threatening by the other power, which then devises its own defensively inspired counter-moves in response. Though India has traditionally viewed the SA-IOR as sort of Indian security zone, although India has not explicitly laid out such a regional doctrine, Indian behaviour in the SA-IOR has conformed such an implicit doctrine.

China's New Submarine Base, a major underground nuclear submarine base at the southern tip of Hainan Island, intended to house the new Shang-class (Type 093) nucleated power attack submarine and the Jin-class (Type 094) SSBNs. This development came as a 'cause for security concern' to Indian Navy officials, who were alarmed by China's growing capability to control the Indian Ocean Region.[63] Indian analysts across a wide spectrum perceive Chinese activity in the SA-IOR at least potentially threatening to India.

The security of China's Indian Ocean lines of communication is a second taproot of Chinese security concern regarding India. About 9 per cent of China's total trade, including 66 per cent of its petroleum imports, transits the Indian Ocean.[64] China's deepening involvement in the global economy would make sea lane security more important for China.. China's exploding foreign trades means that its "dependence on strategic ocean passages through the Indian and Pacific Oceans are greatly in increase. Moreover a portion of Chinese strategic resources such as petroleum, iron ore, and so on are imported and must also transit Indian Ocean sea lanes to reach China. This needs PLA-Navy to be able to ensure that the sea lanes for strategic resources *via* the southern Indian Ocean and *via* the Malacca strait are not cut.[65]

The growth of China's naval position in the Indian Ocean to protect Chinese interests in the Indian Ocean, means that over the past years China has gradually expanded its naval activity in that region. China's warships made their first ever call to foreign ports in November 1985 through January 1986. The first port of call of a squadron made up of a 3,500 tonnes Luda-class destroyer and a 7,500 tonnes underway replenishment ship was the Pakistani port of Karachi. After a five-day visit, the squadron headed east for Colombo, Sri Lanka, and then further East to Chittagong, Bangladesh.[66] In November 1993, a 4,500 tonnes PLA-Navy training ship with 200 naval cadets returned to the region. It again visited Karachi first, followed by Chittagong and Bangkok. The craft also put in at Mumbai during the trip.[67]

South China Sea

Throughout the 1990s, Chinese companies were involved in modernization or construction of a number of facilities along Myanmar's coast in the bay of Bengal and Andaman Sea. Chinese companies undertook the modernization of harbour, wharf, and cargo handling facilities in a number of Myanmar cities, including Sittwe, Bassein, Mergui, and Yangon. Myanmar Naval bases were located in several of these harbours, and the improved facilities were often dual use (i.e., both civilian and military). At Hainggyi Island south of where Bassein River empties into the Bay of Bengal, Chinese companies constructed a new harbour and military base. Situated in a location not appropriate for utilization by deep draft ships, the new base seemed designed for anti-smuggling and anti-poaching operation. Chinese companies also built radar and electronics monitoring facilities on Ramree Island, Cocos Island, and at Zadetkyi Kyun Island off the southern tip of Myanmar's portion of the Kra Isthmus. PLA personnel periodically rotated through the Cocos facility, and electronic intelligence gathered by that facility, presumed to be shared by China and Myanmar. The facility on Zadetkyi Kyun was one of two earth satellite station maintained by China outside of PRC borders. (The other is at Kitabari in the South Pacific.) The electronic monitoring stations at Zadetky Kyun, on Ramree, and the Cocos allow the PLA to keep tabs on Indian military activity on and around the Andaman and Nicobar Islands.[68]

In terms of Chinese interests, sustaining and strengthening Pakistan is essential to maintain the balance of power in South Asia upon which China's security policy toward that region rests. Stronger transport links to the sea *via* countries friendly to China (such as Pakistan) would also facilitate the economic development of China's western regions. In military terms, the Pakistani goodwill generated by China's support for the Gwadar project, laid on top of the long standing Sino-Pakistan *entente cordiale,* makes it likely that Chinese naval forces would be allowed to utilize the Gwadar complex should that military requirement materialize. As both Chinese and Pakistani spokesmen pointed out at the time of the August 2001 agreements, cooperation in the Gwadar project demonstrates that China and Pakistan trust each other as friends and that no power could affect that friendship. By underwriting the Gwadar project, China is trying to influence developments far beyond its borders in an effort to maintain a situation it believes conducive to its security – a situation that has the additional consequence, as indicated by Jervis, of deepening a rival's sense of insecurity.[69]

Nuclear Proliferation

The nuclear modernization in the region continues with the development of longer-range and more reliable delivery systems, as well as qualitative and quantitative increases in fissile material and warheads. Initiatives, such as the Indo-U.S. nuclear deal, have brought renewed focus on this issue due to its potential impact on proliferation in South Asia.

The A.Q. Khan network confirmed the entry of non-state actors into the realm of nuclear proliferation. Lingering questions regarding the network's activities suggest that its impact has not yet been fully assessed. There is still considerable demand for nuclear technology, both through horizontal proliferation from aspiring nuclear states such as Iran, and terrorist networks looking to augment their capabilities. This study will analyze these varied developments and investigate proliferation trends in the region.[70] Threat perceptions based on long-standing security disputes shape nuclear doctrines and proliferation dynamics. The intensity of disputes brings in security dilemmas that ensure continued dependence on nuclear weapons in South Asia.

For countries like India and China, it is important to note that while the goals of nonproliferation (especially at a time of potential WMD-related terrorism) are extremely crucial, perceived national interests are a greater factor in shaping the eventual policy direction. With this motivational framework in mind, one must examine recent proliferation-related developments in South Asia, that are likely to have far reaching consequences both regionally and in terms of the global nonproliferation regime. They include the proposed Indo-U.S. nuclear cooperation, the significance of the A.Q. Khan network, and links between South Asian and Middle East proliferation dynamics. These developments reflect, partly or in whole, the need for the weaker protagonist to correct the perceived security imbalance against the stronger threat.[71]

In addition, though Pakistan's close links with China were of concern to India, specifically with regard to the crucial Chinese help given to Pakistan's nuclear programme, so was Pakistan's role as a proxy for China, as a surrogate state.[72]

Rivalry of Arms Procurements

The security dilemma often results in an arms race, a rapid competitive increase in military power by rival states during peacetime.

Over the past years, the region has proved itself as the global crucible for the design, development, procurement and fielding of combat aircrafts, as well as maintaining its ongoing focus multi-role combat aircraft with programmes such as India's MMRCA and Advanced Medium Combat Aircraft and more established PAK-FA collaboration and China's J-20 Curio, exploring indigenous fifth generation technologies hitherto limited to North America and Europe.[73]

IAF combat squadrons number 33, well below government authorised levels. In addition to PAK-FA of which India plans to acquire around 200 twin-seaters, the Aeronautical Development Agency is also planning to develop the Advanced Medium Combat Aircraft for 2025. The US had indicated openness to offering the F-35 to India. India reported to have requirement for seven EMB-145/MA-1 SIGINT/ELINT aircraft. Indian Navy issued RFI in May 2010 for carrier based AEW&C. First test fire of BrahMos from a Su-30MKI is planned for 2012. Weapons package on IN's MiG-29K purchase has been criticised by Comptroller and Auditor General. Modernisation of Air field Infrastructure India project is preparing IAF bases for new advanced aircraft.[74]

China increased its budget by 12.7 per cent in 2011. The new Y-8 based MPA has seen, and dubbed Y-8X. PLANAF is expected to field J15 (Su33 clone) from 2014 but is experiencing testing problems with the three prototypes. CAIC WZ-10 attack helicopter is still stalled in final development with eight helos reported to be at Nanjing. JZ-8F reconnaissance aircraft are deployed with Air Force and Navy. The Plan Y-8GX8 ELINT platform is due to enter service in 2012, also flight tests are underway on the ShaanxiY-9, the replacement for the Y-8. The Y-20 heavy transport platform is still in development with PLANAF trailing Y-7 based AEW&C ac for carrier operations.[75]

Bangladesh is planning the procurement a further 20-32 fighter aircraft by 2027, and the first batteries of Chinese sourced FM-90/

HQ-70 short-range air defence missiles, similar to the Thales Crotale, have been fielded with the Bangladesh Air Force near Dhaka.[76]

Whereas Sri Lanka's 2012 budget has risen from $1.9 billion to $2.1 billion[77] and Sri Lanka's Parliament has passed its largest ever defence budget with majority of 91, raising the budget from $1.9 billion to $2.1 billion.[78]

Recent reports reveal that Pakistan is interested in acquiring 36 J10/FC-20 aircraft from China and early model F-16s in MLU to get ITT AN/ALQ 211(V) 9 EW equipment. DB-100 recon pods are now equipping F-16s.[79] Also, Pakistan has a total of 34 F-16s purchased mostly in the 1980s and the jets are currently in need of a mid-life upgrade to retain their combat effectiveness. The military had used the F-16s to target Taliban hide-outs in the troubled Bajaur tribal region.[80] Pakistan and China have conducted a bilateral counter-insurgency and counter-terrorism exercise in Jhelum in Pakistan's Punjab province, the fourth in a series of events initiated in 2004.[81] It has been reported that Pakistan has accelerated plans to build nuclear powered submarines with plans for them to be inducted into the fleet in 2017-2020 and likely to be equipped with the Babur cruise missile. The Pakistan Air Force's first F-16 Modernization (Peace Drive II) Programme aircraft has been delivered by Turkish Aerospace Industries on February 8th. The Peace Drive II programme, covering avionics and structural modernisation on a total of 41 aircraft started in October 2010 and is planned to be completed by September 2014. Two P-3C Orion maritime patrol aircraft have been inducted in to the Pakistan Navy, replacing two aircraft destroyed on the ground in a terrorist attack at their Karachi base in 2010.[82]

Future Perspectives and Challenges

The course of discussion of the India's security dilemma leads to a very crucial point of argument that reflects in the understanding of the contours of future challenges against a backdrop of the changing nature of conflict, nuclear proliferation and political the instability. For example, these are likely to take anyone or combination of the following forms:

(a) Conflicts across the entire spectrum of military operations, to include Low Intensity Conflict Operations.[83]

(b) Asymmetric Warfare, to include unrestricted warfare, encompassing a wide arena of networks and systems.[84]

(c) Dealing with spillover effects of instability and violence in neighbouring countries, including the Indian Ocean Region, which mandates an 'Out of Area Contingency Capability'.[85]

Over the past decade, various states as well as non-state actors have continued to find ways and means to develop asymmetric warfare capabilities, which can be applied against any nation-state. Therefore, countering asymmetric threats is an area of high priority for Army, and the development of a more advanced capacity in this regard makes the situation very crucial and elusive adversary is relevant.

Also defence exercises and military cooperation between India and other friendly countries helps to understand the mutual trust and interoperability with these countries. This is also the basis for addressing shared concerns over threats like terrorism, extremism and militancy. The defence cooperation with countries in the immediate and strategic neighbourhood is an area of priority focus for the Indian Army.

As to future challenges in the long-term perspective, there are a r.umber of challenges that need to be met to develop and maintain security and peace in the 21st century. In order to develop desired Force Capabilities, the military planner is, therefore, confronted with the dilemma of improving the Capital *vs* Revenue ratios to meet the objectives and enhance the assurance of the requisite capabilities.

The ongoing process of modernisation in new operational condition in the Army calls for restructuring and rightsizing of the Army, which is to be put in perspective. The challenges that we face in this regard are twofold; firstly, evolving the requisite structures to operate in a joint environment with the other two Services, with least possible turbulence; and secondly, attain the optimum size of the Army without impinging on the manpower intensive requirements of manning unresolved borders and operating in Low Intensity Conflicts. For example, recent conflicts those in Iraq and Afghanistan, and the 'Israel-Lebanon' War, have reiterated the necessity of 'Boots on the Ground'.[86]

86. Kapoor, Deepak (2008), *Changing Global Security Environment with Specific Reference to our Region and its Impact on the Indian Army*, Perspective Winter, Volume 2, Issue 2. http://www.idsa.in/jds/2_2_2008_ChangingGlobalSecurityEnvironmentwithSpecificReferencetoourRegion_DKapoor

The new geo-strategic imperatives, technology and the changing nature of conflict, call upon to enhance the levels of jointness even further. There is ample scope for enhancement of Inter Service cooperation and integration, in related areas of congruence, by optimizing force capabilities in the technological realm and by synthesizing resources and efforts of the three Services.

Conclusion

The 21st Century certainly promises to be momentous for the nation in many ways. Despite the turbulent times and the region that we live in, our democratic credentials remain strong and our economy has shown resilience. The understanding of the Indian security dilemma mainly inclines on strategic thinking and development of external security concerns in new paradigm. Also in this regard, considerable inputs derived from the existing features of the corresponding security system architects gives conceptual framework for further analysis. Moreover, India's quest for security and the presence of major powers especially China and US in the South Asia region convulse the whole geopolitics of Indian security.

The potential rise of India as a major power would require development of all elements of National Power, to secure our interests and enable us to play a more effective role in the regional and global arena. Not only should the country be ever prepared to meet external challenges from its traditional adversaries but also it must continue to retain strategic autonomy in decision-making. The Army, as part of the defence forces, comprises an important component of India's comprehensive national power and has always responded to every challenge successfully and relevant to today's needs and the anticipated challenges of the future.[87]

References

1. Annual Report 2011-12, Ministry of Defence, Government of India, p. 2 http://mod.nic.in/reports/AR-eng-2012.pdf accessed 10/07/2012.

2. *Ibid.*
3. *Ibid.*
4. *Ibid.*
5. *Ibid.*
6. Benjamin Miller, (2007) *Nations and the Great Powers: The Sources of Regional War and Peace States* (Cambridge: Cambridge University Press, p. 18.
7. *Ibid.*
8. *Ibid.*
9. *Ibid.*
10. *Ibid.*
11. Joshi, Sharad, (2007) "Nuclear Proliferation and South Asia: Recent Trends", *Aug. 1,* http://www.nti.org/analysis/articles/nuclear-proliferation-south-asia/ accessed on 18/8/2010.
12. Barnwal, Jayant, ed., SP's Military Year Book 2001 (Guide Publications, New Delhi, India), pp. 258-259.
13. *Ibid.*
14. Kapoor, Deepak, *Changing Global Security Environment with Specific Reference to our Region and its Impact on the Indian Army,* IDSA National Security Lecture Series, July 03, 2008 http://www.idsa.in/speeches_at_idsa/NationalSecurityLectureDeepakKapoorNext.htm accessed on 18/10/2008.
15. *Ibid.*
16. Furnivall, John S., (1948) *Colonial Policy and Practice,,* Cambridge, New York; New York University Press, New York, 1956, 303-312.
17. XIN Benjian (2001) "Security Dilemma, Balance of Power *vs* US Policy towards China in the Post-Cold War era", *Contemporary International Relations,* September.
18. Herz, John H., (1950) "Idealist Internationalism and Security Dilemma", *World Politics,* Vol. 2, No. 2, January, pp. 157-158 as cited in XIN Benjian (2001) "Security Dilemma, Balance of Power *vs* US Policy towards China in the Post-Cold War era", *Contemporary International Relations,* September.
19. Collins, Allen (2000) *The Security Dilemmas of Southeast Asia,* Institute of Southeast Asian Studies, Singapore, p. 13.
20. Herz, John H., (1950) "Idealist Internationalism and Security Dilemma", *World Politics,* Vol. 2, No. 2, January, pp. 157-180.
21. *Op cit.* Collins, p. 10.
22. *Ibid.* p. 18.
23. *Ibid.* p. 18.
24. *Ibid.* p. 3.
25. *Ibid.*
26. *Ibid.* p. 6.

27. Jervis, Robert, (1978) "Cooperation under the Security Dilemma" *World Politics*, Vol. 30, No. 2, pp. 167–214.
28. *Ibid.*
29. *Ibid.*
30. *Ibid.*
31. *Op. cit.* Collins, p. 10.
32. *Ibid.* p. 11.
33. Booth, K. and Wheeler, N. (2008), *The Security Dilemma – Fear, Cooperation and Trust in World Politics*, New York: Palgrave Macmillan, p. 2.
34. *Op. cit.*, Kapoor.
35. *Ibid.*
36. *Op. cit.*, Kapoor.
37. *Ibid.*
38. *Ibid.*
39. *Ibid.*
40. Graver, John W. (2002) "The Security Dilemma in Sino-Indian Relations," *India Review*, October, Vol. 1, No. 4, pp. 3-4.
41. Rajesh M. Basrur & Shiping Tang (2007) "Calming Ruffled Feathers," *Daily News and Analysis*, April 17, www.dnaindia.com
42. *Op. cit.* Garver, p. 3.
43. *Ibid.*, pp. 4 & 5.
44. *Ibid.*, p. 5.
45. Harsh V. Pant, "India's Relations with China" in David Scott (ed.) (2011), *Handbook of India's International Relations*, Routledge; London, p. 241.
46. Schweers, Philipp (2008)*Op. cit.*, Kapoor. "India and Pakistan Trapped in a Security Paradox?" *DIAS-Analysis*, Germany, No. 37, Dec. p. 1.
47. *Op. cit.*, Garver, p. 10.
48. Banerjee, Sashanka S. (2006) *India's Security Dilemmas: Pakistan and Bangladesh*, Anthem South Asian Studies: India, pp. 23-26.
49. Ahmed Rashid, "Pakistan's Worrisome Pullback", *Washington Post*, June 6, 2008:A19.
50. Booth, K. and Wheeler, N. (2008), *The Security Dilemma – Fear, Cooperation and Trust in World Politics*, New York: Palgrave Macmillan, p. 4.
51. Butterfield, H. (1951): *History and Human Relations*, London: Collins, pp. 20-21.
    As cited in Schweers, Philipp (2008) "India and Pakistan Trapped in a Security Paradox?" *DIAS-Analysis*, Germany, No. 37, Dec. p. 2.
52. *Op. cit.*, Booth, p. 45.
53. *Op. cit.*, Schweers, p. 3.
54. *Op. cit.*, Banerjee, p. 153.

55. *Op. cit.*, Banerjee, p. 170.
56. Bhattacharya, Abanti (2009) "China's Inroads into Nepal: India's Concerns", May 18 *http://www.idsa.in/idsastrategiccomments/ChinasInroadsintoNepal_ABhattacharya_180509* accessed 12/2/2010.
57. Susan Hangen (2007) "Creating a 'New Nepal': The Ethnic Dimension," *Policy Studies* No. 34 (Washington, DC: East-West Center).
58. Jayadeva Uyangoda (2007) "Ethnic Conflict in Sri Lanka: Changing Dynamics," *Policy Studies* No. 32 (Washington, DC: East-West Center,.
59. Saran, Shyam, (2011) "Balance of Allies" *Indian Express*, September 29, http://www.indianexpress.com/news/balance-of-allies/853216/ accessed on12/10/2011.
60. Oberoi, Vijay, Global and Regional Military Environment, in Kumar, Satish (2004) India's National Security Annual Review 2003, India Research Press: New Delhi, pp. 40-41.
61. *Op. cit.*, Garver, p. 13.
62. *Ibid.*, pp. 40-41.
63. 'China's Deep Sea Plans Alarm India' *The Times of India*, May 3, 'India Wary of Chinese Subs: Navy Chief', *PTI*, May 5, 2008.
64. Xiaojie Xu, (2000) "China and the Middle East: Cross-investment in the Energy Sector" Middle East Policy, Vol. 7, No, 3, p. 4.
65. *Op. cit.*, p. 12.
66. *Ibid.*, p. 13.
67. *Ibid.*, p. 13.
68. *Ibid.*, p. 16.
69. *Ibid.*, p. 21.
70. *Op. cit.*, Joshi.
71. James R. Holmes, "When Interests Collide," *The Bulletin of Atomic Scientists*, May/June 2007, Vol. 63, No. 3, pp. 21-23.
72. L. Dittmer (ed.) (2005), *South Asia's Nuclear Security Dilemma: India, Pakistan, and China*, Armonk: M.E. Sharpe.
73. Regional Air Force, *Asian Military Review*, February/March 2012, p. 22.
74. *Ibid.*, p. 27.
75. *Ibid.*, p. 25.
76. Asian Military Review, Asia Pacific Procurement Update, Volume 20/1 01-February 2012, p. 66.
77. *Ibid.*, pp. 24 and 35.
78. Asian Military Review, Asia Pacific Procurement Update, Volume 20/1 01-February 2012, p. 66.
79. *Ibid.*, p. 32.
80. US Senate asked to finance upgrade of Pakistani F-16s, *Indian Express*, 16/10/2008, p. 11.

81. Asian Military Review, Asia Pacific Procurement Update, Volume 20/1 01-February 2012, p. 66.
82. Asian Military Review, Asia Pacific Procurement Update, Volume 20/2 02-April 2012, p. 58.
83. *Op. cit.,* Kapoor.
84. *Ibid.*
85. *Ibid.*
86. *Op. cit.,* Kapoor.
87. *Ibid.*

4

Conceptualization of National Security in Changing Paradigm

Bijay Kumar Das

Introduction

"Security" in the discipline of International Relations means 'national security'. Security is both an objective and subjective reality. It is objective in the sense, that it denotes a state of affairs in which freedom from threat, fear and want are secured. It is subjective in the sense that the individual, community, or the state can determine how and when the security is achieved. It is the study of security, that lies at the heart of international relations. Its applicability as a core concept in both national and international affairs became widespread only after the World War II. The development of Nuclear Weapons and balance of terror greatly helped to strengthen the idea of the concern for National Security. While war and threat to use force is part of the security equation, it is not exclusively so. The scope of the threats is sufficiently far reaching that, security encompasses dangers that rang from pandemics such as HIV/AIDS and environmental degradation to the more readily associated security concern of direct violence, such as terrorism and inter-state armed conflict.

The Nature of Security Discussion

The Security of the state closely resembles the security of its citizens and the way they judge whether they are secured under the state or not? In fact, inter-state security relations shape assessments of international system as secure, stable and orderly maintained. In essence, it may be said that, security of a nation consists of its territorial integrity, stability of the regime and safeguarding the life of its inhabitants from any threat, action or situation which damage their way of life. National Security is a relative concept because absolute security or security in any comprehensive sense is beyond the reasonable possibility of attainment. It is beyond attainment because an enormous array of threats, dangers and doubts loom over every nation as A.D. Lindsay remarks, "the search for perfect security defeats its own end"[1].

The meaning and nature of security differ from nation to nation as each one of them is exposed to different kinds of threats depending upon the condition of the nations. When nations are strong, national security can be viewed primarily in terms of protecting or safeguarding the nation from external threats.[2] When the nations are weak, they concentrate on domestically generated threats more than external ones. This has been the condition of majority of the Third World nations which either don't have or have failed to generate a domestically strong political and social consensus to eliminate the large-scale use of force as a major and continuing element in the domestic political and social life of the nations.[3] This is the distinction between nations with serious domestic security problems and those, whose primary security concerns are external.

For the weak nations, principal threats to their security comes from within rather than from outside. Among the domestic threats, internal subversion, according to the Latin American national theoreticians is the most devastating threat to National Security.[4] The domestic threats, in addition to undermining national security opens the door for further threats of external intervention, either as a participant on one side or the other, as Syria and Israel intervened in Lebanon in 1976, or as invaders taking advantage of the latter nation, weakened by internal strife.[5] Therefore, the threats to the security of nations have both internal and external dimensions. But whether the threats are internal or external, both undermine the security of the nation as well as the security of its inhabitants as their security is inter-linked with the security of the nation.

The understanding of national security varies widely in their scope and dimensions. According to John Herz, who introduced the notion of 'Security dilemma' states that the self-help attempts of the nations to look after their own security, leads to the rising insecurity for other nations as each nation interprets its own action as defensive and the actions of others as potentially threatening.[6] In the writing of Michael H. H. Low, national security of a nation includes traditional defence policy and also non-military action of the state to ensure its total capacity to survive as a political entity in order to exert influence and to carry out its internal and international objectives. Arnold Wofer's understanding and interpretation of national security have both objective and subjective connotations. According to him, "national security in objective sense, measure the absence of threats to acquired values, in a subjective sense, the absence of fear that such value will be attacked".[7] A narrower interpretation of the concept 'national security' in the writing of Stanley Hoffman ensures protection of nation from physical attack and safeguarding its economic activities.[8] On the other hand, the positive dimension, according to Henry Kissinger, comprises every action by which a society seeks to assure its survival and to realize its aspiration internationally.[9] Security is indispensable for states as they need to protect themselves from array of threats. It is generally argued that the security of nations cannot be defined in general terms, nor can it be determined objectively. Definitions and interpretations depend on states perception about threat and safety. Therefore, on security issues no precise definition has ever been achieved, and the complexity is also related to the problems of which areas of life are the subject of security. In this regard, theoretical debate occurs between two views of security studies, i.e., the "narrow" *versus* "wide" debate. For the followers of the narrow approach to security, i.e., the traditionalist, who argued, the identifying of security issues is easy as they equate security with military issues and the use of force.[10]

The Narrow Concept of National Security and its Extensions

The traditional theoretical perspective on security issues focuses on security relations among states. As a result, international relations theory and analysis has long, sought to explain the core elements of security relations among states. The traditional international relations approach to security was dominated by the ideas of realism. Realism as applied to contemporary world politics has based on the premise that world politics is essentially and unchangeably a struggle among self-interested states for power and domination. For the realists, state exists in a formally anarchic environment, and no legitimate or legal authority is empowered to control, direct or watch over the behaviour of sovereign states. One concurrence of such a system of sovereign state is that, each state must in the end look out for its own security, protection and survival. States struggle with one another for power and influence and must look out for their own interests and ultimately depend upon self-help which leads to the Security Dilemma.[11] Under anarchy with each competing state pursuing it own national interest, conflicts of interests among states are assumed to be inevitable. Realism also emphasizes the ways in which the anarchical nature of international politics dictates the choice that foreign policy makers calculate their interest in terms of power. It also dictates that the state acquire sufficient military capabilities to defer attack by potential enemies and to exercise influence over others. International politics is as Thomas Hobbes put it, a "struggle for power", a "war of all against all".[12] Economics is less relevant to national security than the military might. The need for military power and the constant alertness as to its accumulation and use by others stems directly from the structure of a system of the sovereign state. Security dilemma is central to many other aspects of inter-state relations and will appear in several different forms, for example, arms races and deterrence. The realist's interpretation appeared particularly pervasive after World War II, given the prevailing pattern of conflictual inter-state relations. States and their incessant competition were seen as the defining element of global reality. At the same time, the threatening international environment demanded that, foreign policy take precedence over domestic problems. As the historical imperatives of 'power politics' gave attention to the threat of war, the logic of real politik asserted that military security was the essence of world politics. Like realism, Neo-realism also emphasizes the anarchical nature of international system and the principle of 'self-help' in which the states ensure their own survival. It also tries to explain why the prospects for international cooperation and change often appears to dim and, why state are naturally wary of others and strive to compete with each other. The anarchical nature of the system compels states to be sensitive to their relative position in the distribution of power. Thus, power remains a central concept in neo-realism. However, the quest for power is not considered an end in itself, as if in realism. Instead, the state always pursues power as a means for survival. As Kenneth Waltz, explains "the means fall into two categories: internal efforts, i.e., move to increase economic capability, to increase military strength, to develop clever strategies and external efforts, i.e., move to strengthen and enlarge one's own alliances or to weaken and shrink an opposing one".[13]

Importance of Military Security

The quest for security through arms and the realists' belief in military force remained widespread during the Cold War period. Even after the end of Cold War the importance of military power in the making of foreign policy has been acknowledged. In fact, it may be more pervasive and more comprehensive than it was in earlier period of history when war was less dangerous. Perhaps it was this conviction which inspired former US President, Bill Clinton to assert the view that, "we have to ensure that the United States is ready to win and superior to all other military forces in the world"[14]

Military security has been pursued in myriad ways – through deterrence (making military threats to prevent an action), defence (developing the ability to successfully fight off an armed attack), offence (initiating armed conflict), balancing internal mobilization of resources or making alliances, bandwagoning (actively supporting a dominant action), promotion of particular norms and ideologies and social system, (such as anti-imperialism, liberal democracy, etc.) creation of positive peace (conflict resolution), treaties and imperial and neo-imperial dominance.

Most of the states still devote vast resources to military capabilities compared to other means of influence. For example, the United States has about 20,000 diplomatic personnel but two million soldiers, and spends about $10 billion a year on foreign aid but about $300 billion on military force.[15] For many states, the reason for this dedication of resources is largely defensive. Military capabilities are maintained in an effort to ensure security. Though the overall utility of military force in international relations may be declining, but in the narrow purpose of repelling a military attack, there is often no substitute for military means. Because of the security dilemma, states believe that, they must devote large scale resources to military capabilities if other states are doing so. The shocking attack on the U.S. homeland in 2001 was understood by many states because of their sense of insecurity and their need to maintain capable and viable military forces.

Beyond defending their territories, states develop military capabilities for several other purposes. They often hope to deter attack by having the means to retaliate. They may also hope to compel the other state to behave in certain ways, by threatening an attack if the state does not comply. Therefore, the size and type of military forces makes particular threats credible and states are increasingly using military forces for purposes other than fighting wars. These purposes include humanitarian assistance after disaster, surveillance of drug trafficking, the repression of domestic political dissent, etc.

The Changing Nature of World Power and Security

Military power has been central in policy makers' conceptualization of national security. However, many analysts now argue that the sources of powers are in general, moving away from the emphasis on military forces and conquest that marked earlier eras. In the realm if international influence and power, factors such as technological development, education and economic growth are becoming more important, whereas geography, population and raw-materials are becoming less important. Military force has often proven ineffectual, notably against belligerent revisionist states as well as politically mobilized nationalist and aggressive ethnic movements. Moreover, awareness of the importance of trade competitiveness to national standing has directed increasing attention to the non-military dimensions of security.

The comparison between military-political and trade strategies as an alternative method for realizing national security in the era of globalization highlights the fact that trade strategy appears more effective as a strategy for acquiring political power and material advancement. Spending on military extract and other opportunity cost as well as retard economic growth and create fiscal deficits. According to the International Monetary Fund (IMF), military spending crowds out both private and public investment. The countries which made sharp cuts in military spending and their overall fiscal deficits have the leverage of boosting social spending.[16] Because, state can afford 'more butter' if they need fewer 'guns' and the two objectives sometimes represent trade-offs, the achievement of one may diminish the realization of others, and the substantial costs of defence can erode national welfare which policy-makers hope to defend with military might. Conversely, commercial clout and trade competitiveness may contribute more than military might to national power and security.

Many governments have slashed military budgets in order to deal with the economic crises, which pose a greater threat to states in the form of inflation, underdevelopment and debt. Leaders in disarming states have began to recognize that in the long run high military spending can reduce a state's industrial growth, weaken its global economic competitiveness and ultimately, undermine its ability to pursue and preserve dominance.[17] As a government cannot satisfy citizens' craving for a promising financial future and a standard of living comparable to that of people living abroad, protest against the state from its citizens can be expected in the form of civil war which leads to political disintegration. No level of military might can guarantee a state's invulnerability and state's primary security problem today lies with internal problems rather external aggression.

In the past military might enabled states to project power, exercise influence and dominate others. Today, Nuclear and advanced (biological and chemical) weapons of mass destruction (WMD) make the use of military might risky. Continuing arms proliferation raises new questions, such as does the acquisition of more weapons increase national security – psychological phenomena? Or are preparations for war and defence responsible for the security dilemma that all countries face? Certain groups of leaders agree with the view of the ancient Greek philosopher, Aristotle who argued that, "a people without walls are people without choice".[18] Thus, they accept the realist premise that preparing war is necessary for peace, yet, the capacity to destroy others does not always make for a convincing threat, especially against countries with capacity to retaliate. Therefore, the threat of force often lacks credibility. Military power has become impotent by its very strength and military might no longer compels others compliance. Currently, in the information age, states are likely to invest in non-military methods of acquiring 'soft power', reasoning that, if the state can make its power legitimate in the eyes of others and establish international institutions that encourages others to define their interest in compatible ways, it may not need to expand costly traditional military resources.[19] That outcome could diminish substantially states traditional faith in the proposition that overwhelming military might is required to play the game of international politics because it gets others to accommodate themselves to the demand of a more militarily powerful state.

The Non-Traditional Dimension

The conceptualization of national security merely in terms of external military threats fails to capture large variety of problems facing nations, particularly Third World nations. Military power has no doubt its own value to security of a nation to the extent that it is required for the elimination of coercive sources of threats to security but it does not serve a better meaning to the idea of national security. The scope and nature of national security was widened after the World War II, both in terms of military and non-military threats, whether coming from outside the border or within the boundaries of nation.[20] In essence, it may be said that security of a nation consists of its territorial integrity, stability of the regime, and the realization of its other national and international interests and safeguarding the life of its inhabitants from any threats, action or situation which damage their way of life in any extent. Therefore, the concept national security must include protection against all major threats to human survival and well-being, and not just military threats.

In the past, 'Security' usually addressed as national security has meant the maintenance of strong military defence against enemy invasion and attack. This approach may have served us well in the past, when such attack was seen as only real threat to national survival, today however, when airborne poisons released by nuclear and chemical accidents produce widespread death and sickness, and when global epidemiological and environmental hazards such as "AIDS and the Green House Effect" can jeopardise the well-being of the entire planet, this perspective appears increasingly obsolete. As individual economies become even more enmeshed in the world economy, every society becomes more vulnerable to a global economic crisis. And, as modern communications brings us all closer together, we are made acutely aware of the pain and suffering of those living under oppression, tyranny and injustice.

Given the fact that our individual security and well-being will depend to an ever-increasing extent on the world's success in mastering complex political, economic, environmental and epidemiological problems, we must redefine security to embrace all of those efforts taken to enhance the long-term health and welfare of the human family. Defence against military aggression will obviously remain a vital component of security, but it must be joined by defences against severe environmental degradation, worldwide economic crisis and massive human sufferings. Given the multiplicity of pressing world hazards, the concept of 'National Security' must be integrated with that of 'world security'. In today's interdependent world, the quest for security is rapidly becoming a positive sum process, whereby national well-being is achieved jointly by all countries. Approach to the study of national security now being frequently advocated puts these non-military dimensions of the problem into the picture. These non-military threats must command attention, as human survival may depend on addressing them.

Meanwhile, there is the emergence of transnational actors, and non-state actors with significant capacities for global action to influence the international arena in decision making. This is an important change in international relations with primary of the interaction between various actors. The twenty-first century also demonstrates more strongly than in previous eras the need to solve the problems of millions of human beings who are adversely affected by enormous and growing political, economic, social, health, personal and cultural insecurities. Consequently insecurity is global, even though the manifestation may differ from region to region and from country to country.[21] A core concern is to progress towards the construction of a new global order capable of placing human beings at its centre, and for states, which continue to be the actors with the greatest relative power, to be able to efficiently guarantee people's security and contribute to overcoming the vulnerabilities and difficulties of hundreds of millions of human beings in acceding to progress and development. Emphasis has been from "an exclusive stress on territorial security to a much greater stress on 'people's security' and from security through armaments to security through sustainable human development". According to the UNDP's Human Development Report 1994, human development is defined as "a process of widening the range of people's choices". And human security means, "that people can exercise these choices safely and freely and that they can be relatively confident that the opportunities they have today are not totally lost tomorrow".[22] More specifically, human security is considered in the realm of seven main categories: economic, food, health, environmental, personal, community, and political security. Economic security requires jobs to be secure for an assured basic income. Food security means that all people at all times have both physical and economic access to basic foods. Health security is to provide healthy environment and health services to meet the challenges of poor nutrition, infectious diseases, and so on. Environmental security is concerned with lack of access to clean water, deforestation, sanitization, air pollution, natural disaster, and so on. Personal security is to protect human lives from threats of various kinds of violence by states and other groups. Community security is about threats like oppressive practices and the ethnic clashes in traditional communities. Political security means the protection of human rights and democratization. Further, the Report refers to the problem of environmental degradation, drug-trafficking and international terrorism.[23] The concept of human security enunciated by UNDP has the advantage of systematically understanding various international assistance in order to provide an overall conceptual map for international coordination. This gives rise to the view commonly shared by both supporters and critics that human security is opposed to "state-centric realism" and challenges the traditional concept of security. It is true that the characteristics of human security mentioned in the Report are intended to be distinct from state centric-view. However, they do not necessarily challenge the state. That is why the UNDP's Report characterized human security as the 'integrative' concept that demands "policies for social integration" and such policies do not deny the sovereign states system upon which the UN relies; they seek to reinforce it. While pluralistic values to respect diversity of states and other actors in international society would be the foundation of such policies, strengthening the function of states is the major course of human security. In the context of small states, the issue of security has multifarious dimensions in the complexities of the state and the region as whole. Hence, the nature and magnitude of security within the state should be considered from various angles, viz., geopolitical, historical, socio-political and economical. Such a holistic approach can only ensure a proper understanding of insecurity dilemmas of small states.

Conclusion

The whole inquiry assumes that threat exists when security is a problem. Security can be pursued either by taking action to reduce vulnerability, or by trying to eliminate or to reduce the threat by addressing their causes at source. The first may be called 'national security strategy', because it is based largely within the threatened state. The second may be called international security strategy, because it depends on the adjustment of relations between states.[24] The concept of national security does not lend itself to neat and precise formulation. It deals with a variety of risks and problems about whose probabilities there is little knowledge. The dilemma and disputes about security questions concern not only the relations between the states and their external environments, but relations within the states. Under the heading of security complex, domestic disputes form the first basic level of inquiry in analyzing security problems. It is the domestic political system in each state, which actually produces national security policy. Because, the whole decision making apparatus of the state is largely set up in relation to domestic interest, the security problem of states cannot be assessed without reference to the system, and the character and dynamics of the system cannot be understood without reference to states. The national security problem turns out to be a systemic security problem in which individuals, state, and the system all play a part.[25] Therefore, Security cannot be achieved by either individuals or states acting solely on their behalf. Some collective measures are necessary among the sovereign members of the system of each to achieve security. From this point of view, security might best be served at all levels by a multi-dimensional approach, because the degree of insecurity which a nation faces depends upon a number of internal and external circumstances.

References

1. A.D. Lindsay, *"Introduction to Leviathan"*, Dent: London, 1914, p. 22.
2. Iqbalur Rehman, *"National Security and the Problem of Unconventional Warfare"*. Delhi, Kanishka Publishing House, 1992, p. 10.
3. Bary Buzan, *"People, State and Fear: The National Security Problem in International Relations"*, Hertfordshire, Harvesten Wheatsheat, 1991, pp. 35-36.
4. J. A. Vieragallo, *"National Security Doctrines and their Impact on Human Rights"*, in J.A. Viergallo (ed.), "The Security Trap: Arms Race Militarism and Disarmament: A Concern for Christians", IDOC/WCC, Rome 1982, pp. 89-90.
5. Iqbalur Rehman, *op. cit.*, p. 11.
6. John H. Herz, "The Idealist Internationalism and the Security Dilemma", World Politics, 1950, pp. 157-80.
7. Arnold Wolfer, "Discord and Collaboration", Batimore: Johns Hopkins University Press, 1962, p. 150.
8. Iqbalur Rehman, *op. cit.*, p. 5 (An analysis of the understanding of National Security by Stanley Hoffman have been reflected).
9. M.N. Rawat, "Concept and Environment of National Security", *USI Journal*, Vol. 113, April-June, 1983, p. 114.
10. Bary Buzan, "Security: A New Framework for Analysis", London, Lynee Rienner Publisher, 1998, p. 3.
11. John H. Herz, "Political Realism and Political idealism", University of Chicago Press, 1951, pp. 18-19.
12. Leo Strauss, Elsa M. Sinclair, "The Political Philosophy of Hobbes", Chicago: University of Chicago Press, 1952, p. 10.
13. Charles W. Kegley, JR & Eugune R Wittkopf, "World Politics: Trend and Transformation", Bedford/St. Martin's, Boston, New York, 2001, p. 37.
14. Majeed Akhtar, "Has the War System Really Become Obsolete?", Bulletin of Peace Proposals, Vol. 22, (December), 1991, p. 420.
15. Joshua S Goldstein, "International Relations", Pearson Education, Inc. 2003, p. 221.
16. Koretz Gene, "Fewer Guns, More Butter", Business Week, (July 1), 22, 1996.
17. Kennedy Paul, "The Rise and fall of the Great Powers" New York, Random House, 1987, pp. 56-57.

18. Charles W. Kegley, Jr. and Eugene R. Wittkopf, "World Politics: Trend and Transformation", *op. cit.*, p. 654.
19. Keohane, Robert O., and Joseph S. Nye, Jr., "Power and Interdependence in the Information Age", in Charles W. Kegley, Jr. & Eugene R. Wittkopf (eds.) "The Global Agenda", Boston, McGraw-Hill, 2001, pp. 26-36.
20. Montor Benkowitz and P.G. Bock, National Security, International Encyclopedia of Social Sciences, The Macmillan Company and Press, 1968, p. 41.
21. United Nations Development Programme, (UNDP), 1999, Human Development Report, 1999, New York, Oxford University Press, p. 90.
22. UNDP, Human Development Report, Oxford University Press, 1994, p. 23.
23. *Ibid.*, pp. 24-37.
24. H. A. Simon, "On the Stability of Layered Hierarchies", Proceedings of American Philosophical Society, Vol. 8, No. 3, 1997, pp. 216-20.
25. Bary Buzan, "People, State and Fear", Chapel Hill: University of North Carolina Press, 1979, p. 218.

5

Natural Hazards/Disasters – Environmental Security: Role of Geo-informatics

Parthasarathi Chakrabarti

Introduction

Environmental security is to tackle the ever increasing menace of ecological/natural as well as anthropogenic hazards/disaster – a global threat to the human being (Table 5.1). In this regard, leaving aside the anthropogenic disaster basic issues reflect on study of bidirectional relationship between human subsystem and physical

Table 5.1: Classification of Extreme Events/ Hazards /Disasters

Meteorological Disaster	Floods
(Exogenous origin— often accentuated by Human activities)	Cyclones/Storm-surges, Heat Wave/ Cold Wave, Hail Storm
	Drought/Desertification (land degradation)
Geo-disaster (Endogenous origin)	Earthquake, Volcanism, Tsunami, Landslide.
Anthropogenic Disaster	Flooding/ water logging due to failure of dam/reservoir/ barrage/ embankment; obstructions on the spill channels; subsidence due to underground mining/withdrawal of groundwater, Industrial-oil /gas spills, Bomb Blast, Electrical/ Road Accidents, etc

environment in the context of rising population, rapid urbanization and industrialization, unplanned use of land and water resources with vulnerability and risk due to natural hazards/disaster (Fig. 5.1). In this respect, the core business is to establish dynamic viewing capabilities for identification of acceptable changes between the Environment (E) and Human Capital and Mobility (HCM) in terms of:

- Conservation and rational utilization of natural resources.
- Agro-ecological characterization and industrial development for ecological stability.
- Setting up of 'Early Warning System' to minimize the adverse effects of natural calamities.
- Prioritization of 'Bio-prospecting zones' for biodiversity conservation.
- Information dissemination for building public awareness to ensure public participation.

Prime Requisite –

- Creation of structural framework for generation of multi-theme spatial information on natural resources and inter-operability with attributable data on societal aspects in GIS platform.
- To generate application specific 'strategic dataset', i.e., Geo-information.

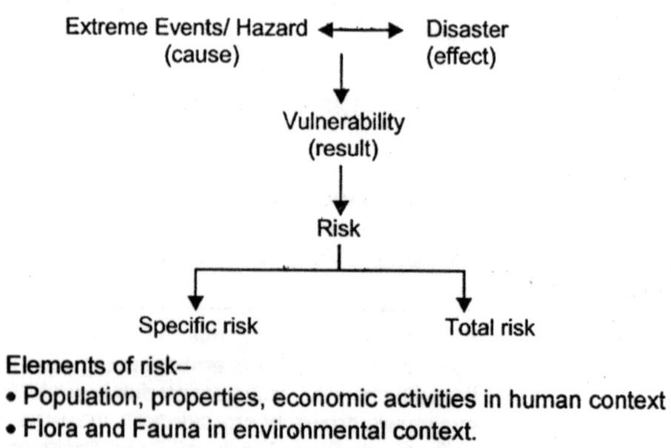

Fig. 5.1: Extreme Events in Socio-Environmental Context

- To upgrade 'ethno-science' practices with 'techno-science' support.
- To provide 'easy-to-access' user oriented database for 'locale specific' planning with regional perspective.

In this regard, Geo-environmental Mapping (GEM) plays a subjective role in Geo-spatial Resources Management (GRM) identifying the factual and functional parameters (Fig. 5.2).

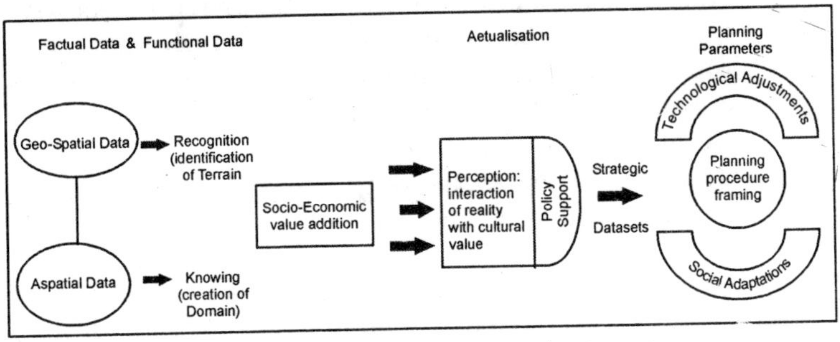

Fig. 5.2: Conceptual Framework of GRM

Geoenvironmental Mapping (GEM)

- unravels the impact of Anthropic developments on bio-physical environment through space and time identifying the factual and functional parameters.
- frame guidelines for rational balance between (E) and (HCM) through 'Technological adjustment' and 'Social Adaptations', e.g., huts with raised platform in flood prone area to minimize loss of lives, etc.

GEM indicates suitability of different terrain units in relation to the existing utilization or selective alternate uses.

'Easy-to-understand' presentation of spatial data in 'Geo-environmental Mapping' requires identification of *Geo-environmental Indicators* (GEI) and *Geo-environmental Unit* (GEU) in relation to Natural System Unit (NSU) /Terrain Mapping Unit (TMU)

GEI: 'Process-sensitive and easy-to-measure' physico-chemical characteristics of dynamic earth which help in identifying the various geomorphic environment in human orientation through space and time. Two types –

- *Qualitative* – to identify the specific characteristics of landform unit(s) in terms of spatial change detection, e.g., landslide/soil erosion /flood prone areas, bank line shifting of a river or shoreline shifting, etc.
- *Quantitative* – supplementary to Qualitative indicator. Numerical attributes related to change detection generated from *in situ* measurements are of basic importance, e.g., round the year beach profiling data to specify the zone of erosion or accretion; sediment monitoring station may generate data on soil erosion; variation in chemical qualities of water in identifying the hydrological characteristics of an area.

GEU: Spatial database with certain entity or bounds as defined by GEI. A GEU may contain one or more TMU (Meijrink, 1988) or Natural System Unit (NSU) and *vice versa*.

To support the Geo-environmental Mapping it is essential to interlink the spatial and non-spatial data using sequential Remote Sensing data and GIS technology to conclude on technical adjustment and societal objectives.

Case History Examples

I. Tsunami on 26th December, 2004

The major shallow focus earthquake (of magnitude 9.0) occurred on the Sunda belt on 26th December, 2004 at 6:18:53 IST, hit the sea off the west coast of northern Sumatra due to movement of Indian Plate and Burma Plate. The epicentre of this earthquake was at 3°24′ N: 95°82′ E and the focus was at 37.0 km. below the sea floor. A vast area around its epicentre was rocked including Andaman and Nicobar islands and parts of the eastern and western coasts of the Indian mainland. It may be mentioned that the 26/12 event resulted in widespread adjustment in Andaman-Nicobar Islands – Survey of India indicates that the northern part of the A & N Islands has uplifted with a eastward tilt.

The other event associated with this earthquake was the most devastating 'Tsunami' in history. The deadly tsunami waves caused widespread damage in eleven countries bordering the Indian Ocean with propagation of waves in E-W direction as the submarine fracture was caused by the earthquake in a nearly N–S direction.

Andaman being nearer to the epicentre of the earthquake is affected both by the earthquake tremors and tsunami. Reflection of this phenomenon is exemplified in the North Andaman by damage due to earthquake whereas combined effect of earthquake and tsunami is present in South Andaman.

The presence of Andaman and Nicobar islands (6° to 14° latitude) saved the Orissa and West Bengal coasts from the tsunami attack. Andaman and Nicobar islands, act as a buffer zone/shock absorber for West Bengal and Orissa coasts whereas the tsunami directly hit the southern fringe of Andhra Pradesh and Tamil Nadu coasts and Sri Lanka.

It may be mentioned that if such a submarine earthquake takes place in Thailand or Burma (Myanmar) it may directly attack the coastal tract of West Bengal. The bathymetric configuration of this coastal tract is not so steep as it is in the case of Tamil Nadu and Sri Lankan coasts due to the presence of the Ganga delta. However, the funnel shaped Hooghly Estuary with 'ridge runnel' bottom topography is likely to be affected by Tsunami 'bore' as mentioned earlier, though the breaker zone, lies near 'sand heads', far off (about 40 miles) from the coast line. The adjacent Medinipur coastal plain may also be affected but not like the Tamil Nadu coast where steep bathymetric configuration exists.

Geo-spatial Information

Comparative study of pre- and post-tsunami Remote Sensing (RS) data supported with ground truthing, interview of the local people and ancillary data collection of the study area demand discussion on damage assessment caused by earthquake and tsunami in two different sectors, viz., physical/natural environment and human orientation (Chakrabarti *et al.* 2006).

The effects of the severe earthquake are very much exemplified on ground as well as on man made structures in the form of cracks as slips/fractures and collapsed structure, etc. in North and Middle Andaman. The main reasons are the physiographic configuration of the area and very specific location of the settlements in the higher ground away from the HWL (High Water Line). Whereas, the devastation in South Andaman (especially in Port Blair and Little Andaman) is more due to the combined effects of earthquake and tsunami. However, it is reported by the Geological Survey of India (2005) that the intensity of earthquake remain same in north, middle and south Andaman. For example:

North and Middle Andaman

- Due to upliftment and shifting of HWL (High Water Line) towards sea (i.e., recession of HWL), deterioration in Mangrove Swamp Zone took place at places, e.g., Aerial Bay, Swarajgram, etc.
- Major damage in the Austin bridge due to Translational movement in NE-SW direction – middle span shifted towards NE by 0.45 m and adjacent span gone down by 0.10 m.
- In Kalipur, Ramnagar, Pokadera/Baludera very gently sloping beach face and beach front dune with 'keya' trees mainly absorbs the thrust of waves though at places sea water ingressed in the cultivable land; no infrastructural damage due to absence of settlements/inhabitated area along the beach-dune complex.
- In Rampur a newly built up double storied building collapsed due to failure of load bearing RC columns of the ground floor.
- In Karmatang area the beach is mainly rocky/bouldery with some sandy patches. Sandy beach, steep in nature with 'berm' and low height dune (with 'Ipomia biloba', 'keya' trees/mangroves); tsunami wave toppled dunes at places but restricted within 25.00 m; insignificant or no damage in the 'Eco-park'.
- In Dasarathpur, Rangat, tsunami wave attack predominant; the reclaimed portion of the Intertidal Flat being waterlogged planted trees uprooted and embankment-cum-road severely damaged (Photo 5.1a, b, c).

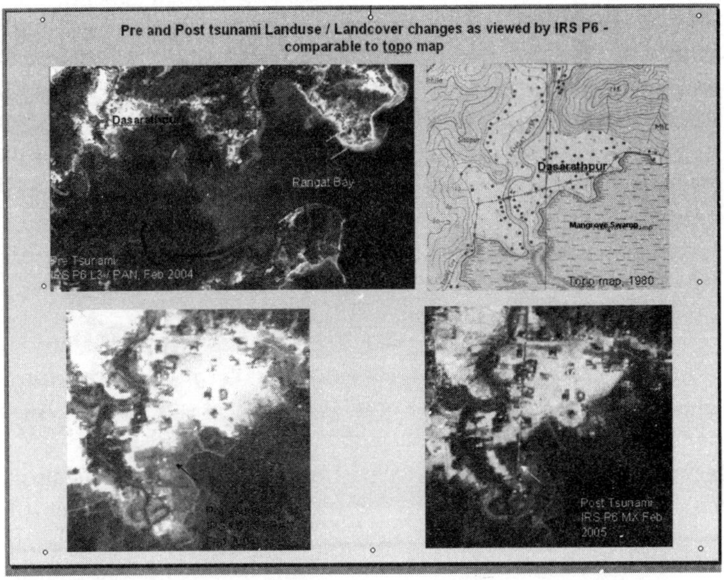

Photo 5.1a: Pre- and Post-Tsunami Land-Use/Landcover Changes

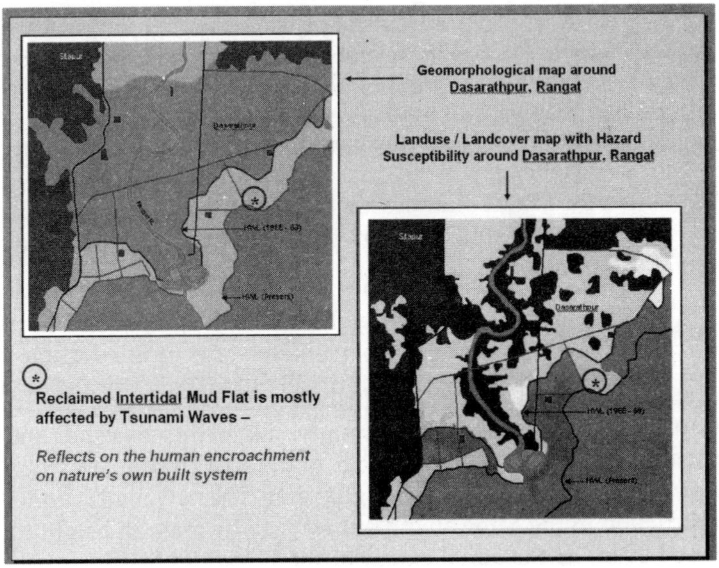

Photo 5.1b: Geomorphological and Landuse/Land cover map with Hazard susceptibility around Dasarathpur, Rangat

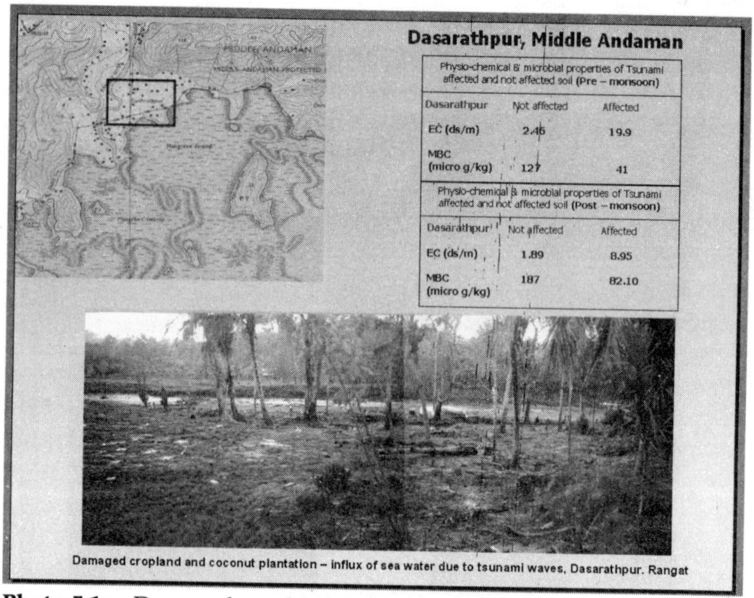

Damaged cropland and coconut plantation – influx of sea water due to tsunami waves, Dasarathpur. Rangat

Photo 5.1c: Damaged cropland and coconut plantation due to Tsunami and entering of sea waster Dasarathpur

- In Nayagarh area, Baratang, tsunami water entered into the cultivated land through Jarwa creek near the Mud Volcano; local villagers reported that immediately after the earthquake two Mud Volcanoes started erupting at 6.35 hrs (Photo 5.2); however, no loss of life and property as no settlement in the surroundings. It may be mentioned that the Mud Volcanoes are located along the crested parts of the Andaman geanticline – zones of fault/thrust (Chakrabarti *et al.*, 2006).

South Andaman

In the Port Blair and Ferrarganj tehsils the effect of tsunami is more conspicuous in terms of sea water ingression in the croplands and agricultural farms as well as damage of the ATR (Andaman Trunk Road) around Ograbaraij and Sipighat area. The new road is under construction in the same alignment with an increase in height by about 1.00 m, as the aerial extent of the Intertidal Flat increased due to rise of the HWL caused by earthquake and tsunami. It may

Photo 5.2 : Mud Volcano, Nayagarh, Baratang, Middle Andaman; effect of Aftershocks (post tsunami feature)

be mentioned that the settlements in the low-lying areas (mostly reclaimed) are worst affected by the tsunami and water logging condition prevails (Chakrabarti, *et al.*, 2006).

It is worth mentioning here that the reclaimed 'Intertidal Mangrove Swamp Zone' is mostly affected in the South Andaman reflecting the unscientific approach towards encroachment of nature's own built buffer zone for such a devastation. *This may be considered as best example of "Technology Push" rather than "Application Pull" which leads to impart/implement technology not appropriate to the terrain condition and social settings – concern environmental security.*

II. Integrated Coastal Zone Management, West Bengal

Two contrasting coastal environs present in the coastal tract of West Bengal, viz., 'Macrotidal Hooghly estuary' and 'Mesotidal Medinipur coastal plain'. In Hooghly estuary, the mangroves play an important role as dominant geomorphic agent (in response to the warm humid climate) in the evolution of the tidal shoals and their eventual accretion to the main landmass resulting in the delta progradation upto recent past. In the existing scenario, the Hooghly estuary becomes the abandoned part of the lower deltaic plain of the Ganga-Brahmaputra within India and is turning destructive as revealed from the beach surveying (Chakrabarti, 1991, 1995). It is estimated that the destructive phase has started, at least, in the early part of the 20th century, possibly due to abandonment of delta growth and global sea level rise.

In Medinipur coastal plain, development of successive rows of dunes with intervening clayey tidal flats is due to the punctuation in the regressions of sea in Holocene times.

In response to the contrasting physiographic configuration, the integration and analysis of the qualitative and quantitative 'base line data' generated from Quaternary geological and geomorphological mapping and beach surveying lead to conclude on 'site specific' action plain in regard to ICZM (Chakrabarti, 1999):

(a) In Digha and Bakkhali-Gangasagar areas safeguarding of the built-up land from coastal erosion is the burning issue which is not present in the Dadanpatrabar-Junput area (the accretional zone in between).
Both in Digha and Bakkhali-Gangasagar area to ameliorate the environmental degradation, an area upto 200 m from 'High Tide Line' (HTL) has been earmarked as 'No Development Zone' by Govt. of West Bengal (1996/2005) though it is not in vogue (Photo 5.3).

Inspite of CRZ Notification construction activities in progress, Bakkhali Beach, Hooghly Estuary, West Bengal

Photo 5.3: Inspite of CRZ Notification construction activities in progress, Bakkhali Beach, Hooghly Estuary, West Bengal

(b) Prawn cultivation in coastal areas is coming up fast as the returns from the aquacultural farming is more than the crop farming. But brackish water pumped inland to rear prawns can infiltrate surrounding soils and render them unfit for cultivation by increasing the salt content and also seep into the underground aquifers and destroy sweet groundwater. In response to that extension of brackish water fish farming in the area under reference should be given prime importance during land-use planning as this particular phenomenon has more socio-economic implication than analytical land evaluation procedure. In such areas GIS may play an important role to provide proper decision, e.g., establishment of typical ditch system for combined rice-shrimp cultivation, as it is in vogue in Mekong Delta, Vietnam.

III. Bank Failure and Flooding in Ganga–Padma River

The lateral migration/oscillation of the Ganga-Padma river in West Bengal down the ages both in prehistoric and historic periods, may be considered as a natural phenomenon in Geological time scale. But in human orientation, this shifting of the river course is causing large scale disaster in terms of flooding, bank failure in Malda and Murshidabad districts, West Bengal, India. In this respect, sequential changes in the courses of this major river system within West Bengal has been studied using IRS 1B/1C LISS II FCC (1996 – 1999)/, IRS-1D, WiFS (1998 – 2002)/, SOI toposheets (1970 series) and PS maps of Bengal Survey (1935-40) with ground truthing for identifying the zone of erosion/bank failure or zone of submergence, etc., for futuristic planning options in terms of technical aspects (i.e., structural means) and social adaptations (i.e., non-structural means).

In the PS/Thana map (1934-40; on scale 1 inch to 1 mile) one may find that the Ganga river after Rajmahal (Jharkhand) enters West Bengal (Maldah district) and flows in SE direction with a straight course. However, the comparative analysis of the Thana map with Survey of India toposheet (1972-73) reveals that the river has shifted easterly for about 8.00 km. in a curvilinear fashion causing bank failure in the Manikchak-Gopalpur area. Active bank erosion/failure is present all along the left bank of the Ganga river e.g., about 700 m shifting of river bank between April 1997 to November 1997. Morpho-arrangement of older meander scrolls are indicative of further eastward extension of the river upto Pagla *nadi* and that has attained in 2002. The Pagla *nadi* – an offshoot of the Kalindri/Phulher river from south-east corner of the 'Bhutnir Char' was flowing in a curvilinear fashion upto Gopalpur and then flows in two branches with broad meandering. Presently, the upper portion of the Pagla *nadi* is cut-off from the Kalindri river but remnants of abandoned channel course is well documented in the satellite images.

It may be mentioned here that one channel bar is now formed along the left bank of Ganga around Manikchak in 1999/2000 and gradually it becomes a prominent feature as exemplified in 2002 satellite image of the area. It seems, with the formation of this channel bar the effect of bank erosion in the left bank of the river in this stretch will be reduced to a great extent.

It is interesting to mention that the comparative analysis of PS/Thana map (1939-40), SOI toposheet (1972-73) and the up-to-date satellite images reveal that the shifting of the Ganga river in the aforesaid area is accelerated possibly due to the anthropogenic activities in terms of construction of circuit embankment around the 'Bhutnir Char' (a permanent channel bar) in 1972 ignoring the play field of such a major river, to accommodate the water spreading during high discharge time instead of confining the flood time flow along the constricted channel enhancing the thrust causing bank erosion.

Further downstream upto Farakka barrage the Ganga river has straightened to a large extent from 1970 and engulfed the meander loop of the Pagla *nadi*. In this sector Ganga has shifted about 1.10 km. towards east between 1970 to 2003. Presently, the most vulnerable zone is 10.0 km. stretch south of Panchanandapur upto Beguntola – Ganga is likely to straighten its course maintaining the river morphology and mav cause severe bank erosion (Nag & Chakrabarti, 2008).

Downstream of Farakka, the Ganga-Padma river becomes a braided river with fabrics of channel bars and the main flow is in the right side of river. In response to that the shifting of river course and bank failure zones are all along the right bank of the river in comparison to the left bank shifting of river course in the upstream of the Farakka barrage. The possible geo-spatial reason is the presence of comparatively hard 'Barind formation' (in Bangladesh) almost all along the left bank of the river.. The most vulnerable areas within India are: Teghari-Paharpur, Akheriganj and Jalangi areas of Murshidabad district.

In Akheriganj area, migration of main flow of the river is towards south with a river island ('Nirmal Char') and there is a tendency to capture the older meander scrolls. It may be mentioned that the earlier branch-off point of Bhairab river is about 6 km. north of the present mouth which rejuvenates only in the rainy season with increase in discharge level. This is an indication of southward smoothening of the curvature of the Ganga river occupying the earlier flood plain. It may be mentioned here that any circuit embankment around 'Nirmal Char' as demanded by the local inhabitants will replicate the acceleration of the bank failure in the Akheriganj area as experienced in the Manikchak-Gopalpur area for the circuit embankment of 'Bhutnir Char' (Photo 5.4).

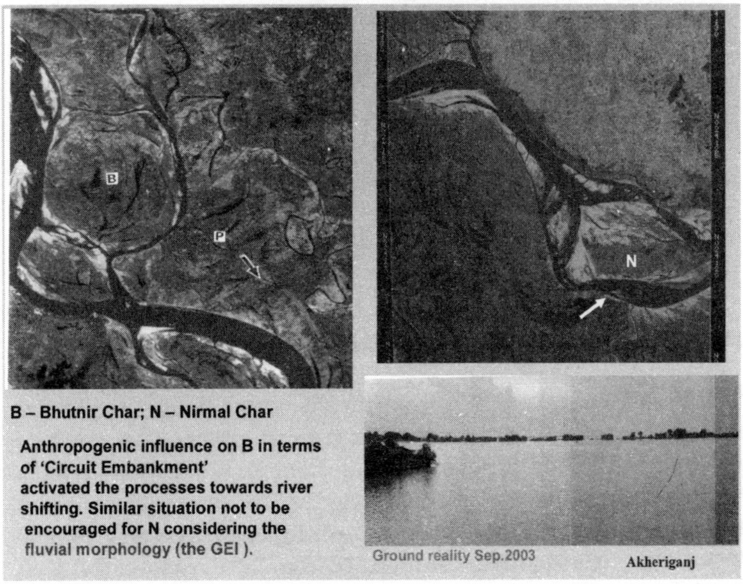

Photo 5.4: Anthropogenic influence on B in terms of 'Circuit Embankment'

Root Cause of Bank Failure

The study of the natural sections of the left bank and right bank of the river upstream and downstream of Farakka respectively, reveals the existence of a sandwiched fine sand layer partings of about 1.0 m within the silty clay sequence. During high discharge time removal of the fine sand/silt layer accelerates the process of bank failure (Photo 5.5).

Photo 5.5: Root cause of Bank failure

IV. Arsenic Contamination in Groundwater, West Bengal

In the Gangetic plain, more specifically, in the Bhagirathi-Padma interfluve arsenic contamination in groundwater is a very striking geo-environmental problem in West Bengal, India. The available technical literature on the issue upto 2007 indicate occurrence of arsenious groundwater in 79 blocks of eight districts, West Bengal, India, viz., Malda, Murshidbad, Nadia, 24 Parganas (N & S), Barddhaman, Hooghly and Howrah districts. It is fairly established so far that arsenic is present primarily in the intermediate aquifer (20-80 m.b.g.l.) and associated with high concentration of Fe.

Arsenious aquifer is dominantly made up of fine sand and clay. It is fairly established that arsenic contamination is 'geogenic' and aggravated by anthropogenic activities through time. In this respect, a comprehensive applied geomorphological approach using RS (Remote Sensing) and GIS technologies unravels the source pathway of the 'geogenic' arsenic contamination in the context of changing geomorphology of the coalescing fans of the Himalayan rivers and Gangetic Younger Alluvial Plain (YAP) alongwith changing land-use (e.g., Summer rice cultivation) and land cover through space and time.

In this respect, integration and analysis of the spatial data on geomorphology, land-use/and cover pattern and chemical analysis data reveal that —

(i) Higher As concentrations are not present in post monsoon/ winter season water samples, in general, where surface water source (e.g., bils/jhils, active meander scrolls etc.) are being used for irrigation of rabi and summer crops.

(ii) The areas where groundwater being extracted for irrigation of rabi and summer crops, higher As concentrations in post-monsoon/winter season are present in the wells.

In this regard, Nadia district could be cited as an example where surface waterbodies are more than other arsenic affected districts and only 26 per cent of the wells showing high As concentration in post monsoon/winter season — reflects on use of surface water sources for rabi and summer crops. Similarly, in 24 Parganas (S) district and in the southern part of the 24 Parganas (N) district, in general, the groundwater are not being used for rabi and summer crop cultivation as near surface aquifers are saline or brackish in nature — upto 160.0 m.b.g.l. (Chakrabarti & Das 2006). This may be considered as a startling revelation in the context of existing knowledge that the concentration of arsenic in a tubewell is diluted during the monsoon/post monsoon period due to natural replenishment of the contaminated aquifer.

In the existing scenario considering the hydrogeological/ geomorphological and hydrochemical conditions for arsenic mobilisation in the groundwater it will be wise to make good use of surface water with appropriate and adequate treatment. It may be mentioned here that the area under interest is with numerous 'bils'/oxbow lakes, etc., one or two such waterbodies may be identified in Gram Panchayat orientation (i.e., Community based Water Supply Scheme) and that could be used as source for piped water supply for drinking purpose after necessary treatment at the source point.

In long term perspective the 'Nadia group of rivers' may be rejuvenated through river interlinking to get all season flow in the rivers and use of the same with necessary treatment for drinking water supply.

V. Drought Hazard in the Western Upland, West Bengal

Regionally, the western upland constitutes the eastern fringe of the Chhotanagpur Plateau with erosional remnants (in the form of isolated hills) exhibiting highly dissected pedimental landscape and lateritic upland with skeletal soil covering Puruliya district and parts of Bankura, Paschim Medinipur and Birbhum districts. The meteorological data reveal that the average annual rainfall is, in general, between 1300-1350 mm — much in the higher side to prevail drought condition. It is established fact that the surface runoff of seasonal rainfall is more in the area due to its terrain characteristics which is also accelerated by existing land use practices. The '*tnar*' and '*baid*' lands (the upper portions of the rolling topography — geomorphologically, Pediment and Buried Pediment Shallow) are being used for kharif paddy cultivation though the productivity is low. This practice accelerates soil erosion and land degradation due to tilling of the skeletal soil. In this respect one should also consider the socio-economic condition — in general, the marginal farmers are the plot holders in the '*tnar*' and '*baid*' lands — there is no alternative for livelihood.

In such areas, developmental planning on micro-watershed basis in sub-watershed orientation may be considered as the best form of maintaining the landscape ecology *vis-à-vis* biological diversity where a compromise is sought between the upstream (catchment area) and downstream bio-physical environment of a river for wise use of natural resources through analysis of traditional and existing land-use. In this regard, the 'base line' database generated by the Geoinformatics and RS Cell, DST, Government of West Bengal reflect on site specific 'Rain water harvesting structures' and targeting 'Potential zones of groundwater'.

It may be mentioned that the 'Pragmatic dataset' generated as stated above are based on the integration and analysis of the spatial information generated through morphogenetic approach and the functional data (i.e., non-spatial data) which includes primarily physico-chemical attributes (e.g., meteorological data, groundwater fluctuation data or chemical analysis, demographic composition etc.) and historical traditional data in societal aspects. However, in implementation of micro-watershed programmes the conflicts present are –

- Natural watershed boundaries *versus* manmade administrative boundaries.
- Implementation of micro-watershed concept in the context of terrain conditions, e.g., whether micro-watershed zonation is applicable in the drainage basins with tributaries (e.g., Pedimental landscape) or distributaries (e.g., Alluvial fan plains) or anastomatic pattern in Deltaic/ Coastal plain.
- Existing land-use pattern in response to the present day societal aspects *versus* acceptance of alternative land-use practices, e.g., marginal farmers are scared to accept alternative practices considering the risk factor over their assured production/income.

In view of the above in micro-watershed development programme one should be very much aware about the terrain condition/geoinformation to achieve the best result (Chakrabarti, 2004) for example –

(i) Construction of 'Rain water harvesting structures' (e.g., check dam, nalabundh etc.) within micro/mini watershed requires very specific detailed ground/*in situ* survey for identification of suitable sites for such structures, e.g., the nalabundh at Kajalpahari Ghat on Kulia Nadi, Abdarpur village, Birbhum district, became useless as the river bypassed the structure. However, suitable site for such structure with rocky basement and side wall, is present about 100 m upstream of the river (Chakrabarti, P. *et al.* 2006).

- Remote sensing data provides site specific geological and geomorphological information for land and water resources management on watershed basis (Chakrabarti, 2004).

(ii) Existence of some lineaments as identified from the multi-temporal satellite images (IRS 1D LISS III), which act either as conduit or barrier depending upon the geological (both lithological and structural) parameters –

(a) in Damodar watershed the major lineament (North Purulia Shear Zone) trending ENE-WSW/E-W, act as a conduit for surface water movement. Actually, a reservoir constructed at Dubrajpur village, Purulia I block is unable to support the beneficiaries in the downstream (i.e., northern side of the reservoir in Para block) as the stored water percolates beneath through the highly fractured and crushed CGC (Chhotanagpur Granite Gneiss Complex) rocks.

(b) in Hura block, Purulia district (in the adjoining parts of the Dwarkeswar and Kangasabati watershed) the identified lineament in the satellite image is actually a dolerite dyke trending E-W in ground. Here the dolerite dyke act as a barrier for movement of groundwater as exemplified by the depth to water level (DWL) data from dug well on both sides of the dyke around Amlator-Chatumadar villages.

(iii) In the Ayodhya hill surroundings (parts of Baghmundi, Balarampur, Arsa and Jhalda blocks) the hill wash deposits (especially 'Accumulation glacis') play an important role in recharging the groundwater table in accordance with the master slope. The hill wash deposits constitute unconsolidated to semi-consolidated materials with varying texture and thickness, which retains a major portion of normal precipitation and has locale-specific significance in surface and groundwater movements. Due to such geomorphic configuration, construction of low height 'horseshoe dyke' is likely to arrest surface run-off for subsequent recharge of groundwater as well as partial utilisation as surface flow.

On the other hand, in coal field area (Andal, Raniganj blocks, Barddhaman district), the areas of subsidence could easily be identified from the 'geomorphic anomalies' and 'drainage deflection' – those areas are not at all favourable for micro-watershed development approach as well as groundwater targeting as the terrain condition is obliterated to a great extent by mining activities (Chakrabarti, 2001).

(iv) In Kashipur block, Puruliya district, the wastelands (land with scrub) with shallow to moderate soil profile (land capability subclass – IVes) and geomorphologically termed as 'Buried Pediment shallow' could be utilized for sericulture purposes considering the local adaptability (due to existence of sericulture farms in the surroundings) – an example of integration of societal parameters in watershed development programme.

(v) In the southern part of Puruliya district in Banduan and Baghmundi blocks 'Babui grass' plantation practised in the wastelands. However, the commercial value of the 'Babui grass' for rope manufacturing, etc., are not so encouraging now-a-days. In those areas instead of 'Babui grass' some other alternative agricultural plantation (e.g., Bamboo, Akashmani, etc.) could be done alongwith agro-horticulture.

(vi) The wasteland (Lateritic upland/erosional remnants) in Suisa-Tunturi area in the southeastern corner of Baghmundi block, Puruliya district may be utilised for siting industrial complex. The area is well connected with the Ranchi and Jamshedpur industrial towns by NH, SH and railways. Added advantage is the availability of surface water from Sanka river and Subarnarekha river (Chakrabarti *et al.*, 1996).

Conclusion

Environmental security may be considered in terms of reduction of adverse effects of natural hazards/disaster – a core component in the framework of sustainable development, as deliberated in the World Summit for Sustainable Development (Rio + 10), 2002, Johannesburg following the Agenda – 21.

The experiences of International Decade for National Disaster Reduction (1999-2000) and the futureframe work for action (2005-2015), UN-ISDR, Yokohama strategy, UNOCHA/UNEP, NOAA have stressed upon the bi-directional relationship between environmental management and disaster risk reduction.

In the present day scenario, the baseline geo-spatial information generated using RS and GIS technologies supported with past history of anthropic development (the 'strategic datasets') emerged as a synergistic tool, reflects on human oriented future directives interlinking food and shelter, education and vision/policy decision, i.e., poverty alleviation and build natural resources assets for environmental security:

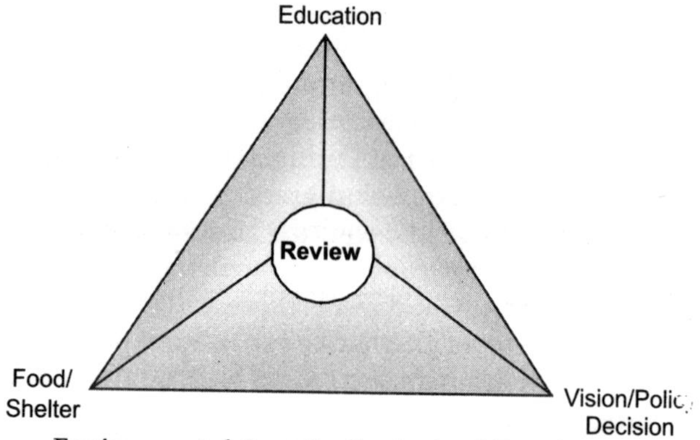

Environmental Security for Societal Development

Acknowledgement

This paper is the enlarged version of the lecture delivered in the seminar on 'Contemporary Security Concepts of India' organized by the Department of International Relations, Jadavpur University on 18th May, 2008. Sincere thanks to Prof. (Dr.) Sumita Sen for personal communication to deliver the lecture.

The views expressed in this paper is author's own and does not reflect the views of the department to which he belongs.

NOTES

Chakrabarti, P. (1991): Process-response system analysis in macrotidal estuary and mesotidal coastal plain of eastern India. Mem. Geol. Soc. India, No. 22, pp. 165-181.

Chakrabarti, P. (1995): Evolutionary history of the Coastal Quaternaries of the Bengal Plain, India. Proc. Indian Nat. Sci. Acad. 61. A. No. 5. pp. 343-354.

— — (1999): Land evaluation — Geoinformation: Pragmatic input for landuse planning. Confer. Vol. "Geoinformatics Beyond — 2000"; IIRS Dehradun, India. pp. 187-196.

— — (2001): RS and GIS: Spatial format for sustainable resource development. MGMI Transactions, 97 (1&2), pp. 29-37.

— — (2004): Geoinformatics for Natural Resources Management *vis-à-vis* Environmental Justice. Proc. Vol. ISPRS (Int. Soc. Photogrammetry & Remote Sensing) XX Congress Vol. B7. VII/3, Istanbul, Turkey, pp. 427-432.

— — (2004): Geoinformatics in Watershed Management. *Integrating Watershed Technologies for Sustainable Development* Ed. B. B. Basu; School of Fundamental Research, Kolkata, pp. 150-55.

— — (2006): Geoinformatics for Water Resources Evaluation and Management: S & T Inputs – West Bengal Scenario. MGMI (Mining, Geological, Metallurgical Society of India Transaction) Centenary Volume. pp. 86-101. Kolkata.

Chakrabarti, P. *et al.* (2006): Earthquake and Tsunami effects, Andaman Islands, *India Geomatics in Tsunami*. Ed. Ramaswamy, Kumanan, Sivakumar & Bhoop Singh. New India Publishing Agency, New Delhi. pp. 37-62.

Chakrabarti, P.; Das, D. (2006): Unpublished Report; Groundwater Quality Assessment and Zonation in the Arsenic affected districts of West Bengal, Deptt. of Science & Technology, Govt. of West Bengal.

Chakrabarti, P.; Nag, S. (2008): Changing course of Ganga/Padma river, West Bengal, India; NNRMS Bulletin – 32. Deptt. of Space, Govt. of India, Bangalore, India. pp. 72-79.

Meijrink, A.M.J. (1988): Data acquisition and data capture through terrain mapping units. *ITC Jour Spl. Issue* (1) pp. 23–44.

Section II

India's Security and its Neighbours

6

India's Nuclear Policy : Regional Ramifications

Binoda Kumar Mishra

India's Nuclear policy has been the most enigmatic of India's policies over the years. There is a style of caution to India's nuclear behaviour. The way she made her nuclear weapons programme known to the world is commendable. From the day of her independence, India has pursued a nuclear programme, which was planned for long and the balance between strategic secrecy and democratic transparency has been well maintained. India informed the world of her Nuclear weaponisation in such a way that the Nuclear five could do nothing but accept India into the Nuclear Club though with Pakistan as an undesirable companion. India has gained a lot from this magical multi-disciplinary weapon. Politically, India is now counted and heard. India now figures in every major strategic calculation. It has also brought in economic opportunities. But the irony is we are not sure whether nuclear weapons have contributed to the primary cause of its development and possession, i.e., security.

Evolution of India's Nuclear Programme

It is not possible to analyse India's nuclear programme within any particular theoretical framework. The evolution of the programme has been influenced by both internal and external factors that call for both realist and organisational theories to explain the evolution of the programme. The non-contiguity between the external and international factors explains the programme being the longest in the world to break the nuclear weapons threshold. Since independence, India has maintained that world peace should be the objective of each nation's foreign policy and all of India's policies are directed towards that ultimate objective. But it is no secret that India pursued a Nuclear Programme that was not entirely peaceful in purpose. It must be kept in mind that when India started her Nuclear programme, China was yet to go nuclear. The reason for mentioning China so early in the discussion is to underline the fact that India's Nuclear programme was never linked to China's nuclear programme as we are made to believe. It was a slow progress in developing nuclear technology without any expressed objective. If we observe the international environment of that time, we get two different trends. Cold War rivalry dividing the world, and a cooperative effort by the major powers to maintain the preponderance of power they had achieved through possession of Nuclear weapons. India on the other hand, represented the sentiment of those who demanded comprehensive Nuclear Disarmament. It must be understood at the beginning that though India argued and worked for comprehensive Nuclear Disarmament, was apprehensive of her efforts yielding any positive results in luring the then nuclear haves to renounce their nuclear weapons. Thus, in the name of "scientific temper", Pandit Nehru initiated the nuclear programme of India. It was Homi J. Bhaba who convinced Nehru that nuclear energy is the futuristic and India has certain advantage in harnessing this source of energy. According to Bhaba, India had a pool of good scientists and a large reserve of thorium, a potential source of fissile material. He even argued that India could gain from exporting nuclear raw materials.[1] This was a convincing argument to Nehru who was interested in putting maximum possible effort to modernise India in a short span of time. Thus began the slow march towards an unknown future.

Interpretations differ about Nehru's preferences regarding the military future of India. But Nehru certainly was excited about the prospects of nuclear technology, in both its civilian and military manifestations, contributing to India's eventual leadership position in the region and beyond. In a speech in 1946 he for the first time talked about Nuclear Weapons. He said:

> As long as the world is constituted as it is, every country

> will have to devise and use scientific devices for its protection. I have no doubt India will develop her scientific researches and I hope Indian scientists will use the atomic force for constructive purposes. But if India is threatened she will inevitably try to defend herself by all means at her disposal. I hope India in common with other countries will prevent the use of atomic bomb.[2]

On the occasion of the 34th session of the Indian Science Congress, on January 3, 1947, Nehru expressed his 'excitement' about Hiroshima and said that nuclear technology has dual face and both are here to coexist side by side.[3] He further stressed on the importance of nuclear technology in "building of a free and self-reliant India."[4] This is the earliest indication of India's plan for building a nuclear bomb. He reiterated his commitment, and this time with more clarity, in a letter to his Defence Minister Baldev Singh in 1948, that:

> The future belongs to those who produce atomic energy. That is going to be the chief national power for the future. Of course, defence is intimately concerned with this. Even the political consequences are worthwhile. The probable use of atomic energy in warfare is likely to revolutionise all our concepts of war and defence. For the moment, we may leave out of consideration except that it makes it absolutely essential for us to develop the method of using atomic energy for both civilian and military purpose. This means scientific research on a big scale.[5]

On 12 August, 1956, in a letter to the Chief Ministers of the provinces, Nehru wrote that "We are living a in the atomic age and if we do not recognise the obvious facts of this age then we are bound to fail as a nation…".[6] Nehru's preference for nuclear weapon is clearly evident from his testing Bhabha's ability to develop the bomb. During a meeting with Major General (Ret.) Kenneth D. Nichols who was an American engineer involved in the Manhattan project and visited India in 1960 to pursue Indian leadership to accept American light-water reactors. He notes Nehru's conversation with Bhabha, which took place in his presence. Nichols writes that Nehru turned to Bhabha and asked:

> "Can you develop an atomic bomb?" Bhabha assured him that he could and in reply to Nehru's next question about time, he estimated that he would need about a year to do it. I was really astounded to be hearing these questions from the one I thought to be one of the world's most peace loving leaders. He then asked me if I agree with Bhabha., and I replied that I know of no reason why he could not do it. He had men who were as qualified or more qualified than our young scientists were fifteen years earlier. He concluded by saying to Bhabha, "Well don't do it until I tell you to."[7]

Thus, it is evident that Nehru not only ideologically supported the weaponisation idea, but also put efforts to operationalise a dual faced nuclear programme. Indian Atomic Energy Commission was created in 1948 to regulate the programme and maintain secrecy.

The External Push

The first external push for seriously considering nuclear autonomy was the refusal of United States of America to carry out nuclear trade with India and provide nuclear aid to India in 1953 on the pretext that India was selling thorium nitrate, a potential nuclear fuel, to China which was prohibited under US domestic laws.[8] Though the problem was solved mutually, it signalled that India cannot rely on foreign support to carry out independent and time demanded nuclear activity. Added to this was the courtship that developed in 1954 between the US and Pakistan, which ensured a steady supply of military aid to Pakistan. This increasing proximity between the US and Pakistan created a kind of security dilemma that assisted the cause of nuclear weaponisation but it was not sufficient enough cause to declare the intent of going the weapons way. But the direction of Indian nuclear programme towards weaponisation was evident from Nehru throwing allusions of going nuclear against threats. But there was a necessity to camouflage the programme from international efforts that were slowly gaining ground to prevent horizontal proliferation of nuclear weapons. Nehru adopted the most effective strategy of campaigning for comprehensive nuclear disarmament. Along with

Homi Bhabha, Nehru invited Bertrand Russell to organise the first meeting of scientists from both sides of the then iron curtain, which was eventually shifted to Pugwash in Canada, to discuss and pursue international community to renounce nuclear weapon. One should not doubt Nehru's commitment to global nuclear disarmament. But Nehru was aware of the reality that given the advantages a nation gets by possessing nuclear weapons, it was not feasible in the near future that those nations who are already in possession of the weapon would renounce it. The cold response to the Pugwash suggestions from the US convinced Nehru that the international efforts towards nuclear disarmament are actually part of a game to deny the developing countries access to the revolutionising technology. Nehru played the same game for denying the developed countries to influence the Indian nuclear programme. Such posturing went well with India's international image as a nation of "non-violent Satyagrahis". This posturing proved to be the most powerful impediment for India to fulfil its desire of possessing the atom bomb and show it to the world. Nehru's immediate successor, Lal Bahadur Shastri could not dare to decide in which way the Indian nuclear programme to be directed as he lacked Nehru's understanding of India's nuclear programme and also lacked the ability to take on the international opinion in the event of India diverted from her made to believe international posture. Shastri failed to notice that Nehru-Bhabha combination had started making it clear that India is not opposed to the idea of nuclear weapons. Bhabha, subtly declared, in the January 27-February 1, 1962 Pugwash Conference in Udaipur, India, that given the threat China poses to her smaller neighbours, it is expedient for India to go the nuclear weapons way.[9]

The best opportunity, that came India's way to break the nuclear threshold or to declare her such intent, was the Chinese test of October 16, 1964. During the period from 1948 till 1964 there remained a silence over the progress of the programme. The critical time came in 1964 after the Chinese tests. The time was critical in every sense. Not long before India had a war with and loss from China. Global attempts were intensifying to prevent horizontal proliferation of nuclear weapons. India had to make a

1962 India-China War

choice. The only important change that had taken place in India's political circle was the death of Nehru by the time the Chinese test took place.

This created a dilemma for the then Indian leadership as to how to respond to the critical situation. One can safely conclude that had Nehru been alive, he would have described this as the "absolutely necessary" situation forcing India to go nuclear. But his own writings and international posturing had created a make to believe impression that India had distaste for the nuclear weapons. He personally stood for comprehensive global nuclear disarmament, movingly wrote and spoke against the use of nuclear technology for weapon purposes and passionately urged the nuclear haves to rescue the entire humanity from the fear of nuclear holocaust by renouncing these frightful engines of destruction.[10] There are some who argue that Nehru was (now we know that he was not) unsure about the utility of the weapon for India's purposes and thus while arguing for nuclear disarmament, had agreed to allow research to proceed in the direction of 'contingent weaponisation'. However, after Nehru's death and Chinese test, the nuclear debate started in the Indian policymaking and academic circles.

There were three distinct positions that emerged regarding the direction India's nuclear programme should take. The first stand was that of abolitionists who out and out rejected the idea of India pursuing the weapons option. They included prominent bureaucrats such as V.K. Krishna Menon, politicians such as J.P. Narayan and Morarji Desai. The rationale of their argument was more political and ideological than technical. According to this view India must show respect to her great tradition of non-violence and commit herself to global nuclear disarmament. The second view was just the opposite. Led by Homi Bhabha himself. This group argued that given the fact that nuclear weapon is the great equaliser, India must lay her hands on this weapon in order to deter the massive Chinese conventional and unknown nuclear stockpile. It was Bhaba's formulation that India can achieve absolute deterrence *vis-à-vis* China with the help of nuclear weapons.[11] The third position was held by security analysts and military personnel who argued in favour of India going nuclear but found no urgency in doing so and wanted to relate India crossing the threshold only in the event of any new strategic/

political threats such as conflict with China or any other unspecified crisis.[12] Without going to the relative merits and demerits of the three positions, we can agree that the Indian nuclear programme followed the third position, i.e., Contingent Weaponisation. But the progress from ambivalence to that of weaponisation to the degree of minimum credible nuclear deterrence was not a handiwork of any single leadership or group. It has evolved after a lot of search for a correct explanation for developing a weapon India stood firmly to eliminate from the earth.

The debate among the three positions remained inconclusive till 1965 war with Pakistan. The war with Pakistan and the Chinese aggressive posturing[13] finally gave the hawks in the Indian establishment the opportunity to push the case of weaponisation more forcefully. It is beyond the scope of this chapter to describe in detail as to what were the exact factors that the Indian hawks capitalised on. It is suffice here to say that the behaviour of China and the US during this time emitted sufficient allusions that India has to achieve self-reliance in defence matters including nuclear weapons. Just as the war with Pakistan was coming to a close, nearly a hundred members of Indian Parliament, across party lines issued a letter to the Prime Minister to decide immediately to develop nuclear weapons.[14] However, Shastri the then Prime Minister chose not to exercise the weapons option rather pledged commitment to nuclear disarmament. But important to notice here that, it was Shastri who had given a go ahead to the Subterranean Nuclear Explosion Project (SNEP), which subsequently contributed to the testing of the fission device under the name of Peaceful Nuclear Explosion (PNE). The exact intention of Shastri behind authorising SNEP could not be known as he passed away shortly after that. His death was closely followed by the death of Homi Bhabha creating a vacuum in the nuclear policy establishment that could have ensured continuity of the nuclear programme. The policy of ambiguity continued for a considerable period before India could finally test her first device in 1974.

From various accounts we come to know that India had all the technical capabilities to acquire a weapon by 1966, but the option was exercised after eight years. Thus, there remains little doubt that India's nuclear (weapons) programme was not as much technologically determined as it was politically. This is corroborated by the position India maintained against the global nuclear arms control and disarmament initiatives. It is true, as Cohen informs us, that the Indian academia, policy makers and military establishment were divided over the nuclear weapons question.[15] But the rejection of Nuclear Non-Proliferation Treaty (NPT) and Comprehensive Test Ban Treaty (CTBT) proves beyond doubt that India wished not to give up the nuclear weapons option. The NPT was branded as an unequal treaty. It certainly is unequal but India, while pointing out this fallacy of the treaty, made its intention clear that India wished to possess the bomb as a moral weapon to protect India from nuclear blackmailing and to force the nuclear haves to renounce it.[16] Similar arguments were put forward to oppose CTBT later. After the first nuclear explosion, India maintained a posture of ambiguity till eventually going nuclear in May 1998. Any single variable would be insufficient to explain India's decision to weaponise. I intend to put forward my interpretation of the event at the end. What is more of a concern to the paper is the security fallout of India's evolving nuclear posture.

The Impact (The Security Fallout)

No sooner than India crossed the nuclear weapons threshold, India tried to communicate to the world her intentions behind possessing them. The then Minister for Foreign Affairs, Mr. Jaswant Singh wrote "these are weapons of self-defence, to ensure that India, too, is not subjected to nuclear coercion."[17] India like any other country, argues her nuclear weapons are for deterrence purposes but, once such weapons arrive in a region it creates various other possibilities that does not keep the function of nuclear weapons limited to the purpose of deterrence alone. In the regional context India's nuclear programme has created such a web of possibilities. The debate over the utility of nuclear weapons is yet to come to a close and there are compelling logics being put forth by both abolitionists and proliferationists that prevent the debate to end. In the academia, Kenneth N. Waltz, the Structural Realist, who makes his argument flow from his theoretical construct of an anarchic world, represents the pro-proliferation stand and Scott D. Sagan advocates the abolitionist stand. I intend to analyse the security scenario that has emerged in India's neighbourhood that has backward and forward linkages to India's nuclear programme and try to see the validity in Waltz's argument and fears expressed by Sagan.

It is almost a firm belief that India's nuclear programme is reactionary and not proactive. But a closer analysis of the nuclear behaviour of India's neighbours would suggest that it is India's nuclear behaviour, that to a large extent created an insecure nuclear environment. It is now clearly established that India's programme was neither related to the Chinese nuclear programme nor that of any other country, friend or foe. But the regional impact of India's nuclear posture is multi-faceted. In a timeline, one can see the evolution of Pakistan's nuclear programme. Pakistan embarked on her nuclear programme in 1951 for peaceful purposes. The programme showed interest in nuclear weapons only as a reaction to India's nuclear weapons programme. The relation is evident from the fact that Pakistan expressed her interest to sign the NPT but with the condition that India does so. In the 16th annual session of the United Nations Atomic Energy Conference held in Mexico in September 1972, Pakistan put forward the proposal to denuclearise South Asia.[18] Again Pakistan repeated the proposal in 1974[19] but India did not respond. There are scholars who argue that Pakistan's pledge to denuclearise South Asia was a camouflage for her weapons programme. Such an interpretation is more a matter of conjecture than analysis. A better interpretation of Pakistani nuclear venture is that Pakistan knew fully well that she was in a position of weakness in relation to India and thus wanted to prevent India from possessing nuclear weapons and had India accepted the Pakistani proposals, the latter would not have pursued the costly nuclear weapons programme. Secondly, India's nuclear programme created a nuclear circle around herself. India's refusal to sign the NPT and subsequent conduct of the PNE made Pakistan desperate. In an attempt to develop deterrent nuclear capability, Pakistan walked into the strategic sphere of China. This provided China with a great opportunity to encircle India with nuclear weapons. China, though a party to NPT chose to violate its provisions in full knowledge of the US and the international community and assisted Pakistan.[20] The Sino-Pakistan collaboration began from 1975 indicating that such partnership was a reaction to India's 1974 PNE. Again as a reaction to India's nuclear programme, China increased her nuclear missile presence in Tibet. There can be no other rationale for China than targeting India, as China has a no strike agreement with Russia[21] and an agreement with the US for not targeting US bases in the region.[22]

The first and foremost effect of formal nuclearisation of South Asia has been that, security is no longer ensured by defensive function of war.[23] Now security is entirely dependent on deterrence posturing of the regional powers that includes China, the non-regional power. Waltz questions the fears expressed by some scholars that more nuclear weapon states would increase the chances of nuclear wars. His argument moves around the logic of utility of wars for states. He concludes that possessing nuclear weapons makes fulfilment of objective prohibitively costly. Thus, states possessing nuclear weapons would prefer de-escalation to escalation of wars to the level of use of nuclear weapons.[24] He further dismisses all fears and suggests, nuclear weapons neither generate war nor do they destabilise the region. Drawing examples from the evolution of the major nuclear powers, he is particularly optimistic that smaller nuclear weapon states like India and Pakistan would each find it necessary to maintain deterrence *vis-à-vis* each other and would not dare to undertake preventive or pre-emptive strikes out of the fear of the consequences in case the game is not played to its perfection.[25] His optimism rests on 'mutual distrust that characterises his constructed international system. On the other hand Scott D. Sagan has identified four requirements for a stable deterrence: prevention of preventive war during periods of transition when one side has temporary advantage; the development of survivable second-strike forces the avoidance of accidental nuclear war; and the ability of keeping the nuclear weapons out of the reach of the terrorists.[26] There are good reasons to endorse his argument that deterrence might fail anytime in a region like South Asia as India and Pakistan cannot ensure (or may not choose to ensure) the four mentioned requirements.

The nuclear stability in South Asia is said to be maintained by dyadic behaviour patterns that India and Pakistan are expected to maintain. But the dyadic patterns are irrelevant in explaining the security situation in South Asia since it is more complex – it involves China the non-dyadic party, and there is a remote but realistic possibility of non-state actors of the region laying their hands on these weapons of mass destruction.[27] Currently, India finds herself in such a volatile situation that her security is guaranteed only if deterrence works and never fails in an India-China-Pakistan triangular face-off. In a hypothetical analysis of the possibilities Kanti P. Bajpai presents an alarming picture. He envisages three principal dangers to the region: a three-way arms race, crisis instability and accidental war.[28] Arms race can occur in a triangular fashion in the absence of transparency and mutual distrustful perception leading to limitless pile of warheads in each of the three sides on the rationale that each may view the others nuclear weapons to be in excess than his own.[29] Secondly, there is enough possibility of conventional conflicts between India with either of the other two parties escalating into a nuclear confrontation and the third party taking an opportunistic advantage of the situation.[30] In this case the most vulnerable is India as the possibility of China-Pakistan conflict and its escalation is remote. Finally, accidental nuclear use can occur by human as well as mechanical failures.[31]

The thought of the consequence of any of the three possibilities mentioned above will scare anybody. Some scholars of the region and in the West try to get solace by accepting the Chinese official position that neither China belongs to the region nor are her (Nuclear) policies directed towards the region. Notwithstanding the dangers if the Chinese official position is accepted and China is excluded from the South Asian nuclear framework, the strategic scenario of the region fares no better. There are sufficient chances that nuclear weapons can be used. Optimists argue that the presence of nuclear weapons has brought durable stability to the region. This optimism is based on the assumption that there is an operational deterrence between India and Pakistan[32] and on the belief that there is a "tacit convergence of India and Pakistani interest to avoid nuclear war as an intended outcome of their strategic competition."[33] Both, the assumption and the belief however carry implications of instability. What if deterrence fails? What are the chances of an unintentional nuclear war?

There are evidence that the nuclear weapons of Pakistan are vulnerable and the chances of deterrence failing in the bilateral equation between India and Pakistan are high. Fool proof nuclear deterrence is not possible in case of India and Pakistan, because deterrence must work not only against rational and sympathetic adversary but also against irrational and hostile opposition.[34] Considering the fact that Pakistan regularly lapses into political instability, the chances of deterrence failing increases manifold. The four criteria mentioned by Sagan for an operational nuclear deterrence are conspicuously absent between India and Pakistan. There are enough proof of temptations on Indian side to take advantage of the relative preponderance of nuclear power and plan to attack the Pakistani nuclear establishments. Days before Mrs. Gandhi's assassination, she was advised by the then Army Chief, General Arun Shridhar Vaidya to launch a nuclear attack on Kahuta, the Pakistani uranium enrichment facility.[35] Similar thoughts were entertained by General Sunderji in 1987.[36] Currently, neither Pakistan *vis-à-vis* India nor India *vis-à-vis* China has a fool-proof protection for their nuclear arsenal from possible counterforce attack. Such difference in capability may lead to uncertainty[37] and temptations of pre-emptive attack. The Kargil episode casts doubt over the effectiveness of nuclear weapons in deterring conventional military engagements between the two countries. One can even argue that the presence of nuclear weapons has increased the chances of conventional war between the two countries.[38] Even otherwise, the chances of conventional war escalating into nuclear exchanges are high. During the Kargil war it emerged as a distinct possibility. The incendiary statements issued by the leaderships of both sides were chilling enough to apprehend a pre-emptive strike from either side. Even in a conflict situation that emerged after the attack on Indian Parliament in 2001, there were threats from use and counter use of nuclear weapons by Pakistan and India. General Musharraf declared that in the event of Indian troops "took even a step across the international border or Line of Control, we will not only be in front of them, we will surround them. It will not remain a conventional war.[39] Similar reaction was issued from the Indian side army chief S. Padmanabhan. In January 11, 2002 statement he said that his force was "fully ready" for war. He warned that although "nuclear weapons are not meant for war fighting", India would severely punish any state that is "mad enough to use nuclear weapons against any of our assets". Padmanabhan added, "The perpetrator shall be so severely punished that his very existence will be in doubt. We are ready for a second strike."[40]

It is fairly established that the radical Islamists are in search of an opportunity to lay their hands on the nuclear weapons and there are fair possibilities of them to succeed. Though there are no indications to show any lapses from the Indian side to make it possible for extremist forces getting access to nuclear technology or material, the same cannot be said about the Pakistani nuclear establishment. In Pakistan, the "vulnerability of the nuclear weapons and materials stem from the country's volatile domestic political situation and history of Pakistan's military support for radical Islamists."[41] The nexus between the Inter Services Intelligence (ISI) and the terror outfits such as Taliban is well documented and the presence of rogue elements in Pakistan's nuclear establishment is an open secret. Therefore, the chances of nuclear weapons reaching the hands of radical Islamist groups is clear and increases as political instability in the country increases.

Conclusion

The security environment around India has certainly become more volatile and India is partly responsible for adding the dangerous nuclear dimension to this volatility. The question becomes all the more important as to why India pursued nuclear weapons knowing fully well that they are not going to help India's security needs? There have been organisational, cultural and domestic political explanations to this question. While each of the explanations may be useful in explaining phases of India's long nuclear programme, none of the explanations provide an answer to the basic question as to why at the first place India chose to pursue the nuclear weapons policy? The ultimate nuclear posture of India suggests that her nuclear programme is not directed towards any specific country. In the words of Rear Admiral (Retired) Raja Menon, "India is in a "dumb" place, like a submarine that is neither on the surface where it can fight nor deep below where it can hide."[42] This kind of posturing can only imply that India never seriously thought of nuclear weapons as weapons of war and she must achieve the ability of fighting and winning a nuclear war. There can be only one explanation to India's nuclear programme which is related to her notion of international system and the role India intended to play in that system. The international system that emerged after the end of World War II closely proximated the Hobbessian anarchy and India, lacking an indigenous world view, became captive of the western world view. The experience at birth created a structural dilemma for India that reinforced India's belief about the self-help nature of international system. Probably, the explanation of India's nuclear weapons lies in a cognitive factor. Jacques E. C. Hymans suggests it is a sense of "oppositional nationalism" by which a nation defines her national identity *vis-à-vis* an external enemy that is thought to be fundamentally threatening to the nation's security and values and entertains pride of independence in thought and action.[43] In Indian case, this cocktail of fear of the enemy and pride of self-determination of international image put India within an insecurity dilemma *vis-à-vis* her neighbours that necessitated possession of nuclear weapons. The enemy remained a perceptual and invisible one which changed with time. However, India's quest for and possession of nuclear weapons has given India a sense of elevated regional and global image, at the same time has substantially increased the insecurity dilemma of India and her neighbours and has put security in the region on a "short fuse"[44] of mythical deterrence that can fail anytime.

REFERENCES

1. Stephen P. Cohen, *India: Emerging Power*, New Delhi: Oxford University Press, 2002, p. 158.
2. Dorothy Newman (ed.), *Nehru: The First 60 Years*, Vol. 2, New York: John Day, 1965, p. 264. Cited in George Perkovich, *India's Nuclear Bomb: The Impact on Global Proliferation*, New Delhi: Oxford University Press, 2000, p. 14.
3. Bharat Karnad, *Nuclear Weapons and Indian Security: The Realist Foundations of Strategy*, New Delhi: Macmillan, 2002, p. 182.
4. Arjun Dev, *Jawaharlal Nehru, Years of Struggle: Selected Readings*, New Delhi: National Book Trust, 1989, pp. 169-70. Cited in, Bharat Karnad, *Nuclear Weapons and Indian Security: The Realist Foundations of Strategy*, New Delhi: Macmillan, 2002, p. 182.
5. Quoted in Raj Chengappa, *Weapons of Peace: The Inside Story of India's Quest to be a Nuclear Power*, New Delhi: Harper Collins Publishers, 2000, pp. 71-72.
6. S. Gopal, *Jawaharlal Nehru: A Biography, Vol II*, p. 203. Bharat Karnad, *Nuclear Weapons and Indian Security: The Realist Foundations of Strategy*, New Delhi: Macmillan, 2002, p. 198.
7. Kenneth D. Nichols, *The Road to Trinity*, New York: Morrow, 1987, p. 352. Cited in *Perkovich, op. cit.*, p. 36.
8. *Perkovich, op. cit.*, p. 22.

9. *Perkovich, op. cit.*, pp. 60-62.
10. *Cohen, op. cit.*, p. 161.
11. Homi J. Bhaba, "The Implications of a Wider Dispersal of Military Power for World Safety and the Problem of Safeguards," cited in Chapter 6 Footnote 5 of *Cohen, op. cit.*, p. 341.
12. *Cohen, op. cit.*, p. 164.
13. On September 17, 1965, China issued an ultimatum to India to remove construction works in Tibet or face grave consequences. See, *Perkovich, op. cit.*, p. 109.
14. *Perkovich, op. cit.*, p. 111.
15. *Cohen, op. cit.*, p. 157-97.
16. *Ibid*, p. 169.
17. Jaswant Singh, "Against Nuclear Apartheid," *Foreign Affairs*, Vol. 77, No. 5, September-October 1998. cited in Gaurav Rajan and Michael Vannoni, "Battlefield Nuclear Weapons in South Asia: The Case for Restraint," *South Asian Survey*, Vol. 12, No. 1, 2005, p. 92.
18. *Dawn*, October 4, 1972, cited by Savita Pande, *Strategic Analysis*, Vol. 22, No. 11, February 1999, p. 1681.
19. General Assembly draft resolution, a/c.1/L. 682.
20. Ashok Kapur, *Pokhran and Beyond: India's Nuclear Behaviour*, New Delhi: Oxford University Press, 2001, p. 194.
21. Sino-Russian Detargeting and No-First-Use Agreement, September 1994.
22. US-China Non-targeting Agreement, June 1998.
23. Raju G.C. Thomas, "India's Security Environment", in P. Sahadevan (ed.), *Conflict and Peacemaking in South Asia*, New Delhi: Lancer's Books, 2001, p. 64.
24. Kenneth N. Waltz, "The Spread of Nuclear Weapons: More May Better", *Adelphi Paper*, No. 171.
25. Kenneth N. Waltz, "The Spread of Nuclear Weapons: More May Better", *Adelphi Paper*, No. 171.
26. For a detailed discussion on the reasons for failure of deterrence in South Asia, see Scott D. Sagan, "Nuclear Dangers in South Asia", *Forum on Physics & Society*, April 2004, http://iis-db.stanford.edu/pubs/20573/sagan_nuc_sasia.pdf.
27. Ashley J. Tellis, "Nuclear Stability in South Asia," in P.R Chari, Sonika Gupta and Arpit Rajan, *Nuclear Stability in Southern Asia*, New Delhi: Manohar, p. 20.
28. For a detailed discussion, see Kanti P. Bajpai, "Managing a Strategic Triangle: India, China and Pakistan", in P. Sahadevan (ed.), *Conflict and Peacemaking in South Asia*, New Delhi: Lancer's Books, 2001, pp. 81-105.
29. *Ibid*, p. 87-88.
30. *Ibid*, 88-91.
31. *Ibid*, p. 91.

32. The argument of operational deterrence moves with the assumption that mere possession of nuclear weapons by two adversaries refrains both from undertaking a nuclear attack.
33. Syed Rifaat Hussain, "Analysing Strategic Stability in South Asia with Pathways and Prescriptions for Avoiding Nuclear War", *Contemporary South Asia*, Vol. 14, No. 2, June 2005, p. 142. (pp. 141-53).
34. *Cohen, op. cit.*, p. 186.
35. William E. Burrows, Robert Windrem, *Critical Mass*, New York: Simon & Schuster, 1994.
36. George Perkovich, p. 280.
37. Scott D. Sagan, "The Perils of Proliferation," *Asian Survey*, Vol. 41. No. 6, Nov-Dec. 2001, p. 1066.
38. Paul Kapur argues that the possession of Nuclear weapons has embolden Pakistan to increase cross boarder activities in Kashmir as it believes that Pakistan's nuclear weapons will deter Indian conventional attack on Pakistan. *Stanford Daily*, November 10, 2005, http://cisac.stanford.edu/news/.
39. "Warning forced India to pull back troops, says President," *Dawn*, December 31, 2002. Cited in Michael Krepon, Ziad Haider and Charles Thornon, "Are Tactical Nuclear Weapons Needed in South Asia," in Brian Alexander and Alistair Millar (eds.), *Uncovered Nukes: Tactical Nuclear Weapons and the Challenge of Arms Control*, Washington DC: Freedom Forum, 2002, p. 191.
40. Praful Bidwai, "India Sharpens Nuclear Claws," *Asia Times*, January 31, 2002.
41. Charles D. Ferguson; William C. Potter with Amy Sands; Leonard S. Specter and Fred L. Wehling, "The Four Faces of Nuclear Terrorism," *Monterey Institute for Non-Proliferation Studies*, Nuclear Threat Initiative, 2004. cited in Garima Singh, *Pakistan's Nuclear Disorder: Weapons, Proliferation and Safety*, New Delhi: Observer Research Foundation, Lancer Publishers, 2006, p. 25.
42. Rear-Admiral Raja Menon, *A Nuclear Strategy for India*, New Delhi: Sage, 2000. Cited in *Cohen, op. cit.*, p. 183.
43. Jacques E. C. Hymans, "Why Do States Acquire Nuclear Weapons? Comparing the Cases of India and France," in D. R. Sardesai and Raju G.C. Thomas (eds.), *Nuclear India in the Twenty-first Century*, New York: Palgrave-Macmillan TM, 2002, pp. 144-45.
44. Praful Bidwai and Achin Vinaik, *South Asia on a Short Fuse: Nuclear Politics and the Future of Global Disarmament*, New Delhi: Oxford University Press, 1999.

7

China as a Major Security Threat to India in Post-Cold War Era

Bhagaban Behera

Introduction

India and China are emerging powers in international politics and the relationships between two countries are based on declining values of trust. It is an observation that the duality of India – China security perception is always meant to be understood in terms of suspicion and mistrust because of ambiguous statements made through media and other sources, which creates anxiety and tension and chaos between the two emerging powers. India and China always had been apprehensive about each other through strategic and diplomatic understandings in the region. Indian Defence Minister George Fernandes described China as "Enemy Number One" in May 1998, a few days before India shocked the world with a series of nuclear tests.[1] This was a disturbing reminder of the state of bilateral relations after a war in 1962 and several bloody border skirmishes in 1967, 1986 and 1987.[2] Cold relations between the two Asian giants, however, stand in the way of addressing major threats from common elements, such as foreign-sponsored terrorism in Kashmir and Xinjiang. Though largely ignored, there are other areas of aligned interest as India and China, among the fastest growing economies in the world, seek to enter a global trade environment where the rules have already been set. A radical rethink of each country's strategic focus is essential to address critical political, military and economic issues facing the two Asian countries in the 21st century.

The progressive strengthening of India's post-Cold War policy of *de'tente* towards China led the two Asian giants to commit in 1996 to a constructive cooperation. After the Atal Bihari Vajpayee government took office in 1998, however, it referred to China as India's greatest threat, citing it as justification for conducting nuclear tests. This implied a turn for the worse in India's China policy, and that the two countries had entered a new era of antagonism and hostility. But the situation changed again when the Vajpayee government began making overtures towards China, and the two countries reached consensus on comprehensive bilateral cooperation in 2003 during Prime Minister Vajpayee's visit to China. Manmohan Singh's government later established a strategic partnership with China geared towards peace and prosperity, but at the same time promoted nuclear agreement and joint military exercises with the United States and strengthened strategic cooperation with both the United States and Japan. Authoritative sources on Indian strategy interpret this as an explicit move to balance China. This article takes India's security concept as a starting point, exploring the influence of India's security strategy on its China policy, and interprets the substance of changes in India's post-Cold War China policy and the direction of its likely evolvement.

Background

George Fernandes' identification of China as India's primary security threat seems to be well founded. China does not recognize the incorporation of landlocked Sikkim into India and some 150,000 square-kilometres of land are still disputed between the two countries; meetings between Chinese and Indian delegations breakdown the moment differing versions of border maps are produced. The People's Republic of China (PRC) also periodically issues statements against Indian "regional hegemonism that presumes to block the natural and rightful expansion of China's relations with India's neighbours."[3] Much of Pakistan's nuclear programme, targeted at India, was allegedly developed and financed by China[4] and the perception of a Sino-Pakistani umbrella over India's land borders sends shivers down the spines of Indian military strategists and ordinary citizens alike. India, for its part, hosts the Dalai Lama and the Tibetan government-in-exile a mere

200 miles from the Chinese border. Increased military and naval cooperation between India and countries such as the USA, Japan and Australia also makes China uneasy; many observers suspect that the increasing warmth between India and Western powers has less to do with an overdue recognition of India's increasing stature and more with a policy of containing China.[5]

Since the establishment of PRC in 1949, the Sino-Indian relationship was relatively stable. In 1954, the two governments declared the *Five Principles of Peaceful Coexistence* in the Agreement on Trade between India and the Tibet region of China. India acknowledged that Tibet was an integral part of China. In 1959, the Dalai Lama, the religious leader of Tibet, escaped from a Chinese military attack and fled to India. Since then, the Dalai Lama's use of India as a home base for campaigns against Chinese control in Tibet has remained a source of tension between the two countries.[6] Territorial disputes are another irritant in Sino-Indian security relations. China rejects the so-called McMahon Line, drawn by the British in 1914 to separate China and India, as an unjust colonialist manipulation. In 1962 War, the defeat of Indian troops by the Chinese army left continued tensions and distrust along the border, as each side still claims that territories rightfully belonging to it are occupied by the other.

In 1964, China exploded its first nuclear device. China worried about possible nuclear strikes by either or both nuclear superpowers and began to develop its own nuclear arsenal in defence. China's development of a nuclear capability two years after the border war triggered India's own nuclear aspirations. Among the reasons cited by India for its rejection of the Nuclear Non-Proliferation Treaty in 1968 was its concern with China's new status as a nuclear power. India's first detonation of a nuclear device in Pokhran in 1974 acclaimed public support. However, M. J. Desai, former Secretary General of the Ministry of External Affairs, said that a nuclear race with China would retard India's economic and social programmes, weaken the country internally, and eliminate its political influence in Asia and Africa.[7] During the 1970s and 1980s, Sino-Indian relations continued to deteriorate. The two sides conducted eight rounds of talks between 1981 and 1987 but failed to find a common ground. In 1988, the then Prime Minister, Rajiv Gandhi visited China and Sino-Indian relations began to improve. Both sides agreed to establish a China-India Joint Working Group to develop conditions for "a fair and reasonable settlement" and "to maintain peace and tranquillity in the border region." Bilateral relations improved markedly after Prime Minister Narasimha Rao visited Beijing in 1993 and the two governments signed an Agreement on the Maintenance of Peace and Tranquillity along the LAC.[8]

In the light of the gradually improved Sino-Indian security relationship, the world was puzzled to see the Indian nuclear tests justified by references to the "Chinese threat." The Chinese assessment of India's nuclear development was that a nuclear bomb programme is technically feasible, politically highly desirable, strategically inescapable and economically not only sustainable but actually advantageous.... India's nuclear programme has always been strongly influenced by the China factor.[9] According to Xinhua News, India's 1998-1999 defence budget increased by more than 14 per cent from the previous year's $9.38 billion to $10.70 billion.[10] Further China is aware of India's potential to target it with nuclear weapons and as a senior Chinese official said that, "from mutual confidence we have now moved to mutual apprehension."[11]

China's Perception of India's Post-Cold War Security Scenario

Chinese analysts believe that India's post-Cold War security scenario remains based on the conviction that military might is all-decisive, and that any conceptual adjustments are merely tactical.[12] India's entrenchment in the traditional concept of security is, according to this view, manifest in three ways:

First, India persists in the antagonistic, zero-sum perspective that held sway during the Cold War, whereby threats emerge primarily from disparities in strength, specifically military strength. For instance, India has since the end of the Cold War regarded China's overall military and economic superiority as a twofold threat. From the military perspective, India has expressed concern over China's drive to modernize its defences, and interpreted China's cooperation with Pakistan, Myanmar and other neighbouring states as moves towards isolating and encircling the subcontinent. From an economic point of view, India regards the economic threat China poses as consisting in its economic strength being transfigured into military strength; also in the stiff competition with Indian commodities that those from China constitute in domestic and foreign markets.[13]

Second, India's definition of national security is confined to the traditional spheres of military and territorial security. Its post-Cold War security strategy evinces a thoroughgoing geopolitical logic whose primary focuses are upon guarding against and containing Pakistan and China—its territorial rivals—and upon establishing and safeguarding rights of control in the Indian Ocean.[14]

Third, India continues to expand its military strength as a means of maintaining national security, the main planks of its strategy being expansion of forces, development of nuclear weapons and fortified sea power.[15] India has moreover borrowed on the strength of major powers to compensate for its weak position relative to China in the balance of power and thus contain its neighbour. For instance, after attempting to restore its traditional relationship with Russia after the Cold War, India exploited the US inclination towards containing China by actively improving and developing its relationship with the superpower. It achieved the same result, albeit through different means, during the Cold War when it took the chance offered by Sino-Soviet differences to form an alliance with the USSR.[16]

India's Security Perception *vis-à-vis* China

Analysts in India believe that an obvious change occurred in India's security concept in the aftermath of the Cold War, whereby a kind of neo-liberalism replaced the so-called Nehruvianism predominant in Indian strategic thinking since independence.[17] The neo-liberal stress is on globalized development, deepening international interdependence, the high dividends of economic association as compared with those of competition, and the greater appeal to nations of mutually beneficial cooperation than zero-sum antagonism. In the globalized era it is economic rather than military strength that gives states a voice in international affairs. This theory holds that expanded economic strength is more effective in protecting India's security and interests than military strength or the use of armed forces, and India has indeed carried out domestic free market policies and participated in international free trade to improve its economic relationships with other states and expand its economic strength. In short, India's economic development, modernization and integration into the global economy should become the core of its security strategy in the post-Cold War era.[18]

India's security has traditionally been thought about in terms of domestic, regional, continental and systemic challenges. Domestically, India's security is threatened primarily by insurgencies, separatist violence, terrorism, and communalism. At the regional level, the greatest threats to India are China and Pakistan. Both are military threats to India at the nuclear, conventional, and sub-conventional levels. Continentally, the rise of China is a concern for India.

The rate of growth of Chinese power suggests that it could be the hegemony of the continent in the decades to come, seeking to push out the United States altogether and reducing India and Japan to acquiescent status. At the level of the international system, India must keep an eye on China. China is not just an Asian power any longer. Its moves in Africa and Latin America and its massive economy, hard currency reserves, manufacturing base, and emerging technological capabilities suggest that it will be a superpower with the ability to project hard power beyond Asia and to exerrise influence globally. Both China and the US are a structural challenge to Indian security in the sense that as the two greatest powers on earth they will strive to manage world politics in ways that suit their interests. In doing so, they may affect India's security adversely. India must, therefore, be attentive to the military and economic power balance with both China and the US.

India and China's Security Strategy

China's overture to India in recent years was an effort to prevent the latter from falling into the US camp. As China expands into South-East and Central Asia, India will have to develop a strategy to contend with the possibility of Chinese dominance. China will also want to become more involved in South Asian affairs, while India would like to exclude China.[19] In nuclear arms and doctrine, China will continue to upgrade its second-strike capability, which may lead India into an arms race. Once China has full confidence in the capabilities of its missile systems, the situation in the Asian region may develop toward one of Chinese hegemony. India will continue to be inspired to compete with China. However, India may not have the will or the capability to persevere in an arms race with China. In order to avoid an expensive arms race, India instead may try to form alliances with the United States, Japan, and ASEAN members against China.[20]

India's interests will feature an increasing need to protect trade routes as trade continues to grow, and to guarantee access to rising supplies of oil and gas as the economy and population expand.[21] India is participating in protecting commercial traffic in the Straits of Malacca and the Indian Ocean in cooperation with the United States and other powers. India needs a significant naval presence in order to (1) protect against sea piracy and fisheries poaching; (2) ensure the rights to disputed islands; and (3) provide security against infiltration into the Indian Ocean by Malaysia and other states.[22]

India may participate in protection of the Gulf, the Red Sea, and the South China Sea in near future. Eventually, India and China could clash over the South China Sea, the Straits of Malacca, or the Indian Ocean. India may form partnerships and alliances with Iran, ASEAN, Korea, and Japan.[23] India is already a leading member of the South Asian Association for Regional Cooperation, the Indian Ocean Rim-Association for Regional Cooperation, and the ASEAN Regional Forum. In order to defend its interests, India could forge a partnership or alliance with the United States. It is also likely that India will forge close relations with Iran.[24] On the other side of the argument, there are those Indian strategic thinkers who argue in favour of self-reliance and free agency. Some hawks even advocate targeting ICBMs at Washington, Moscow, and Beijing to enhance India's great power stature.[25]

It has been suggested that India's military posture towards China may need to be upgraded from dissuasion to deterrence. As long as India's posture remains manifestly defensive, making it more secure—but not at China's expense—the security dilemma is unlikely to be exacerbated. Depending upon whether India has a credible minimum deterrence against China both with respect to conventional and nuclear forces, it can be concluded that India's relative restraint is indeed optimum rather than suboptimum. The failings that produced the outcome of 1962, and the steps taken to address those failings, will provide valuable insights to evaluate whether the offence-defence balance has shifted in India's favour since then.

Although this source of insecurity can be substantially moderated by the reassurance deriving from India's own capabilities pending a final settlement, it can be further influenced by knowledge of China's intentions. The military doctrine of China as well as its past uses of force could offer relevant insights about the instruments that it may seek to employ to address the territorial dispute with India.[26] The circumstances behind China's decision to attack in 1962 need to be re-examined in order to conclude whether those circumstances were unique, or whether they could obtain once again in the future. Both sides have taken a number of confidence building measures in order to make this possibility remote, and it remains to be seen whether the CBMs have run their course, or more steps can still be taken.

While China's growing military capabilities have inadvertently reduced India's security, the same is not necessarily true of China's relationships with a number of India's neighbours, notably Pakistan, and, to a lesser extent, Myanmar, Nepal, Bangladesh and Sri Lanka. India can very well live with these relationships as long as they are not targeted against it. There are two sources of insecurity here. One is about China using these relationships to magnify its own profile and in the process constrain India's freedom of action in what was hitherto India's zone of influence, especially in the Indian Ocean. However, there is an alternate narrative, which explains this in terms of China's desire to safeguard its sea lines of communication that transport its vital energy supplies, as well as to connect its landlocked hinterland to the sea, the so-called 'string of pearls' strategy. To the extent that this is the underlying motivation behind China's actions, India can accommodate China's interests in the Indian Ocean.

In the face of China's growing ties with India's periphery, primarily its *entente cordiale* with Pakistan, India's restraint *prima* facie appears to be sub-optimal. The strategic partnership of recent vintage with the US can be viewed as a tentative response. There is also the proposed framework for a quadrilateral strategic dialogue between the major democracies of the Asia-Pacific, including Japan and Australia. While this could provide useful leverage, an attempt to overplay this hand could result in heightened competition rather than cooperation. The other option for India is to impress upon

China the opportunity costs of such actions in terms of the unfulfilled potential of Sino-Indian cooperation.

On the other hand, India still remains uncertain about China's intentions, which stems from a perceived lack of transparency in China's actions. This is despite China's efforts to reassure its neighbours that it follows a policy of peaceful development. The US has counselled China to demonstrate its good intentions by playing the role of a responsible stakeholder in regional peace and stability. India has to ascertain China's intentions with greater confidence, since India's insecurity derives from the uncertainty shrouding China's intentions.[27] If China's intentions were known to be benign with reasonable confidence through an expanded CBM regime, it would automatically moderate India's insecurity. China could telegraph its benign intentions towards India in a less ambiguous manner which could lead India to reciprocate, producing a dynamic that is the mirror image of the security dilemma by which both sides take mutually reinforcing cooperative measures that enhance mutual security.

The prospects for the strategic partnership between the two countries metamorphosing from vision to reality depends on progress on the underlying insecurities, including an expeditious border settlement, India upgrading its conventional and nuclear deterrent in the face of China's military modernization, China moving towards greater equidistance between India and Pakistan, as well as India reassuring China on its relationship with the US and its Tibet policy. If they are not addressed, a ceiling will remain on how far the bilateral relationship can rise. But CBMs can raise the floor on how far the bilateral relationship can fall. These include trade, people-to-people contact, cooperation on energy and maritime security, and cooperation in several regional forums.

The main reason for India's upgraded security environment was the changed balance of international power at the turn of the century. China's rapid rise brought major adjustments to Asia's power structure, accentuating differences between the United States and China. In this background, India began to receive more attention and to be entrusted with the important new role of acting as a 'swing state in the global balance of power'.[28] In other words, the major powers compete to have India on their sides in the process of the construction of a new world order. As Prime Minister Manmohan Singh said in August 2007, while celebrating the 60th anniversary of Indian independence, "the world today wants India to do well. The world community wishes us well. Our external situation is benign and favourable."[29]

Changes in India's China Policy

The growth of the sub-continent's comprehensive strength and improvements in the international environment in the late 1990s presented India a real possibility of realizing its unprecedented and available strategic opportunities.[30] In this backdrop, reconciliation with China and the unchanged overall direction of the relationship produced several new adjustments to the positions and goals of India's China policy. India also saw China neither as enemy nor friend, believing that cooperation could coexist with competition between the two countries. India still considered China as constituting no threat in the short term, but began focusing on long-term trends in the balance of power. The emphasis of the goals of its new China policy are on ensuring that future Sino-Indian relations are of benefit to India by making China a positive factor in the process of its rise. Maintaining the stability of Sino-Indian relations remains fundamental.

Converging Economic Interests

India and China share interests on many key trade issues. At first glance, there may appear little in the way of Sino-Indian complimentarily as exists with US capital and comparatively cheaper Chinese labour. However, while areas of bilateral interest may not exist at present between the two countries, the growing importance of India in international trade as well as the existing strength of the Chinese economy suggests that the two countries together could form a powerful lobby to address shared external interests. Tariff barriers, access to developed markets, environmental policy and patent protection are major irritants in both countries' relations with the G8. India's extensive lobbying efforts in this regard have already started to yield positive responses, particularly in the field of pharmaceuticals. Coordinated efforts between the two countries could generate greater tangible success, with significant economic implications.

Balance of Power between India and China

As India continued to abide by the principle of checks and balances after the Cold War, its China policy still emphasized the desire for parity. The obvious power gap between India and China motivated Indian leaders' decision in the 1990s to emulate China by expanding comprehensive national strength and restoring a balance of power between the two countries.[31] The race to overtake China thus subtly began in India, and continues to the present day. But unlike the arms race of the Cold War period its progress is measured in comprehensive national strength. India has at the same time sought new partnerships to adjust the balance of power between the two countries which led to actual parity with China. For instance, against backdrop of China's rise India's strategic relationships with the United States and Japan have strengthened and its Look East policy both deepened and expanded. It is India's hope that these relationships might bring new strategic space to its relations with China.[32] Similarly, although Indian officials deny any intent to contain or isolate China behind the first strategic dialogue among the United States, Japan, India and Australia in May 2007, or the joint military exercises in September of the same year held by the United States, Japan, India, Australia and Singapore in the Bay of Bengal, Indian strategists nonetheless admit that they will use such relationships to balance China and at the same time raise India's regional influence and international standing.[33] India does not believe that these new partnerships will reach the level of alliance as their advantage lies solely in their ability to check China; they will have no impact on improved Sino-Indian relations.

Conclusion

Changes in post-Cold War India's security strategy towards China were thus the result of both domestic and foreign factors. The first change during the early post-Cold War period was triggered by passive reactions to transformations in the nation's domestic and international situation that, in turn, prompted a passive transformation of thinking and understanding, manifest in passive defensiveness of India's foreign policy, specifically its China policy. The security concept that appeared during the late 1990s was comparatively proactive. The expanded strength of India's domestic economy and improvement of its external environment compelled a new understanding of security issues, as expressed in the proactive change in its security concept. This assertiveness was manifested in strategy and in an active, enterprising foreign policy. Seizing the historic opportunity to realize India's rise had become the common security objective of both major Indian political parties. Decentralization of political power and expanded openness of the foreign policy-making process, however, caused India's old and new security concepts to bind into one, and the resultant duality of India's hybrid security concept since the Cold War's end is reflected in its China policy. As India's dual security concept will continue into the foreseeable future, the duality of its China policy will be difficult to change.

REFERENCES

1. *Asia Week*, May 22, 1998.
2. Neville Maxwell, "Sino-Indian Border Dispute Reconsidered", *Economic & Political Weekly*, Vol. 34, No. 15, April 10-16, 1999.
3. *Peoples' Daily*, April 6, 1995.
4. Rory McCarthy, "Pakistan's Nuclear Nation Building", *The Guardian*, March 30, 2001.
5. John W. Garver, *Protracted Contest: Sino-Indian Rivalry in the Twentieth Century*, (University of Washington Press, 2002).
6. "1959: Dalai Lama escapes to India", *BBC*, available at *http://news.bbc.co.uk/onthisday/hi/dates/stories/march/31/newsid_2788000/2788343.stm*.
7. "India's Nuclear Tests: Sino-Indian Mutual Concerns", available at www.carnegieendowment.org/files/ChinaChanging_CH2.pdf.
8. S. Mansingh, "India-China Relations in the Post-Cold War Era", *Asian Survey*, Vol. 34, No. 3, March 1994, pp. 285-300.
9. Kotera M. Bhimaya, "Nuclear Deterrence in South Asia: Civil-Military Relations and Decision-Making", Asian *Survey*, Vol. 34, No. 7, July, 1994, pp. 647-661.
10. "India's Nuclear Tests: Sino-Indian Mutual Concerns", *op. cit*.
11. *Ibid*.
12. Li Li, "India's Security Concept and Its China Policy in the Post-Cold War Era", *Chinese Journal of International Politics*, Volume 2, Issue 2, 2008, pp. 229-261.

13. Lan Jianxue, "Post-Cold War Sino-Indian Relations: Normalization and Strategic Harmony", *South Asian Studies*, No. 2, 2005, pp. 9-10.
14. Wei Ling, "On Indian Security Strategy and Sino-Indian Security Relations", *Journal of People's University of China*, No. 6, 2005, pp. 95-105.
15. *Ibid*.
16. *Ibid*.
17. Kanti Bajpai, "Indian Strategic Culture", in Michael R. Chambers, ed., *South Asia in 2020: Future Strategic Balances and Alliances* (Carlisle Barracks: Strategic Studies Institute, Army War College, 2002), pp. 245-303.
18. *Ibid*. pp. 252-253 and 255-266.
19. John W. Garver, *Protracted Contest: Sino-Indian Rivalry in the Twentieth Century* (Seattle: University of Washington Press, 2001), pp. 384-389.
20. Amit Gupta, "India's Third-Tier Nuclear State Dilemma: N Plus 20?" *Asian Survey*, Vol. XLI, No. 6 (Nov-Dec, 2001), pp. 1044-1063.
21. Dilip H. Mohite and Amit Dholakia, *India and the Emerging World Order: Foreign Policy and Security Perspectives* (Delhi: Kalinga Publications, 2001).
22. Kuldip S. Ludra, *The Defence of Andaman and Nicobar Islands* (Chandigarh: Thakur Strategic Research Centre, 1999).
23. K.V. Kesavan and Lalima Varma, eds., *Japan-South Asia: Security and Economic Perspectives* (New Delhi: Lancer Books, 2000).
24. Mohammed Ayoob, "South-West Asia after the Taliban," *Survival*, Vol. 44, No. 1 (Spring 2002), pp. 51-68.
25. Bharat Karnad, *Nuclear Weapons and Nuclear Security: The Realist Foundations of Strategy* (Delhi: Macmillan, 2002).
26. Robert Jervis, "Cooperation Under the Security Dilemma", *World Politics*, Vol. 30, No. 2, January 1978, p. 187.
27. Charles L Glaser, "The Security Dilemma Revisited", *World Politics*, Vol. 50, No. 1, October 1997, p. 192.
28. C. Raja Mohan, "India and the Balance of Power", *Foreign Affairs*, July-August 2006.
29. Manmohan Singh, "Prime Minister's Speech on the Occasion of 60th Anniversary of India's Independence", 15 August, 2007, New Delhi, available at http://pmindia.nic.in/speeches.htm.
30. C. Raja Mohan, *Crossing the Rubicon: The Shaping of India's New Foreign Policy* (New Delhi: Penguin, 2003).
31. *Ibid*., pp. 149-150.
32. *Ibid*., pp. 211-217.
33. K. Subrahmanyam, "New World, If Only China Could See", *The Indian Express*, August 14, 2007.

8

Is Indo-Naga Peace Process moving towards National Integration?

Herkan Neadan Toppo

The prevailing orders of North-East India have diverse issues related to ethnic resurgence, migration, and ethnic conflict and autonomy movements of various ethnic groups along with insurgency. The causes for continued unrest in the North-East India as can be identified in ethnicity, economic development and elections. Also reflected in and maintained that improper handling of the situation by successive governments for narrow political mileages have further aggravated the situation. The emergence of the trend of ethnic identity with an idea of sovereign ethno-nationalism along the political boundaries has been viewed from a different perspective. The politics of autonomy in North-East India in general and Nagaland in particular, has not been successful in fulfilling the aspirations of various ethnic Naga-groups. It is said that by invoking the right to self-determination on the basis of their 'distinct ethnic identity and unique history, the Nagas defied the Indian State that sought to make them a constituent part of the post-colonial Indian Union.[1] India's geo-strategic interest of keeping its eastern frontier intact, especially the Naga territories, is undoubted and indisputable. An equally important aspect of the truth is that the resolution of Naga homeland issue on the basis of exercising genuine self-determination can only provide a stable security corridor and economic growth for India's quest for a dominant role in Asian power theatre.[2] Besides this, Government of India (GOI) seems likely to continue using localized autocracy to manage the North-East that involved massive economic transfers, a security presence to counter the greatest threats and secure the borders.[3] In addition the GOI's reliance on local autocracy to maintain a modicum of political stability is fraught with long-term, potentially negative consequences. This negative shock to India's coercive capacity in the region is easily exploited by militants tapping into the areas of complex economic grievances and identity-based rivalries. It is observed that there was failure to find an agreement or come to solution, which is a significant one on the part of successive governments that in more than seven decades of democracy have failed to ensure all sections of society in the region into political mainstream. Thus, the potential for the re-emergence of severe insurgency movement continues. As in the past, such violence probably did not pose an existential threat to India, but the potential costs are certainly not negligible, especially in terms of the quality of India's democracy and the well-being of citizens in the North-East.[4]

Many theories have been propounded and suggestions have been put forward by academicians, scholars and researchers for finding lasting solution to the insurgency-induced conflicts in the region. A. Lanunungsang Ao relates the emergence of Naga Insurgency movement to self-determination and argues that 'whatever the conflict, it must be sorted out first within the Nagas themselves before their national political agenda is placed before New Delhi in India for discussion to reach a point of agreement for bringing final settlement'.[5] Bethany Lacina discusses in her essay, 'Rethinking Delhi's North-East India Policy' that "those who put forward such easy solution do not address the embedded nature of rebel groups in the political process of the North-East. Only concerted efforts to establish the rule of law, a system of accountability and faith in the formal institutions of governance can break the cycle of violence".[6] She believes that a political system less ambivalent towards the rule of law in theory as well as in practice can marginalize these groups relatively easily and also the Armed Forces Special Powers Act (AFSPA) applicable in the North-East does harm than benefit by encouraging the public dissent or resentment.[7]

India's basic interest in Naga areas is border, which is seen as strategic and defensive. But of late with the emergence of many struggling people asserting their right to self-determination India fears that any settlement with the Nagas on this line will encourage them and jeopardize the integrity of India.[8] Therefore, North-East India is seen as an area of concern for national security.

Beyond this, as concerning to political development, out of suffering a convention was emerged known as the Naga People's Convention. The main objective of this convention is understood as to how best the Naga political settlement could be achieved through dialogue and negotiations. This convention was held in three successive years and they adopted a 16-point resolution. Finally it became the so called 16-point Agreement between the Naga people's Convention and the Indian Government. The main salient feature of this convention was to form a separate State within the Indian Union: with a Governor, a Legislative Assembly and Council of Ministers. The outcome of which is a full fledged State of Nagaland was formally inaugurated on December 1, 1963.[9]

Despite creation of a separate State of Nagaland, the struggle for self-determination continues for decades in search of amicable solution to the quest of Naga nationalism and it has been South Asia's longest running guerrilla campaign.

Naga-Insurgency and Movement for Self-Determination

The Naga insurrection posed the first major challenge to India's post colonial nation-building process and development since the time of Japanese invasion of the World War II. The first definite expression of the Naga desire for self-determination goes back to the visit of the Simon Commission in 1929. The Naga Club (established with British patronage in 1918), the first political group among the Nagas, told the Commission in a memorandum that the British should 'leave us (Nagas) alone once you leave so that we determine for ourselves as in ancient times'. In June 1945, the Naga Club subsequently became the Naga National Council (NNC) and demanded an autonomous State for the Naga dominated area in a memorandum presented to the British Government.

Meanwhile, in June 1946 when the Cabinet Mission Plan was announced the NNC through its resolution demanded for autonomy within Assam. However, Nehru insisted that Naga should form a part of India and Assam. As a result in December 1946, the NNC decided to claim for sovereignty for all Naga Tribes. In 1947, the Indian Advisory Committee on the Aboriginal Tribes visited Kohima, and the NNC put forward a four-point proposal for the right of self-determination:

- A ten-year interim government for the Naga people with full powers in respect of legislation, executive and judiciary;
- Full power for revenue collection and expenditure;
- An annual subvention by the guardian power to cover the revenue gap; and
- A force maintained by the guardian power for defence and to aid the civil power.

But no agreement was reached between the Advisory Committee and the NNC. The Assam Governor, Sir Akber Hydari's subsequent hard work brought back the Nagas to the path of reconciliation.[10] Though the NNC accepted the Hydari agreement, but dispute had arisen on some provisions among the Nagas. Whereas the claim took a new turn as India's independence approached, Angami Zapu Phizo took over the organization of the NNC and immediately declared Naga independence, a day before India became free and set the Nagas on a path of conflict with India.

However, on 11 December, 1950, Phizo was elected as the President of the NNC succeeding Visiar Angami and in his leadership NNC rejected Sixth Schedule and refused to send any member to the Parliament. Instead it held a plebiscite and according to its claim 99 per cent of the Nagas favoured severance from India and self-government. But the Union Government did not give any importance to it.[11] Besides in December 1951 Nehru, who was on a visit to Assam, advised five-member delegation of NNC to accommodate their demands within the Constitution of India which was refused by the Nagas. Further, under the leadership of Phizo NNC boycotted the General Election of 1952 and as a result of NNC's declaration, no one contested the election to the District Council, Assam Assembly or Indian Parliament.

Nehru visited Kohima on 30 March, 1953 with the then Prime Minister of Burma U Nu. Due to a 'misunderstanding', the crowd that gathered in the hall left where the Prime Minister was supposed to address the gathering. The NNC was denied right to present a welcome address which led to the walkout. Nehru lashed out at 'outsiders' (Christian missionaries) for misleading the Nagas.

The Federal Government of Nagaland or Hongking was announced in Tuensang on 18 September, 1954 and consecutively inter-tribal feuds also broke out in the area which complicated the situation. The Government of Assam used its repressive measures to contain the situation. But it worsened in March 1955 when fierce fighting broke out between Assam Rifles and the Hongking Army in the Tuensang area. The Naga delegation consisting of Phizo, Jasokie and three other leaders met Bshnuram Medhi, the then Chief Minister of Assam in Shillong signed a declaration condemning terrorism and promising that the NNC would use peaceful means in achieving its goal issuing leaflets espousing peace and had a number of public meetings. Thus, moderates who had lost the leadership to Phizo were again gaining grounds.

In January 1956, T. Sakhrie, the cousin of Phizo, who opposed the violent doctrine of Phizo was abducted from his house, tied to a tree and murdered brutally by the extremists with a view to striking terror in the hearts of the moderates.

On 22nd March, 1956 The Phizo group declared the establishment of the Federal Government as a *de facto* government in a ceremony held at Phensinyu village in Rengma area. The Naga National Flag bearing red, green and white with three blue stars was hoisted with great traditional ceremony and feast. The Naga Movement had thus the metamorphosis: from an overground activity the Naga Movement had become underground insurgency.

The Reform Committee which was formed within the NNC by the moderates under the Chairmanship of Thepfulo Nakhro issued a statement opposing violence, military method and pledged to restore peace and order by trying to win over the 'hostiles'. It expressed its confidence on Prime Minister's assurance that a separate unit of administration would be constituted to preserve the rights and customs of Naga people. It also expressed its desire to send representatives to Indian Parliament.

Naga People's Convention was held on 22nd-26th August, 1957 under the chairmanship of Dr. Imkongliba. It was participated by around 2,000 participants representing different Naga inhabited areas. It also had the endorsement of about 1765 traditional representatives of the different Naga tribes. It espoused the cause of the political settlement of Naga imbroglio and on 1st December, 1957. According to the Act of Naga Hills—Tuensang Area Act 1957 which was passed by the Parliament of India, a single administrative unit was created.

Meanwhile on 4th-5th May, 1965, the Nagas came up with the fresh demand that Phizo should be associated in the next higher level talks. The Government of India agreed to this proposal but Phizo refusd to come to India for talks. The venue was shifted to New Delhi as the Nagas had desired the talks should be upgraded to ministerial level. There were as many as six rounds of ministerial level talks between the Government of India led by the Prime Minister of India and the underground Nagas led by their Prime Minister Ato Kilonser. The talks spread over a period from February 1966 to October 1967.

At the same time on 3rd May, 1966 External Affairs Minister Dinesh Singh announced in Rajya Sabha that Rev. Scott had been served with orders to leave the country immediately. In an earlier occasion, Scott had questioned the legitimacy of India's rule over Nagaland and asked for the setting up of an Indo-Naga Commission to investigate the 'crime-sheet' prepared by him in 1964-65. Scott's exit weakened the morale of the Nagas considerably.

Subsequently on 27-29 October, 1966 Kukhato, the leader of the Naga delegates, submitted the 14-point agreement to the Prime Minister. The Government of India rejected allowing sovereignty but they were assured however that Nagaland could have maximum autonomy within the Indian Union. The Naga leaders were permitted to meet Phizo in England and accordingly Suisa and Vizol went to meet Phizo and consult with him before any final decision is reached upon. It is believed that Phizo gave the two Naga leaders a cold reception refusing to meet them and snubbing Suisa with whom he was very annoyed.

It is on 8th August, 1974 Naga Peace Council (NPC) submitted a four-point memorandum to Governor L.P. Singh. It resulted in the Shillong Accord in 1975, which created major discord among the underground Nagas. A section of the leaders denounced the Accord and issued a stern warning to the signatories of the Accord. The ambiguous position of Phizo alienated him from his former colleagues. In the mean time, the inter-tribal rivalry between the various Naga groups reached a new height. The leadership of the underground movement shifted form the hands of the Semas to the Tangkhul Nagas which itself was a cause of resentment in the feud ridden Naga society. [12]

As the Government of India banned the NNC in 1972 under the Unlawful Activities (Prevention) Act of 1967 and launched a massive counter-insurgency operation. On November 11, 1975, the Shillong Accord was signed between NNC and the Government of India where the NNC cadres accepted "without condition, the Constitution of India". However, a section of the NNC rebelled against the accord and formed the National Socialist Council of Nagaland (NSCN) in 1980. Tribal differences led to a split in the NSCN in 1988 leading to the birth of Isak-Muivah faction (NSCN-IM) and the Khaplang faction (NSCN-K). Both these outfits continued their movement with an avowed objective of establishing a Nagalim (greater Nagaland) comprising Naga inhabited areas of Nagaland, Assam, Manipur, Arunachal Pradesh and neighbouring Myanmar.[13]

Nevertheless, in 1987 the NNC split and the breakaway faction NSCN emerged to give Naga rebel movement a fresh lease of life. Subsequently, in 1988 the NSCN also split into two factions, namely NSCN (Isaac-Muivah) and NSCN (Khaplang) because of the long history of insurgency in Nagaland, the NSCN factions are some of the most sophisticated militant outfits in the region in terms of their access to weapons and funding, level of training, and network of safe areas. One of the significant steps taken by NSCN is the shift of policy and strategy from guerrilla warfare to mass warfare, from machine gun warfare to computer warfare and from armed confrontation to political negotiation, so both the factions are now in negotiations with GOI.

But the fragile peace process in the Naga Hills has been shattered by internecine conflict. This is ironical because the ceasefires between the GOI and its armed forces, including the paramilitary, and the two factions of the NSCN remain in place. In 2008 assembly election political parties along with the Congress had raised the issue of 'integration of Naga-inhabited areas', but the voters were perhaps not convinced about its intention as the party talked about the implementation of the unimplemented clause of the historic 16-point agreement signed between the Government of India and the erstwhile Naga People's Convention in July 1960.[14] Clause 13 of the agreement states that "the other Naga tribes inhabiting the areas contiguous to the present Nagaland be allowed to join Nagaland if they so desire", but there has been no direct commitment from the Centre about its implementation.[15]

Dialogue Initiatives and Peace Process

During the course of Naga National struggle for sovereignty major agreements and initiatives have been made to restore peace and facilitate talks between the GOI and Nagas. The Naga Peace Mission (NPC), which came into existence due to the efforts of the Nagaland Baptist Church Council resulted in the signing of the first Ceasefire Agreement in September 1964 between the GOI and Federal Government of Nagaland (FGN) to facilitate peace talks, realizing the necessity of bringing peace to Nagaland (as there was an undeclared war going on between the Indian Armed forces and the Naga Army). But this agreement was once again abrogated like the other previous agreements by the GOI on August 31, 1972.[16]

The Indian Government made a major policy-shift towards the Naga insurgency in 1990s and made several attempts to negotiate peace with the insurgent groups appeared to be as intractable. The Union Government had several rounds of peace talks to solve the Naga insurgency within as well as outside the country with the NSCN-IM which is the principal militant formation in Nagaland.

Eventually, the process of negotiations resulted in the Ceasefire Agreement of 1997, signed between the GOI and NSCN-IM with the sole objective to continue the peace process during which the Naga political talk could be held and believed solution could be worked out and in July 1997, a ceasefire was declared between the GOI and two Naga insurgent groups, though talks were first initiated by the then Prime Minister P. V. Narasimha Rao in Paris on June 15, 1995. In this wake, the wide-scale violence subsided to certain extent, but fratricidal killing continued until the intervention of civil societies led by Forum for Naga Reconciliation (FNR). At the behest of FNR the "Covenant of Reconciliation" was signed among the warring Naga insurgent groups at Chiangmai, Thailand. The declaration of Indo-Naga ceasefire had corresponding impact on India's border frontier as the other insurgent groups subsequently entered into peace talks with the State and Union governments. However, the issue of sovereignty and the demand for the creation of a 'Greater Nagaland' (Nagalim) comprising Naga-inhabited areas of Assam, Arunachal Pradesh and Manipur, remained as bones of enduring contention after all these years of negotiation. The Ceasefire between the GOI and NSCN was effective from August 1, 1997. It was also agreed that the ceasefire agreement is between the GOI and NSCN as two entities without territorial limits (Joint statement on June 14, 2001) and later negotiated a similar cease-fire agreement with Khaplang faction of NSCN in 2001.

Consecutively, in May 6-10, 2002, in its third Naga consultation meeting held in which 73 Naga delegates representing Naga Hoho, the Churches and mass based civil society organizations solemnly declared that they fully support the ongoing political negotiation between the Government of India and the NSCN.[17]

Whereas in its fourth Naga people's consultation to strengthen the Indo-Naga political talks in January 20-21, 2005, Naga people and their civil society organizations covering across the length and breadth of the Naga Homeland reaffirmed their fullest support for an honourable and acceptable solution to the Indo-Naga political issue on the basis of the uniqueness of Naga history and situation.[18] From the Centre's perspective, the NSCN-IM and NSCN-K ceasefires have had real benefits.

There has been a dramatic decline in security force fatalities. From 1992 – 2001, an average of 24 government troops were killed each year in Nagaland. In contrast, there have been a total of only nine such deaths from 2002 to 2008.

NSCN factions have reduced their logistical and manpower support to other militants groups attacking security forces. Some of the insurgent groups that appeared in the 1990s had the capacity to attack State forces only in conjunction with NSCN fighters. Those groups have declined since the NSCN ceasefires.

Although passivity toward factional and inter-communal violence in Nagaland has been called a product of indifference, the centre may actually believe that allowing a local autocrat to emerge from the factional violence is the most efficient way to achieve temporary stability in the otherwise volatile region.[19]

The hard earned Indo-Naga peace process has endured many ups and downs to the point of testing the limits of both sides on more than one occasion. But to the credit of both the GOI and the NSCN, the greater cause for a peaceful resolution of the Indo-

Naga political problem has ensured that the peace process has survived the rough weather till today.[20]

One of the basic flaws in the ceasefire agreement is the ambiguity in the 'territorial scope' of the ground rules and whether cease fire extends beyond Nagaland. While it is understandable that given the sensitivity of other North-East States involved, for the GOI to clearly spell out the scope of the ceasefire beyond Nagaland State, yet the question now is whether it is time to clearly point out the same because it does not make sense to confine a ceasefire agreement to Nagaland State alone. The NSCN operates in other Naga areas contiguous to Nagaland. So does it then mean that the GOI and NSCN ceasefire in Nagaland but continue to fight militarily elsewhere? If this is the logic, then how can the peace process sustain? One can almost guess that having a ceasefire agreement with territorial limit is illogical. What is distressing is the dilly dallying by the political establishment in Delhi over the territorial scope of the ceasefire.[21]

It may be recalled that Mr Kaushal Swaraj, the former representative of the Prime Minister of India officially declared in public that the "matter relating to cease-fire has been considered by the GOI at the highest level. It is not limited to Nagaland State as was earlier interpreted". He goes on to state that the cease-fire area coverage is without any geographical limitation". This was sometime in June 1998 at the initial stage of the ceasefire. But Delhi went back on its official line. The GOI's flip flop is further evidenced by the fact that K. Padmanabhaiah, the interlocutor in the Naga peace talks, in a letter to the NSCN (IM) Chairman reiterated that the ceasefire agreement cannot be extended beyond the current boundaries of Nagaland. Yet again on June 14, 2001, while extending the cease-fire with the NSCN (IM), Delhi extended the area of coverage into the Naga inhabited States of the North-East region thereby giving legitimacy to the term 'ceasefire without territorial limits'.[22]

An interesting point that should be noted here is that the text of the ceasefire ground rules agreed between Delhi and the NSCN-(K) begins at the top by clearly writing that the ground rules will be valid only for the State of Nagaland. No such thing is mentioned in the ground rules between Government of India and NSCN-IM. Obviously one can, therefore, infer that the GOI has taken a liberal view on the matter of coverage of the ceasefire. But then unless there is a clear mention of this in the text agreement there is bound to be confusion and misinterpretation on both sides. A news report states that "according to ceasefire ground rules NSCN-IM cannot set camps anywhere outside the territory of Nagaland". But nowhere does it mention in the ceasefire agreement about setting up of designated camps in Nagaland or outside of it. The only point mentioned is that the NSCN will notify list of all its camps to the Ceasefire Monitoring Group (CFMG) who after due consultation would declare them as the designated camps. If this is so, there is no reason why such a camp should not be 'designated' as such in Shiroi. After all there is already three other designated camps in Manipur. Having another one at Shiroi or some other place in Ukhrul district should not become a bone of contention for either side. This can be mutually agreed through the CFMG.[23]

In July 31, 2007 Cease-fire extended indefinitely. The 40-page booklet, titled "Healing and Reconciliation" was released at a meeting of representatives of various organizations. October 10, 2007: Union Ministers Oscar Fernandes, Prithviraj Chavan, S. Regupathy and interlocutor K. Padmanabhaiah, held talks with a eight-member IM team headed by Muivah in New Delhi. The Federal Assembly of the Naga Hoho reiterated its earlier resolution pertaining to reconciliation and unity, integration and peace process and reaffirmed to support the ongoing Indo-Naga political dialogue, strengthened the reconciliation and unity process amongst the Nagas as well reactivate (effort) towards integration.[24] Also during the election campaign in the State of Nagaland in 2008, Prime Minister Manmohan Singh made a commitment that the Congress Party was 'willing to go the extra mile' to find an honourable solution to the vexed Naga problem and bring long lasting peace to the State.[25] As a consequence on 22nd January 2009, in a goodwill gesture and to foster peace and understanding amongst the Nagas, the GPRN/NSCN today released 6 members of NSCN (IM) unconditionally in the presence of the Forum for Naga Reconciliation (FNR) and other Civil Societies at a brief function at Khehoi designated camp. Befitting to the gesture, the NSCN (IM) reciprocated with a hope-giving and heartening response of gratitude to the "GPRN/NSCN." The realization of Naga reconciliation will hasten the will of the people. Therefore, it is the responsibility of every Naga to sensibly respond and demonstrate their active solidarity and participation for Naga reconciliation.[26]

On June 1, 2010, Centre and NSCN (IM) held peace talks for the first time in Nagaland at Kohima, where the issue of integration of Naga-inhabited areas, as demanded by the outfit, was discussed. However, the Centre ruled out change in boundaries of states without the consensus of political parties. Both sides came to an understanding on some issues and expressed their commitment to explore all possibilities to arrive at a consensus on other sensitive issues.

On June 4, 2010 Muivah moved to Pfutsero in Phek district on a "Goodwill Mission". In the same month he visited Jotsoma village near Kohima, Pughoboto in Zunheboto district, Tuensang and Peren as a part of his peace mission where he held consultations with civil society leaders on the Naga talks issue. Two more rounds of talks were held in Delhi with the Centre on July 23 and July 29, 2010 with both the sides expressing satisfaction over the way the talks are progressing.[27]

Civil Society Participation

The participation of civil society in the Indo-Naga peace dialogue is a significant measure in managing the intricate conflict in Nagaland. Also it has been traditionally effective with the Church's active involvement as a very important player in peace making among the insurgents. The civil society organizations in Nagaland such as the Forum for Naga Reconciliation, the Naga Hoho, and many other women's and students' organizations like the Naga Mothers' Association (NMA) have played an important role in laying the groundwork for the emergence of lasting peace in the region and have worked towards reconciliation among the warring factions. These are the actors who are working as a bridge between the various regions which comprises Nagalim, in Nagaland, Arunachal Pradesh, Assam, Manipur and parts of Myanmar; and without any substantial political overtones. They have been successful in reaching out to communities, both Naga and other ethnic tribes, and promoting dialogue and understanding at the civil society level between contesting aspirations of communities in the region, which the political outfits engaged in talks have not been able to do. They have joined efforts to talk to top rebel leaders to stop fratricidal killings among Naga insurgent factions and extortions and threats, and to include more women in the peace talks.

Even the tribal councils belonging to the different tribes in the State including the Ao Senden, the Sumi Hoho have tried to establish unity among the NSCN-IM and NSCN-K, albeit without much success. Also organizations like the Naga People's Movement for Human Rights (NPMHR) that periodically highlights the alleged abuses by the security forces, are seen as placating the interests of the NSCN-IM and have no influence on either the NSCN-K or the NNC.[28] The citizens of the State have been taking initiatives for bringing peace in the State. On 20 May, 2008, a reconciliation meeting of the Naga factions, mass-based Naga organizations and tribal Hohos was organized by the Naga Reconciliation Forum, headed by Baptist clergyman Wati Aier, Baptist World Alliance and a UK-based Quaker group, at Chiang Mai in Thailand. But, the NSCN-K rejected the offer made by the rival NSCN-IM for a dialogue outside the country and the move failed.[29]

The marginalization of civil society organization creates conditions for increased factionalism and violence, as demonstrated by the emergence of NSCN (U) (Unification) and the resultant increase in fratricidal killings. The Forum for Naga Reconciliation recently called for turning swords into plowshares, and for working creatively towards ensuring enduring peace and a lasting solution to the Naga question. The Church-led Naga Reconciliation Forum (NRF), with representations from 42 community groups as well as the militant outfits, organized several reconciliatory meetings both within and outside the country. Two such meetings were organized at Chiang Mai in Thailand in June and September 2009.[30] The long-drawn war of attrition has been waged under the camouflage of extended cease-fire agreements, which the Union of Government signed with the NSCN-IM in 1997 and the NSCN-K in 2001.

The initiative of the State in declaring the Indo-Naga ceasefire and the role of civil society in the peace process, therefore, assumed a considerable importance in the regions' quest for peace. More importantly, however, the participation of civil society in the peace process has virtually helped dispelling the sense of insecurity in

Nagaland, torn apart by the seven decades old violent armed conflict.

Despite these difficulties, the Naga civil society movements with support from civil voices in India have openly demonstrated for early solution to the Indo-Naga political process reflects the people's continued yearning for a united purpose and reconciliation within the national resistance to gain a just, honourable and lasting settlement. Will the Government of India respond with understanding and amicably resolve the unique case of the Naga nation diplomatically or will it relaunch another deadly phase of military assault in its most sensitive regions under occupation?[31]

Centre and Nagaland : A Step towards National Integration

The GOI has tried many things in order to resolve issues in the North-East in terms of the conflict. It has tried throwing the army in the security forces and heavily armed the police giving them special training in counter insurgency to deal with the insurgents but all this has not worked. And the reason is that it cannot deal with a political issue or problem by using brute force to come to a discussion or negotiation that enables the resolution of the problem.[32]

The AFSPA (Armed Forces Special Power Act) for instance, shows the inability and reluctance of the government to solve the conflict with adequate political measures. The AFSPA was passed on 18 August, 1958, as a short-term measure to allow deployment of the army to counter an armed separatist movement in the Naga Hills, but it was extended to all the seven States of the North-East region in 1972 (with the exception of Mizoram). It was part of a bundle of provisions, passed by the Central Government, to retain control over the Naga areas, and NNC demanded further autonomous rights. The AFSPA became a powerful measure for the Central and the State Governments to act against actors challenging the political and territorial integrity of India. As a result, the Indian army for the first time since its independence was deployed to manage an internal conflict. But, instead of resolving the problem, it led to an ongoing escalation of the conflict by bringing it on a military level. The regular violations of human rights has led to a radicalization and militarization of the region and weakened also the supporters of a political solution. Among the lessons that have emerged from the phase of the Naga conflict is a realization by the central government and the Naga group's that dialogue is more fruitful than force or violence. The system must now enact laws to control the situation peacefully and involve communities and civil society in increasing the democratic space.[33]

The ongoing political talks between GOI and NSCN have been based on the following ceasefire principles: that the talks are unconditional; they took place at the highest level of the Prime Minister and they convened in a third neutral country. These talks indicate the Indians government's *de facto* recognition of the Naga people's sovereignty. In July 2002, the recognition of the "uniqueness of Naga history and situation" by the National Democratic Alliance (NDA) Government in New Delhi under Prime Minister Vajpayee paved the way for serious negotiations between the two entities to begin. During his meeting with the NSCN leaders in Osaka, Vajpayee invited Isaac Swu and Muivah to visit India. They are reported to have told the Prime Minister that it was he who should remove obstacles such as arrest warrants that prevented them from visiting Delhi. Besides, they pointed out that their organisation was a banned one. "We have no problems about visiting India, particularly when Vajpayee himself has invited us and expressed his sincerest desire to settle the Naga issue. What we need is a congenial atmosphere for talks and negotiations," they said.[34]

The Nagaland Government has withdrawn all criminal cases that were pending against Isaac Swu and Muivah, including the one relating to the armed attack on Chief Minister S.C. Jamir's convoy. The move to withdraw the arrest warrants is seen as an attempt by the government to facilitate the continuation of peace talks in Delhi. The last round of talks was held between the Centre's emissary and NSCN leaders in Kuala Lumpur.[35]

Meanwhile, there is tremendous pressure on the NSCN (I-M) leaders from different Naga groups to settle the decades-old insurgency issue and restore peace. The Naga Hoho, an apex body of all Naga tribal councils, has launched a "reconciliation campaign" throughout the State. The Naga Hoho, which believes that the settlement of the Naga problem is not possible without the unity of the 52 Naga tribes, has initiated the campaign in order to help end the clashes between the different extremist groups operating in the State and to bring together all Naga sections, particularly the underground outfits, for the "greater cause of rebuilding the Naga family and ending years of blood-letting." The Church in Nagaland, which plays a significant role in the State's tribal society, has for years been making efforts in this regard without any apparent success.[36]

In 2003, the Naga resistance leadership visited New Delhi for the first time after many decades of living in exile, at the personal invitation of the Prime Minister of India. Also in December 2004, they came for a second visit, this time at the invitation of the new Prime Minister of India with the United Progressive Alliance (UPA) government in power. The NSCN leaders visit to India also gave them the opportunity to come to Nagaland where extensive consultations with the Naga public for preparing future substantive talks were held.

Besides this, it provided them the space to intensively negotiate with the Indian Government representatives and the talks were upgraded from a bureaucratic interlocutor to a political level through the appointment of a Group of Ministers headed by Oscar Fernandes from the GOI had created a more conducive atmosphere for continuing the dialogue. Political parleys continued over the past 9 years with the ceasefire agreement being extended every one year at a time, except in July 2005. The ceasefire extension period was shortened to six months at the insistence of the NSCN after seeing no tangible progresses in the talks with the Government of India were occurring.[37]

The talk of an interim solution to the Naga question was raised at intervals by the Central Government, the State Government and the NSCN (I-M) ever since the year 2004, and the idea of an interim solution took five long years to gain any sort of fruition as the next round of talks at Zurich in Switzerland by end of March 2009. The interim proposals are still being discussed and reworked, and the stage for a possible confrontation has been set by the declaration by NSCN (I-M) leader Isaac Chisi Swu that any relationship within the ambit of the Indian Constitution is unacceptable.[38]

On 29 June, 2009, Naga Hoho in its press release said that it "is overwhelmed to see a spark of hope over the new development with renewed vision particularly between NSCN (K) and (IM) in Chiangmai, Thailand, owing to the timely initiatives of peace makers along with the unflinching support of peace activist from

America, England and Canada under the banner of Forum for Naga Reconciliation." Towards this 'noble endeavour,' the Naga Hoho expressed strong feelings that Nagas should take this effort seriously having missed many opportunities in the past due to petty differences and, therefore, not allow adversaries to derail the Naga's destiny. Simultaneously, the Naga Hoho said it was disturbed "to see the excessive actions of both the NSCN be it the leaders or cadres generating restlessness and enigma in the minds of the common people which has culminated over the burning down of properties worth crores of rupees and turning Vihokhu camp into ashes and most of all, loss of precious lives." The Nagaland Peace Centre (NPC) lauded the symbolic gesture made by "General (Retd.)" V.S. Atem, emissary to the collective leadership of the NSCN (IM) and Y. Wangtin Naga, Dy. Kilonser of "NSCN/GPRN" at Chiang Mai Naga Peace Summit in Thailand. More than 40 students' leaders of NSF, federating units and sub-units are part of the mission. Some of the leaflets of the NSF read, 'Reconciliation our path of freedom,' 'Reconciliation has no tribalism,' 'Reconciliation our hope our future,' 'Reconciliation power of the powerless' and 'Reconciliation our strength.' To pave the way for realization of "The Covenant of Common Hope," the Naga political groups and the Forum for Naga Reconciliation, in the deepest desire of the Nagas, have agreed to work out details of "turning swords into plowshares" ("ceasefire") at the earliest time frame.[39]

In the interim, in February 2010, the Union Government appointed former Union Petroleum Secretary R.S. Pandey as the new interlocutor to negotiate with the NSCN-IM. The Government had earlier decided not to extend the term of former Union Home Secretary K. Padmanabhaiah as interlocutor with the Naga outfit. Padmanabhaiah had been appointed for one year as peace interlocutor in July 1999, but had continued to hold this position till his replacement by Pandey. Since the appointment of the new interlocutor, three rounds of negotiations (two in New Delhi and one in Kohima) have been held between the Union Government and NSCN-IM.[40] The NSCN-IM's demand for integration of the Naga-inhabited areas for creation of Nagalim and a separate constitution to protect the 'unique identity' of the Naga people were, unsurprisingly, rejected by the Union Government, and were turned down on the second day of the first round of negotiations in this phase. The Union Government was, however, willing to discuss the issue of expanding the scope of federalism to give greater powers to the State of Nagaland for the management of natural resources, within the framework of the Constitution[41]

But in Indian context the terms 'within the Constitution' is a vague political notion which can also mean nothing substantial. And it was used as the operative concept to mean that a political solution must be on the basis of Nagas acceptance of union with India or to quote the Nagaland Peace Mission, 'the Nagas participation in the Union of India on their own violations'. These legal notions would become the political impediment in the present Indo-Naga Peace process.[42]

There have been many versions of the possible motives behind these never-ending parleys between the GOI and the NSCN (I-M). Accusations have been made of the Central Government deliberately delaying the move towards a solution and at the same time working towards destabilizing the NSCN (I-M) by engineering splits and factional fights within. The NSCN (I-M) has also been accused of trying to establish its dominance across Nagalim, and eliminating its opposing factions, before it reaches a final settlement. Also it is argued that the involvement of the NSCN (K) faction in a separate ceasefire with the Central government and its role in an ultimate political solution has been intensely contentious. The conspiracy theories may be many, accusing the Central Government, the State Government, the NSCN (I-M) and the NSCN (K), of delaying the peace or derailing the peace process, but the fact remains that the ultimate casualty is the peace process itself.[43]

The peace talks on 30 July, 2007 between the GOI and the representatives of the Naga people reflected on ten years of negotiations that have brought both parties much closer to a solution than have four decades of conflict.

The current talks, which started in March 2010, are still not concluded as other actions are in progress. Two issues—"sovereignty" for Nagaland and the integration of all Naga-inhabited areas—have become difficult to resolve. The claims also include a sort of "sub-constitution" and a "Naga army", though either side knows constitutional and legal challenges that such propositions present.

In a way, this new development is being regarded as the federal principles enshrined in the Constitution allow a great deal of flexibility relating to "autonomy" of particular areas and people. The conspiracy theories are many, variously accusing the Indian government, the Nagaland government, the NSCN (I-M) and the NSCN (K), for prolonging the peace talks with vested interests.[44] It is also being pointed out that the NSCN (I-M) have an excellent opportunity to hold on to what the Indian government has offered, which is the 'special federal relationship', under which the present talks are progressing. Yet pragmatism and the imperatives of peace demand that the ultimate target of a permanent and full scope agreement should not suffer once again. In fact, the need for circumspection is greater now than ever before. The current phase of peace parleys should not be left half-way for yet another future attempt.[45] However, the peace process was initiated by the Forum for Naga Reconciliation (FNR) headed by Rev. Wati Aier, a Baptist clergyman, and still it is being supported by various Naga organisations, State government and international organisations[46] to prolong the truce and continue this dialogue through which progress has been made.[47]

Conclusion

In conclusion it can be said that understanding the nature of autonomy movements and conflict situation in North-East India especially Indo-Naga peace process for national integration needs elaborate study and discussion. Moreover the system of granting autonomous council for particular ethnic group in a State having diverse groups sharing the same geographical area has created more problems than solving ethnic problems. The idea of integration of Naga inhabited areas of Arunachal Pradesh, Assam and Manipur, and seeking due recognition for the Naga people living in Myanmar have already been made popular issue by the NSCN (IM) in the course of its peace negotiations with the centre needs realistic approach without violating the norms and sanctity of the Indian Constitution for any development activity and peaceful co-existence in the region.

Managing these new challenges in the North-East India and beyond borders would require enlightened and sustained Naga leadership. India had sent mixed signals regarding the ongoing peace process which requires co-operation on a broad range of issues that extend beyond the military realm for sustainable peace in the region. The process should be more meaningful to the various stakeholders in the region, most prominently the Naga people to safeguard their culture, identity and fundamental rights

India's other major internal security challenge occurs in the North-East of the country. The insurgency movements in Nagaland, Mizoram, Manipur, Tripura and Assam have tied down India's security forces over a long period of time. In these States, a variety of movements have been fighting for more political control or independence. Their demands spring from the continued lack of attention by India's power elite to developing these regions economically, as well as from porous borders that allow the groups to get training from outside, including from Nepal, Bangladesh, and Myanmar. India's response, resorting to coercive military means to quell the unrest, seems to have helped to increase alienation in the region.

REFERENCES

1. Srikanth, H. & Thomas, C. J., (2005) "Naga Resistance Movement and the Peace Process in Northeast India" *Peace and Democracy in South Asia,* Volume 1, Issue 2, p. 57.
2. N.P. Ariiphre-ou, (2007) "Colours of Naga Struggle and the World", *The Morung Express,* 6 July, p. 7.
3. Bethany Lacina, (2009) "The problem of political stability in northeast India Local Ethnic Autocracy and the Rule of Law", *Asian Survey,* Vol. Xlix, No. 6, November/December, p. 999.
4. *Ibid.*
5. Ao, A. Lanunungsang, (2002), *From Phizo to Muivah: The Naga National Question in North East India,* Mittal Publications New Delhi, p. 12.
6. Bethany Lacina, (2008) 'Rethinking Delhi's Northeast India policy: Why neither counterinsurgency nor winning hearts and minds is the way forward.' In Baruah, Sanjib (Ed.), *Beyond Counterinsurgency: Breaking the Impasse in Northeast India,.* New Delhi: Oxford University Press.
7. *Op. cit.,* Bethany (2009).
8. Chamroy. N., "Some thoughts on the Indo-Naga Peace talks", *http://www.e-pao.net/epSubPageExtractor.asp?src=news_section.opinions.Opinion_on_Manipur_Integrity_Issue.Some_thoughts_on_the_Indo-Naga_Peace_Talks accessed on 13/11/2010.*

9. *Op. cit.* Ao, A. Lanunungsang, p. 53.
10. *http://www.c-nes.org/nycu/539.html accessed on 12-02-2011.*
11. Chronology of Naga Movement, *http://www.safhr.org/index.php?option=com_content&view=article&id=195:chronology-of-naga-movement&catid=120:chronology-of-events&Itemid=408 accessed on 15/6/2011.*
12. Nag, Sagal (2002) Contesting Marginality: Ethnicity, Insurance and Subnationalism in North-East India, Manohar Publications, New Delhi, p. 271.
13. Overview: Insurgency & Peace Efforts in Nagaland http://cdpsindia.org/nagaland_insurgency.asp accessed on 13/7/2011.
14. Talukdar, Sushanta (2008) "Chance for Peace" *Frontline,* April 11, p. 35.
15. *Ibid.*
16. *Op. cit.* Ao, A. Lanunungsang, Pp. 64-65.
17. *Op. cit.* Chronology of Naga Movement.
18. http://www.unpo.org/downloads/155.pdf accessed 15/3/2011.
19. *Op. cit.* Bethany (2009).
20. Along Longkumer, Ceasefire Flaw or End Game?, *http://www.morungexpress.com/political_affairs/13120.html* 5/12/2011.
21. *Ibid.*
22. *Ibid.*
23. *Ibid.*
24. *Op. cit.* Chronology of Naga Movement.
25. Talukdar, Sushanta (2008) "Chance for Peace" *Frontline,* April 11, p. 35.
26. *Op. cit.* Chronology of Naga Movement.
27. *Op. cit.* Overview: Insurgency & Peace Efforts in Nagaland *http://cdpsindia.org/nagaland_insurgency.asp.*
28. *Op. cit.* Overview: Insurgency & Peace Efforts in Nagaland.
29. *Ibid.*
30. *www.satp.org/satporgtp/countries/india/../nagaland/index.html* - accessed on 21-12-2010.
31. NP Ariiphre-ou, (2007) Colours of Naga Struggle and the World, *The Morung Express,* 6 July, p. 7.
32. "Seeking solutions in India's North-East." http://southasia.oneworld.net/weekend/seeking-solutions-in-indias-north-east.
33. Charles Chasie and Sanjoy Hazarika, "The state strikes back: India and the Naga insurgency", *Policy Studies* 52, #2835, 24 March 2009.
34. Kalyan Chaudhuri, (2002) "A step towards peace", *Frontline,* Volume 19 - Issue 15, July 20 - August 02.
35. *Ibid.*
36. *Ibid.*

37. NP Ariiphre-ou, (2007) Colours of Naga Struggle and the World, *The Morning Express,* 6 July, p. 7.
38. Mirza Zulfiqur Rahman, Naga-Peace Process: Which Way Forward? http://www.ipcs.org/article/india/naga-peace-process-which-way-forward-2835.html.
39. *Op. cit.* Chronology of Naga Movement.
40. Sandipani Dash, "India's Nagaland: Intractable Talks" - *South Asia Intelligence Review,* Monday, 14 June 2010. http://www.eurasiareview.com/201006143199/indias-nagaland-intractable-talks-south-asia-intelligence-review.html accessed on 21-09-2010.
41. *Ibid.*
42. *Op. cit.* Chamroy. N.
43. *Ibid.*
44. N.K. Das, "Naga Peace Parleys: Sociological Reflections and a Plea for Pragmatism", *Economic & Political Weekly,* June 18, 2011, Vol xlvi, No. 25, p. 77.
45. *Ibid.*
46. Nagalim: Positive Developments in the Ongoing Naga Reconciliation Process, *The Calcutta Telegraph.,* Tuesday, April 12, 2011, http://www.unpo.org/article/12509.
47. *Ibid.*

9

Emerging Security Dynamics : India's Security and South-East Asia

Homen Thangjam and *Konthoujam Indrakumar Singh*

India and countries of South-East Asia are geographically, culturally and strategically linked. It is needless to emphasise the importance of South-East Asia in the security of India. Next to South Asia, South-East Asia constitutes the vital security parameter of India because of its geographical location. A close look at the Atlas indicates the strategic position of South-East Asia *vis-à-vis* India's security. To be more precise the region is located between the Indian and Pacific Oceans, and some of the countries of South-East Asia have boundaries with India and China, two of the major powers of Asia. Again there are close cultural and civilizational bonds between India and South-East Asian countries. India has exerted a great cultural influence on South-East Asia which was evident from the nomenclature of Indianised kingdoms such as Khmer, Sailendra, Funan, Sri Vijaya, Angkor etc.[1] Thus India and most countries of South-East Asia shared deep cultural and civilizational linkages in the historical past. Consequently India under Nehru's leadership tried to forge a good rapport with the countries of South-East Asia particularly Burma, Indonesia, Vietnam, etc. In line with the great power ambition, India under Nehru tried to promote Asian solidarity and regionalism in the 1950s and 1960s. In 1967, India even suggested the formation of an Asian Council[2] believing that such "a broad based economic organization of all countries in Asia should be formed so that no single country or group of countries from Asia or outside can dominate any country in Asia".[3]

However, in spite of having many cementing factors such as geographical proximity, ancient cultural and economic ties and shared colonial heritage the relation between India and countries of South-East Asia more particularly ASEAN 5[4] (Association of South-East Asian Nations) did not develop into the expected level due to the onset of Cold War and its subsequent impacts upon the political and security landscape of South and South-East Asia. The Cold War politics shaped the nature and pattern of relationship between India and most of the countries of South-East Asia. There were fundamental differences in terms of economic ideology, political outlook and security perceptions between India and ASEAN 5 during the Cold War period. India's policy of non-alignment, her tilt towards USSR and India's closed and inward oriented development strategy were coldly received in South-East Asia. Moreover India's support for North Vietnam, recognition of the Khmer Rouge regime of Heng Samrin in Cambodia and India's support for Vietnam in Cambodian Crisis hampered former relations with non-communist countries of South-East Asian countries. On the one hand pro-American policy of ASEAN 5, their participation in SEATO (South-East Asia Treaty Organization)[5], Indian perception of ASEAN as an extension of SEATO, etc. were contrary to India's foreign policy principles. It can be argued that the presence of unfavourable politico-economic realities during the Cold War period seriously hampered India in its pursuit for deeper engagement with South-East Asian countries particularly ASEAN 5. More importantly certain geo-political development in the South Asia during the Cold War era had restricted India into a sub-continental balance of power politics with Pakistan[6].

However, there have been drastic changes taking place both at regional and global levels since the end of Cold War. Among the significant changes were the resolution of Cambodian conflict, the rise of China as a major regional power and its increasing influence not only in SEA region but also in South Asia, withdrawal of Russia and the USA military from their respective military bases in South-East Asia and emergence of ASEAN as a stable and strong regional organization. Unlike in the Cold War period, new regionalism in SEA region has developed as outward looking, non exclusive and multidirectional in function[7]. This trend has facilitated India to rethink its policy towards the SEA region. Besides, India's own domestic economic reform through liberalization and privatization and failure of the SAARC (South Asia Association of Regional Cooperation) as a regional organization due to the rivalry between India and Pakistan; and other smaller neighbours' suspicion of India's hegemonic design in South Asia. These crucial geo-political and economic shifts at the regional, global and domestic spheres have collectively influenced India to "realign its foreign policies and implement, what it refers to as a move towards big power strategy with the characteristics of a multi-directional foreign policy[8].

India's Look East Policy (LEP) initiated under Narasimha Rao government in the early 90s is one of the foreign policies outcomes of such strategy. LEP signifies India's determination to engage actively with SEA countries at various levels; at the same time it also reflects India's recognition for emerging geo-strategic developments in South-East Asia which are crucial to India's security. India's relations with SEA countries in general and ASEAN in particular has developed significantly since the implementation of LEP. As a result of LEP, India today is very much part of the strategic landscape of SEA region. Present article briefly explores India's relations with ASEAN in the post Cold war period, at the same time exploring India's strategy to consolidate her foothold in SEA both at the bilateral and multilateral forums. Secondly, the article looks at the rise of China as a major power and its expansion, particularly maritime expansion, into the Indian Ocean (IO) and South China Sea (SCS) region as offsetting a new security dynamics in the Asia-Pacific region. While the article also deals with India and ASEAN 10 economic relations, focus is given on the security issues and cooperation throughout the article with special reference to maritime dimension. Present article tries to locate India and ASEAN's security issue at the larger security dynamics of Asia-Pacific region.

India in South-East Asia : Engaging ASEAN Region

The changed security and geopolitical environment made India, under the leadership of Prime Minister Narasimha Rao, to initiate a conscious effort in 1991 to forge greater economic and strategic ties with ASEAN. As a result India became a sectoral dialogue partner in 1992 and full dialogue partner of ASEAN in December

1995. While sectoral dialogue partnership was meant to promote trade, investment and tourism relations that of full dialogue partnership had a broader agenda for cooperation in various fields such as security, political, economic and culture. The momentum of this policy initiative was maintained by the successive government at New Delhi. Such trend indicates the broad consensus among the political parties of diverse nature in India towards the strategic importance of South-East Asia to India's security. India's sustained effort bore fruit with India becoming a member of ASEAN Regional Forum (henceforth ARF) in 1996. ARF is an important forum for discussing security related matters among the member countries. Thus India began participating in the ASEAN Post-Ministerial Conference and the ARF (ASEAN Regional Forum) since then. India and ASEAN relation was upgraded to summit level partner in 2002. During the First ASEAN-India Summit in November 2002 in Phnom Penh, India offered to start free talks and to have a working free trade agreement (FTA) by 2012. India made the offer, a day after ASEAN and China signed an agreement to have an FTA by 2010. During the second ASEAN-India Summit at Bali in 2003 India ASEAN signed three significant documents such as (i) The Framework Agreement for Comprehensive Economic Cooperation; (ii) The accession document to the ASEAN Treaty of Amity and Cooperation; and (iii) Adoption of the Joint Declaration on Cooperation in Combating International Terrorism. Again at the Third ASEAN-India Summit held in November 2004 in Vientiane, India and ASEAN signed the "ASEAN-India Partnership for Peace, Progress and Shared Prosperity" document, setting out a road map for long-term ASEAN-India engagement. India's participation in the East Asia Summit in 2005 in Kuala Lumpur was a significant step in "India's drive for stronger linkages with East Asia as well as in ASEAN's effort to have India strategically and economically engaged in the affairs of the region and to play a counter-weight role *vis-à-vis* China"[9]. India's strategy *vis-à-vis* its relation with ASEAN is to engage the region through web of linkages both at the bilateral and multilateral level. Through ASEAN India is also hoping to join the Asia-Pacific Economic Cooperation (APEC) grouping and the Asia Europe Meeting (ASEM). At the bilateral level India is forging greater linkages to enhance political, diplomatic and economic ties with special focus on the new member-states of ASEAN such as Cambodia, Laos, Myanmar and Vietnam (CLMV) because of their proximity with India as well as China. India is also participating actively at various multilateral forums hosted by ASEAN such as ARF, East Asia Summit (EAS) to consolidate its hold in the Asia-Pacific region. It can be argued that membership and focus of multilateral forums such as ARF and EAS are extended to the Asia-Pacific region and they are becoming an effective security dialogue forum for Asia-Pacific region. Secondly, India is trying to forge greater linkages with strategically vital SEA countries through the creation of sub-regional groupings such as BIMSTEC (Bangladesh, India, Myanmar, Sri Lanka and Thailand Economic Cooperation also known as Bay of Bengal Community Initiative for Multi-sectoral, Technical and Economic Cooperation) and Mekong-Ganges River Cooperation. BIMSTEC was initiated at the instance of Thailand in 1997 with a view to create a free trade area by 2017 with advance countries, India, Thailand and Sri Lanka by 2012 and the rest by 2017. Its agenda also include agreement for fighting terrorism, cooperation in the field of energy and environmental issues. Significantly Nepal and Bhutan were also inducted into the BIMSTEC. Through BIMSTEC India can hope to pre-empt further Chinese influence in the South Asian region at the same time isolate Pakistan. Secondly, this sub-regional grouping can provide a convenient forum for India to initiate confidence building measures with the member-states in South Asia and SEA whose troubled relations with India in the past had given room to external power like China to spread its clout for the regions with vital security implications for India. Again in 2000 under India's sponsorship the "Mekong-Ganges River Cooperation Project" between India and five riparian states of Mekong such as Vietnam, Laos, Cambodia, Myanmar and Thailand was initiated to promote cooperation in tourism, culture and education in this sub-region. These five riparian states not only form the mainland SEA but are also strategically located due to their proximity to China as well as India. Due to this fact India accorded special focus to these countries. The main driving forces of these sub-regional groupings are the economic potentials of member-states and the concern for overwhelming Chinese clout over the SEA region. Same is the case with India and ASEAN relations.

India's linkages with SEA countries are equally crucial from economic dimension as enhancing economic partnership with ASEAN can increase India's share in world trade. The ASEAN region presents an opportunity for India to expand its trade as well as source for Foreign Direct Investment (FDI). At present combined total income of ASEAN stood at US$ 737 billion and US$ 720 billion in external trade. Besides, India and the ASEAN states are located in a geographically contiguous market that has more than 1.5 billion people with 300 million middle-class consumers in India alone.[10] SEA 560 million people form a US $330 billion consumer market and the region holds 40 per cent of oil and gas resources in the Asia-Pacific[11].

This will go a long way in realizing India's policy for a regional approach to pressing energy needs. Thus India and SEA region hold a tremendous opportunity for economic cooperation. Along with growing political and diplomatic relations, India and ASEAN bilateral economic relations is also showing great momentum. This can be understood from the fact that India's trade with ASEAN stood at mere 2.4 billion US dollars in 1990 but has grown to 23 billion US dollars in 2005 and cross 30 billion US dollars in 2007. India is targeting to increase this trade with ASEAN member-countries to $50 billion by the end of 2010 and is expected to US $100 billion by 2015. The India-ASEAN Trade-in-Goods Agreement under a Free Trade Agreement, which came into force on January 1, 2010, has opened new opportunity to enhance trade relations with ASEAN. The Trade-in-Goods Agreement, which was signed after six years of intense negotiations in 2009, focuses on mainly trade liberalization on mutually, agreed tariff lines from India and ASEAN, which aimed at eliminating 80 percent of existing trade tariffs. Under the agreement India has to reduce tariffs to zero on some 3,666 imported items from Indonesia and nine other ASEAN countries by the end of 2012. So far India, Singapore, Malaysia and Thailand have ratified the agreement[12]. The signing of FTA by India with ASEAN can be located within the broad context of India's desire to join APEC and to integrate its economy with other regional groupings in the Asia-Pacific region, which was referred to as 'arc of advantage'[13] by the Prime Minister of India, Dr. Manmohan Singh. The total income of the Asia-Pacific community would rival that of European Union's in near future. In terms of trade it would be bigger than the North American Free Trade Agreement comprising that of United States of America,

Canada and Mexico and the combined foreign exchange reserves of the Asia-Pacific region would be greater than those of the European Union and NAFTA[14]. From ASEAN's perspective FTA with India is part of its strategy to contain growing China's economic challenges to the region. Besides, ASEAN's leaders at the October 2003 ASEAN Summit in Bali had pledged to form an ASEAN Economic Community (AEC) by 2020. AEC is conceived as a single regional market and production base in which goods, services, investments, capital, and labour will flow freely[15] to balance challenges posed by growing China's economy. Precisely China's economy, which is growing at a rate of approximately 10 per cent at present, is expected to overtake Japan's economy by 2020. Growing economy of China has effected economy of SEA in the form of diversion of FDI from South-East Asia. Moreover there is a fear of cheaper Chinese goods flooding into SEA, overwhelming local industries because of increasing competitiveness of China's economy and its entry into the World Trade Organization (WTO)[16].

Emerging Security Dynamics : India's Security and South-East Asia

The end of the Cold War saw the emergence of new security dynamics in the Asia-Pacific region. The rise of China, India and Japan, and the United States of America's (USA) re-engagement with SEA after the 9/11 terrorist attack in the USA characterized the unfolding security dynamics of post-Cold War SEA region and Asia-Pacific. The future relationships of China-Japan, India-China and USA-China will determine the course of this dynamics. In this unfolding security dynamics ASEAN holds a key strategic pillar for India's security calculation. There is a synergy of perception between India and ASEAN over the rise of China that provokes anxiety both in India and states of SEA. Studies by the US Central Intelligence Agency and others have projected that China will be a first-rate military power and will rival America in global power by 2020[17]. As ASEAN grows in strength and size, incorporating India's strategically vital next door neighbour Myanmar[18] and massive Chinese influence in military ruled Myanmar and most of the countries in the region, India has to accord cognizance of strategic importance of SEA and danger of ever increasing Chinese influence over the region to India's long term strategic interests. India, therefore, has to make efforts to engage this growing regional association which is so vital to India's national interest from various perspectives.

China's continental and maritime expansion during the last two decades and security dynamics generated as a result of it has created China threat perception both in India and South-East Asian countries; and it is one of the main reasons for India's sustained effort to generate deeper and meaningful political, strategic and economic relations with ASEAN. In this regard India's strategic interest to check Chinese influence and dominance in the region in the eventual reduction of the presence of superpowers coincided strikingly with similar thinking within the South-East Asian community[19]. From the ASEAN's perspective, its relations with India an emerging techno-military and economic power can act as credible balancer against any eventual Chinese expansionism in future.

For India a strong and stable South-East Asia can provide a space wherein India can constructively engage China, Japan and USA through various multilateral forums such as ARF, East Asia Summit (EAS). At the same time India can expand its trade and commerce with Japan, South Korea, Australia and China itself. India's overseas trade is growing and it is likely to cross $ 1 trillion by 2020. Almost half of it will be moving to and fro eastern destinations, most of it by sea[20]. Securing sea lanes of communications (SLOCs) connecting India with these countries from any hostile element is of paramount necessity to India. The growing economic and military power of China and its likely impact upon the security architecture in the Asia-Pacific region, her naval foray into the Indian Ocean and South China Sea, dispute over Spratly Islands group, and rising incidence of piracy in the vital SLOC of South-East Asia are some of the areas where India and South-East Asian countries have common interest. It has been argued that from a geo-political perspective, the strategic horizons of many of the East Asian countries converge with those of India in the eastern Indian Ocean[21]. The location of Indian Ocean is of great strategic importance for the security of India as well as its littoral states in South-East Asia such as Myanmar, Thailand, Malaysia and Indonesia. In fact the security calculi of both India and South-East Asia have significant overlaps in terms of China.

On the one hand, China's domination of the sub-region and even its overbearing military presence in the South China Sea (if its maritime claims were to materialize) would be undesirable for India since this would facilitate China's power-projection into the Bay of Bengal. On the other hand, its presence in Bay of Bengal may be perceived to be detrimental to South-East Asia's interests since this would enable Beijing to straddle the strategic Malacca Straits[22].

The China's maritime expansion and inroad into Indian Ocean is a cause of worry to India. The end of Cold War led to the withdrawal of the United States' military presence from the region with the dismantling of Clark and Subic Bay bases in the Philippines and Soviet forces from Camranh Bay in Vietnam had provided China an opportunity to expand its maritime 'sphere of influence' in South China Sea and Indian Ocean. India's concern for growing Chinese naval power is accentuated by the China's assertion that Indian Ocean is not 'India's Ocean' signalling its intention of increasing naval presence in the Ocean. Secondly, China's growing naval capability and its expanding influence around the littoral states of Indian Ocean, more particularly in Myanmar and Pakistan, is equally a cause of great concern to India. In terms of operational ability, Chinese navy ranks third in the world after the United States and Russia. In early 1995, reports appearing in the Japanese media stated that China had decided to embark on a decade long programme beginning from 1996 to build two aircraft carriers[23]. There has been report of Chinese assistance to Myanmar in the construction of five ports from Sittwe in the north to Victoria Point in the south, a radar station, an airstrip and naval base in Great Cocos Island and a 800-mile Irrawady river link connecting China to the Bay of Bengal[24]. China is also helping Myanmar in the construction of a new naval base on Hianggye Island at the mouth of the Bassein River. Access to these areas and facilities would enable the Chinese Navy to monitor shipping activity *of navies of India and South-East Asian countries* and enable Chinese warships to dock, resupply and carry out routine maintenance tasks, etc[25]. Besides, China's technical assistance and about 80 per cent funding for the Gwadar port in Baluchistan, Pakistan and Pakistan's indication of willingness to provide base facilities to the Chinese Navy in the Gwadar port would give a pretext for China's naval presence in the Indian Ocean besides using it as a transit terminal for oil import.[26] This would enable China to "monitor US naval activity in the Persian Gulf, Indian activity in the Arabian Sea, and future US-India maritime cooperation in the Indian Ocean". Again the port of Gwadar, which is located at the mouth of the Gulf of Hormuz, sit astride the energy routes and can be used to threaten India's supplies in the event of a conflict between India and China in future[27]. China's strategy with regard to India is to make India confine to the South Asia by assisting Pakistan and other countries in the region. "Be it Nepal, Bangladesh or Burma, China has actively sought to contain India all around its periphery"[28]. In April 2005, China signed a comprehensive agreement with Sri Lanka which provides Chinese navy access to Colombo's prized ports and thereby to the Indian Ocean.[29]

China's foray into the Indian Ocean may be driven by the security of its energy 'lifeliness' as its economy and foreign trade is growing momentously but it has security implications for India. India's concerns for growing Chinese naval strength and its foray into the Indian Ocean particularly Bay of Bengal side stem both from the security of energy lifelines as well as possibility of China's nuclear submarines, missile-craft and strike aircraft using the bases/ facilities in Myanmar to threaten India's eastern ports, strategic SLOCs and the widely scattered 572 Andaman and Nicobar Islands[30]. India's apprehension is corroborated by the report of China's submarines modernization[31] and growing China's naval activities in the Bay of Bengal. It can be discerned from the fact that in August 1994 Indian Coast Guard vessels apprehended three Chinese trawlers, flying the Myanmar flag, in Indian waters off the Narcondam Island. The trawlers had on board several detailed charts depicting hydrographic details of the waters surrounding the Andaman Islands[32]. Again in October 2004 Indian navy captured a trawler Yu Man Shing, which came in the guise of fishing near the Andaman and Nicobar Islands. Indian analysts perceived that the trawler having predominantly Chinese crew was meant for intelligence gathering and possibly, oceanography survey for submarine operations around the waters of Andaman and Nicobar Islands[33]. There is no denying the fact that China today is part of the Indian Ocean's strategic landscape and for decades Indian security analysts have expected Beijing to expand its strategic and maritime influence in the Indian Ocean and its littoral[34]. This expansion can be seen as a natural outcome of growing power of China. As China is emerging both as major economic and military power, its security horizon is expanding in order to sustain and consolidate its national interest and momentum of economic growth, just as India's security horizon is expanding as it emerges as a major economic and military power. It is against this context that India's establishment of unified strategic command at Port Blair in 2001 and New Delhi's hosting of biennial congregation of littoral navies including warships from South-East Asian nations, called Milan since 1995, has to be located.

Besides, India is also trying to make its presence felt in the South China Sea (SCS) in order to counter Chinese naval presence in the Indian Ocean and secondly to secure its energy lifeliness. India currently is importing oil from Sakhalin (Russia) and it is investing in Vietnam for oil exploration project. In this context it can be argued that India's naval presence in the SCS can be possible by having deeper relationship with the countries of SEA particularly Vietnam, Malaysia, the Philippines, Singapore and Indonesia. Here India can leverage a mutually compatible strategic and diplomatic rapprochement with above countries of SEA due to their conflict with China over the claims in the Paracel and Spratlys Islands in the SCS. The maritime disputes in the SCS are influenced by economic, strategic and political interests. The free navigation of commercial vessels in the SCS is essential for regional and international trade. Moreover, the SCS is rich in fishery resources, and it is widely believed to hold enormous oil and natural gas in its bed. Over the next 20 years, oil consumption is expected to rise by 3.9 per cent annually on average, with nearly half of that increase coming from China. Exploding energy needs have marked recent political and strategic priorities. Therefore, much political attention has been given on the exploitation of oil and gas resources beneath the sea at large scale[35]. Strategically, if Beijing ever succeeds in achieving its territorial claims, China would be able 'to extend its jurisdiction some one thousand nautical miles from its mainland so as to command the virtual Mediterranean or maritime heart of South-East Asia with far-reaching consequences for the strategic environment'. This will pose threat not only to the Philippines, Vietnam but also to Brunei, Indonesia and Malaysia.

A Declaration on the Conduct of Parties in the South China

Sea was signed at the ASEAN summit in Phnom Penh on 4 November, 2002 between China and ten members of ASEAN which is regarded as a positive step to reduce tensions and pursue their claims by peaceful means. But the declaration only expressed intention of the claimant states; it is not legally binding and its future effect remains to be seen[36]. The political declaration also made no reference to its specific geographical scope, primarily because China opposed any mention of the Spratly Island[37]. Declaration did not alter China's territorial objectives in the SCS[38]. Due to this fact enhancing maritime cooperation between India and ASEAN has become more important not only to counter China's maritime expansion but also to prevent sea bound terrorist activities and piracy as many of the vital SLOCs such as the Malacca Strait, Sundra Strait, Ombai Strait and the Timor Sea are located in the region.

Conclusion

With the end of Cold War politics, the barriers which were dominantly present between India and most countries of South-East Asia have also faded away. As former India's Prime Minister Atal Bihari Vajpayee said that "the Cold War moulds have been broken and this has enabled us to strengthen our links without ideological barrier"[39] Today both India and countries of South-East Asia are beginning to recognise and respect each other's importance, role and security needs. In fact there is a growing convergence of interests between the two entities. India can now exploit the advantages of geographical proximity, cultural and civilizational linkages with the SEA countries. In short India's LEP was initiated in 1991 when India faced a number of successive strategic and economic challenges which threatened its political survival.[40] In the opinion of Visvam (1997) India's LEP adopts a three pronged approach. First, it is an attempt to renew political contacts with the ASEAN partners; secondly it aims to increase economic interaction (trade, investment, science and technology, tourism, etc.); and third, it seeks to forge greater defence links with ASEAN partners as a means to enhance political and strategic interests and understanding.[41]

The end of Cold War was followed by the outbreak of the first Gulf War in 1991. It made India realize that she cannot always rely on the Gulf region for sources of its ever increasing demand for oil as India's economy expands. In order to prevent shortage of energy, India had to explore viable alternative source for energy. India's own domestic economic problem compelled India to open up her economy in order to attract foreign investment. Besides, the break-up of the Soviet Union deprived India of its main trading partner, source of cheap imported oil[42] and a trusted guarantor for India's security. The rise of China as a major regional power and its expanding influence over SEA and SA during the early 90s was an important factor that had tempted India to a major policy shift with regard to SEA region in the post-Cold War period. Besides, India's policy shift is an attempt to counter increasing Chinese influence in SEA and more particularly in South Asia. In this regard India's relations with ASEAN, in a way, can divert China's attention from South Asian balance of power politics, which China is engaging at the moment through Pakistan. Moreover as India strengthened its economy through liberalization since the early 90s followed by technological and military prowess, it is but inevitable for India to forge greater linkages with SEA countries because the region form an important strategic component in India's pursuit for a 'super regional power'. As India's Prime Minister, Dr. Manmohan Singh commented that India's strategic footprint as a 'super regional power covers the region bounded by the Horn of Africa, West Asia, Central Asia, and South-East Asia and beyond, to the far reaches of the Indian Ocean.'[43]

India can now assert its power and role with more weight, effectiveness and vigour in shaping regional geo-political environment to enhance her national interests *vis-à-vis* South-East Asia and Pacific region than before due to the unfolding factors of convergence between India and member of ASEAN. With a relatively better economic structure and advanced military technology and prowess, which it lacked earlier, India, today, is in a much better position to engage SEA region more actively.

REFERENCES

1. Christopher Jafferlot, "India's Look East Policy: An Asianist Strategy in Perspective" in *Review* Vol. 2, No. 1 (April). London: Frank Cass.

2. Zhao Hong, "India and China: Rivals or Partners in Southeast Asia?" in *Contemporary Southeast Asia,* Vol. 29, No. 1 (2007) p. 121.
3. Kripa Sridharan, The ASEAN Region in India's Foreign Policy. Dartmount Publishing. p. 46. England.
4. The Association of South East Asian Nations (ASEAN) was originally established by the five non-Communist countries of Indonesia, Malaysia, Philippines, Singapore and Thailand on August 8, 1967. Subsequently, Brunei Darussalam joined on January 18, 1984, Vietnam on July 28, 1995, Laos and Myanmar on July 23, 1997 and Cambodia on 30 April 1999. Thus by 1999 all the ten countries in the Southeast Asia had become the constituent member of the ASEAN. It has both economic and political objectives, although focus was given on economic character of the organization. The main objective of ASEAN is "to create peaceful, prosperous and resilient community through joint cooperation with a view of strengthening the economic progress and social stability as well as promoting closer cultural ties among the respective member countries". For details aims, objectives and origin of ASEAN see Dr. Shri Prakash Mani Tripathi, *India and ASEAN–10.* New Delhi: Jnanada Prakashan (P & D), 2000.
5. SEATO was formed consequent to the 1954 Geneva Agreement on Indochina. Delegates from Australia, France, New Zealand, Pakistan, the Philippines, Thailand, Britain and the United States, meeting in September 1954 agreed on a South-East Asia Collective Defence Treaty. It was a brain-child of John Foster Dulles, the US Secretary of State. See: Nicholas Tarling, "The Cambridge History of Southeast Asia" Volume 4. Cambridge and New York: Cambridge University Press, 1999. p. 275.
6. Indo-China rivalry since the mid 50s, Sino-Soviet rift from 1960, subsequent Indo-China war in 1962, Indo-Pak war of 1965, 1971 and Chinese strategic ties with Pakistan can be cited as vital geo-political developments during the Cold War which locked India within the confine of South Asia.
7. Leszek Buszynski, "ASEAN's New Challenges" in *Pacific Affairs,* p.555.
8. *Op. cit.,* Zhao Hong, 2007 p. 122.
9. *Op. cit.* Zhao Hong, 2007. p. 124.
10. S.D. Naik, "India and Asean: Towards enhancing economic partnership". *Business Line,* India, 16 October, 2002.
11. Charlyle A. Thayer, "Southeast Asia's Marred Miracle". *Current History,* Vol. 103, No. 672, April 2004. p. 177.
12. "India aims to enhance ties with ASEAN through FTA", *The Jakarta Post,* New Delhi edition. August 08, 2010.
13. *The Hindu,* editorial. December 4, 2004.

14. *The Hindu*, December 4, 2004.
15. *Op. cit.* Charlyle A. Thayer, 2004, p. 179.
16. *Op. cit.* Charlyle A. Thayer, 2004, p. 178.
17. Christopher Layne, "China's Challenge to US Hegemony". *Current History*, Vol. 107, No. 705, January 2008. p. 13.
18. Myanmar (formerly Burma) along with Laos were admitted into ASEAN on 23 July, 1997, which brought ASEAN at the doorstep of India.
19. G.V.C. Naidu, "Whether the Look East Policy: India and Southeast Asia", *Strategic Analysis*, Vol. 28 No. 2, April-June 2004, p. 338.
20. P.S. Das, "India's Look East Policy". *Foreign Affairs Journal*. Vol. 2, No. 2, April-June 2007, p. 19.
21. Rajiv Sikri, "India's Look East Policy." *Foreign Affairs Journal*, Vol. 2, No. 2, April-June 2007, p. 4.
22. Gurpreet S. Khurana, "Cooperation among Maritime Security Forces: Imperatives for India and Southeast Asia" *Strategic Analysis*. Vol. 29, No. 2, April-June 2005, p. 19.
23. Dr. Anil Kumar Singh, "India's Maritime Security: Challenges Ahead", *Indian Defence Review*, p. 29.
24. Gurpreet S. Khurana, *Cooperation among Maritime Security Forces: Imperatives for India and Southeast Asia*, p. 305.
25. Dr Anil Kumar Singh, *India's Maritime Security: Challenges Ahead*, p. 30.
26. Harsh V. Pant, "India in the Asia-Pacific: Rising Ambitions with an Eye on China" *Asia-Pacific Review*, Vol. 14, No. 1, 2007, p. 60
27. P.S. Das, p.19.
28. Harsh V. Pant, *India in the Asia-Pacific: Rising Ambitions with an Eye on China*, p. 61.
29. Zhao Hong, *India and China: Rivals or Partners in Southeast Asia*, p. 130.
30. Gurpreet S. Khurana, *Cooperation among Maritime Security Forces: Imperatives for India and Southeast Asia*, p.305.
31. See for China's submarine modernization and development programme in Amrish Sahgal, "Plan's Plan – II China's Submarine Programme", *Indian Defence Review*, pp. 145-149.
32. Dr. Anil Kumar Singh, *India's Maritime Security: Challenges Ahead*, p. 30.
33. Gurpreet S. Khurana, *Cooperation Among Maritime Security Forces: Imperatives for India and Southeast Asia*, p. 305.
34. Donald L. Berlin, *The Indian Ocean and the Second Nuclear Age*, Orbis, Winter Vol. 48, No. 1. 2004, p. 67.
35. *Ibid.*, pp. 7-8.
36. *Ibid.*, p. 10.

37. Rralf Emmers, "Maritime disputes in the South China Sea: Strategic and diplomatic *status quo*", in *Maritime Security in the Southeast Asia,* edited by Kwa Chong Guan and John K. Skogan. London & New York: Routledge, 2007. p. 57.
38. *Ibid.*, 56.
39. *India and ASEAN – Shared Perspectives,* Speech by Prime Minister of India, Atal Bihari Vajpayee, Kuala Lumpur, Malaysia, 16 May, 2001.
40. B. Rao, 'Indian Economic Reforms and ASEAN : India Economic Relations'. *Journal of Asian Economics* 7, no. 4. 1996, p. 763.
41. Quoted in Konthoujam Indrakumar, "Mapping India's Look East Policy: Shifting Alignments". *Look East Policy & India's North East* (Polemics and Perspectives) edited by Thingnam Kishan Singh. New Delhi: Concept Publishing Company, 2009. p. 31.
42. Zhao Hong, p. 122.
43. Rajat Pandit, 'India to 'Arm' Itself for Strategic Interests'. *Times of India,* 27 October, 2004.

Section III

Social Dimensions of Security

10

Contemporary Security Concerns of India: Religion and Security

Chandreyi Alam

Security has been defined by the Shorter Oxford Dictionary as "Free from doubt or distrust; feeling sure or certain; confident in expectation". When we consider security concerns from the religious aspect, we have to consider the lives of the people or the individual. If life is free from doubt or distrust, one feels sure or certain and confident in expectation from this angle. It is worthwhile mentioning that the life of an individual is governed by his religion, customs and practices. A note of caution must be sound that when there is a state of equilibrium in the life of an individual we need not necessarily conclude that such equilibrium has a positive influence on Indian society and there is no reason to be alarmed at such equilibrium in India.

Religious practices find their roots in the primitive religions where the consecration of life is involved in (1) education (2) government, (3) food supply, (4) kinship, (5) family (6) sex, (7) personality. Presently we shall confine ourselves to the question of family and sex since this is a cause of gross violation of social security. Encyclopaedia Britannica states that "Women for certain physiological reasons is always for primitive peoples hedged round with sanctity, whilst man does all he can do to inspire awe to his powers in women in keeping religion largely at his own hands." (Emphasis added). The result so far as the woman is concerned is that in company with those males who are endowed with sacredness in a more than ordinary degree. She tends to lose in freedom as much as she gains in respect. (Emphasis added). This is also India's experience. She is *Mata, Devi, Shakti* – worshipped idolized yet a victim of incessant violence, humiliation and discrimination in innumerable forms.

What is most significant is that all religions are democratic, the woman treated with dignity and respect as well as humiliated. Faced with such contradictions, we find that the balance of Indian society tilts heavily in favour of values that are discriminatory to women and society seeks refuge of the religion's texts to justify its actions. But religious texts must be considered in the context of the prevalent social conditions. With the passage of time and the existence of a Constitution that enshrines justice – social, economic and political in its preamble and equality before law as a fundamental right, our society does face situations that disturb its equilibrium and the reactions therefrom give rise to security concerns.

Thus the comfortable degree of *status quo* in Indian family life is that the man is the lord and master, or in modern parlance, the head of the family. The women's position is inferior to him, therefore, she can be rightly subjected to discrimination and insubordination and all the religious communities unanimously accept this position. When women react differently to the normal behavioural pattern in the family that sends ripples in the family equilibrium. The seeds of doubt and distrust germinate, thereby threatening the erstwhile "security" prevalent in the family.

Presently in India, the personal laws of the Hindu, Christian and Parsee communities are codified. The personal laws of the Muslim community are not codified. When laws are codified, it is explicit – the courts, lawyers, the litigants or the people have positive do's and don't's and need not depend on interpretations; injunctions from the religious texts. Furthermore, the codified laws in India have to be in consonance with the basic structure of our Constitution and international covenants like the Universal Declaration of Human Rights 1948, The International Covenants on Civil and Political Rights 1966, The Convention on the Elimination of All Kinds of Discrimination Against Women 1979, etc. Hence, these laws have to ensure that the rights of the people in the present social context are protected. For example, prior to 1956, the Hindu Law of Succession totally obliterated the family of the predeceased son from inheritance of the father's property.

Presently in Hindu Law the family of the predeceased son or daughter is entitled to the share of their father's property. The plight of the Muslim community in India is the same as suffered by their Hindu counterparts prior to passing of the Hindu Succession Act 1956. Yet, Pakistan, had promulgated Muslim Family Laws ordinance 1961 and paragraph 4 thereof clearly states that *"In the event of the death of any son or daughter of the propositus before the opening of succession, the children of such son or daughter, if any, living at the time the succession opens, shall per stirpes receive a Share Equivalent to the share which such son or daughter as the case may be, would have received if alive"*. Yet Muslims in India suffer while those in Bangladesh and Pakistan are protected, *vice versa* for the Hindu community in Bangladesh and Pakistan.

This is only one example out of many. The feeling of certainty in the family – where it is 'right' to deprive another gives sufficient reason that the time has come for Indians to shed their "secured" position, take stock of the situation and demand necessary reforms – even though such thoughts and demands are bound to upset the present equilibrium prevalent in the community and would obviously result in a security concern. But in order to ensure that security that is free from doubt or distrust, practices derogatory to the people and women in particular have to be ended – even though it brings about a sense of insecurity amongst a section of the people who are unable to visualise any change in their present state of equilibrium.

The case of Shah Bano Begum is a classical case where the nation had risen from its slumber and demanded a change in the present state of equilibrium.

In 1985, the Hon'ble Apex Court had delivered the judgment in the case of Mohd. Ahmed Khan *versus* Shah Bano Begum (AIR 1985, SC 865). This case is very significant since the battle lines were drawn between the women's movement who demanded that even though Shah Bano was a divorced wife but as the definition of "wife" in section 125 of the Criminal Procedure Code 1973 includes a "divorced wife" until she remarries – Shah Bano Begum counsel argued that she was entitled to maintenance from Ahmed Khan until she remarries. Shah Bano Begum's former husband had rallied the Muslim Personal Law Board to press his case. They differed on the score that according to the Muslim Personal Law, a husband is bound to pay maintenance only during the period of *iddat,* i.e., the period of three menstrual cycles where the wife has the right of residence in her matrimonial home only to ascertain whether there is any pregnancy. A verse from the Holy *Quran* directing that even divorced wives have that right to maintenance – that it is the duty of the 'Righteous', sparked the arguments. The women's movement claiming that the Holy *Quran* permits the divorced wife to receive maintenance whilst the opponents claimed that the world 'Righteous' is not confined to the husband alone but to all. In this connection the Apex Court observed thus – *"it is also a matter of regret that Article 44 of our Constitution has remained a dead letter. It provides that "The State shall endeavour to secure for the citizens a uniform Civil Code throughout the territory of India"*. There is no evidence of any official activity for framing a common Civil Code for the country. A belief seems to have gained ground that it is for the Muslim community to take a lead in the matter of reforms of their personal law. A common Civil Code will help the cause of national integration by removing disparate loyalties to laws which have conflicting ideologies. No community is likely to bell the cat by making gratuitous concessions on this issue. It is the state which is charged with the duty of securing a uniform Civil Code for the citizens of the country and, questionably, it has the legislative competence to do so. A Counsel in the case whispered, somewhat audibly, that legislative competence is one thing, the political courage to use that comptence is quite another. *"We understand the difficulties involved in bringing persons of different faiths and persuations on a common platform. But, a beginning has to be made if the Constitution is to have any meaning. Inevitably, the role of a reformer has to be assumed by the Courts because, it is beyond the endurance of sersihir minds to allow injustice to be suffered when it is so palpable. But piecemeal attempts of Courts to bridge the gap between personal laws cannot take the place of a Common Civil Code. Justice is all is a far more satisfactory way of dispensing justice than justice from case to case."*

The Shah Bano case revealed a glaring contemporary concern of India – a glaring example of religion and security. Since the courts call for a uniform civil code and the interpretation of the Holy text awakened the Muslim community, some people felt extremely insecure with any change, some welcomed the change and as a whole there were discussions, meetings, debates – people from different communities expressing their views and solidarity with whichever side they supported.

But this decision was an eye opener. The government in the desperate attempt to keep the vote bank intact accepted a Private Members Bill in Parliament, and enacted the Muslim Women's (Protection of Rights upon Divorce) Act 1986 in order to negate the historical judgment. And as to the women's movement and members of the Community, the fact that their tales could be narrated within the Community. Also the opportunity to interact and share their experiences with others to learn the true spirit of one's religion should be informed of the codified laws and to speak out. In fact this decision ushered in an era of spreading awareness among the people regarding their personal laws and existing codified laws. Initially such attempts were confined at a micro level within the community – very often facing resistance. But today such awareness programmes are accepted by all officials as well as non officials – and now it is a moment for all to be proud to hear the voice of the voiceless.

Indian society is passing through a transitional stage. It feels safe in gripping on to feudal values. We still have a very strong dowry system that has spread its roots even amongst religious communities that did not have any system of dowry. The Dowry Prohibition Act 1961 has virtually been confined to the Statute Books.

The increase in the dowry deaths or violence perpetuated on women on account of dowry is another contemporary security concern. Even though amendments have been made in respect of the Indian Evidence Act (Sec. 113A, Sec. 114A) or the Indian Penal Code 1960 (Sec. 304B, Sec. 498A) but we are reluctant to bid adeiu to the dowry system, according to the Report of the Committee on the Status of women 1974 – "The young and educated generation of India are also interested in the dowry system. The existence of the Dowry system has made Indian Society feel very "secure" – to the extent that she has a population of "25 million missing women" –whose lives were snuffed out just to avoid payment of dowry in the future. Perhaps the greatest shame of India is the enactment of the "Prenatal Diagnostic Techniques (Regulation and Prevention of Misuse) Act 1994, which, within a span of one year was changed into 'The Preconception and Prenatal Diagnostic Techniques (Prohibition of Sex Selection) Act 1994."

To add insult to injury, this shameful phenomenon in Indian society is prevalent mainly amongst the urban population; with more educated people. The sex ratio in some of the metropolis in our country during the last census reveals a sorry picture.

Name of the Metropolis	*Sex Ratio in relation to 1000 males*	
	1991	*2001*
Greater Mumbai UA	828	823
Calcutta UA	830	869
Delhi UA	829	828
Chennai UA	933	950
Bangalore UA	902	906
Hyderabad UA	930	938
Ahmedabad UA	889	885
Pune	903	896
Surat	839	760
Kanpur	822	868
Jaipur	868	875

Source: Population of India in the New millenium: *Census 2001 Mahendra K. Presis. National Book Trust, India*

Our caste system is another contemporary security concern. Unfortunately the Renaissance in Indian society stopped after Independence. Unfortunately, in her 'Tryst with Destiny, India has fallen back to the 'secured' confines of this system. Thus the Supreme Court, in the case of Lata Singh (AIR 2006, S.C. 2522) held *"The caste system is a curse on the nation and sooner it is destroyed the better. In fact it is dividing the nation at a time when we have to face the challenges before the nation unitedly. Hence, inter-caste marriages are in fact in the national interest as they will result in destroying the caste system (Emphasis added) However, disturbing news are coming from several parts of the country that young men and women who undergo inter-caste marriage are threatened with violence or violence is actually committed on them" .... "We sometimes hear of honour killings of such person who undergoes inter-caste or inter-religion marriage of their own free will. There is nothing honourable in such killings, and in fact they are nothing but barbaric and shameful acts of murder committed by brutal, feudal minded persons who deserve harsh punishment. Only in this way we stamp out such acts of barbarism ...". "... We, therefore, direct that the Administration/Police authorities throughout the country will see to it that if any boy or a girl who is a major undergoes inter-caste or inter-religion marriage with a woman or man who is a major, the couple are not harassed by any one or subjected to threats or acts of violence, and anyone who gives such threats or harasses or commits acts of violence either himself or at his instigation, is taken to task by instituting criminal proceedings by the police against such persons and further stern action is taken against such person as provided by law..."* (Emphasis added)

The case of Rizwanur Rahaman is a classical case in this regard. It revealed the wrath of the society both for and against the right to inter-religion marriages. The courts, relying heavily on Lata Singh's case (supra) have directed that criminal proceedings be instituted against those involved, including the police personnel who had desperately tried to maintain the equilibrium of the family opposing the marriage.

In order to ensure a sense of religious security in our multi-religious country – we will have to develop a sense of respect for the other religions. It must be remembered that to each individual his religion is the best and others are of a lesser value. This leads to a sense of intolerance towards the other. In order to ensure religious security we must realise that to our friends professing a religion different to ours, their religion is the best to them and we have to appreciate their sentiment and exchange views and ideas amidst a high degree of tolerance and respect for each other. As stated earlier the clarion call of the Hon'ble Supreme Court in the Shah Bano case has opened the issue of contemporary security concerns in India – which is being discussed and debated since then. The Rizwanur case revealed the active role of the civil society in dealing with the contemporary security concerns of our country from the proper perspective. It is hoped that a conscious society will persevere to do away with the social vices ailing the communities resulting in discrimination and perpetration of violence amongst the people and eventually bridge the gap between the different streams of Indian society so that the people of India really become "WE the People of India".

11

Migrations in North-East India and its Implications for the Strategic Security of India

Lianboi Vaiphei

Introduction

North-Eastern part of India covers a total area of 255.08 million hectares, constituting 8 per cent of the total land mass. It is also the sentinel of the Indian sub-continent. It is strategically located between the countries of South and South-East Asia, connecting with the rest of the country through a narrow stretch of plains known as Siliguri Corridor, which is sometimes referred as chicken-necked region. The geographical location of the North-Eastern region gives the region an insularity, which has isolated from her natural borders as she shares more than 2000 km of boundary with the South and South-East Asian countries. In fact, out of the seven international boundaries which India possesses, five of the international boundaries are located in the north-east region, namely with Bangladesh, Bhutan, Myanmar, China and Nepal, except for Pakistan and Sri Lanka.

That is also the reason why the geopolitics of India's neighbours' has strong and definite consequences on India's north-east besides what happens in the rest of the country. One of the changing political phenomena that affect India's neighbouring countries is closely related with the strategic concerns that India has. For the change in the political scenario is a pointer to the need for the strategic change as the domestic challenges in the South Asian countries made it necessary to not only examine, but also rethink over some of the issues which are termed as 'security issue' in contemporary India as they are both the conventional and non-conventional 'security issues'. This has been caused due to the challenges that have taken place in her neighbourhood along with the progress of human development.

Besides that, security has increasingly become more Asian-centric than Euro-centric as many of the political dynamics that led to changes in the internal dynamics within the country has influenced the South Asian region and has had political consequences that affect globally.

The aim of this chapter is to analyse the social phenomenon of migration within the region that constitutes North-East India and its implications in the security which are of contemporary concerns in India today. It is in this regard that this chapter seeks to study migrations from two countries of two regions – South Asia and South-East Asia, namely Bangladesh and Myanmar *vis-à-vis* the States of Tripura and Mizoram and how these migrations have influenced the political dynamics within North-East India and contributed to contemporary security concerns in India.

I. Geostrategic Locations of North-East India and Migrations

The geostrategic location of the North-East of India is unique in the fact that by virtue of its regional location, it has developed as a peripheral region to the Indian subcontinent. The reason being that more than 80 per cent of the North-East region has international boundaries with the countries of South and South-East Asia and is connected with the rest of the country only through a narrow stretch of plains which is known as Siliguri Corridor. This narrow stretch of land is sometimes referred as chicken-necked region since it connects with the rest of the country.

The North-Eastern Region covers the eastern Himalayas and the river valley system of the Brahmaputra, which is around an area of 255,144 sq km.[1], which is roughly 7.7 per cent of India's total land surface. With 383 million people in the region, it constitutes 3.72 per cent of the total population in the country, according to the 2001 Census.[2]

The diversity of the North-East region is unique in the sense that it is not only diverse from the rest of India but also within the region as it is located in the Assam Himalayas of the regional classification of Himalayas as made by Sir Sidney Burrard of

Canada, who divided the Himalayan Mountain into four segments from the west to east directions, according to the river valleys[3]. According to which, the North-East India is located in the Assam regional division of Himalayas. Besides, the Assam Himalayas, which has been classified for the easternmost, the other divisions include from the west, are Punjab Himalayas, Kumaon Himalayas and Nepal Himalayas.

Besides, the diversity of the North-East is reflected in terms of agro-ecosystem, socio-cultural mixture of the people, a blend of multiplicity of ethnicity and geo-topographical variability. This is because the North-East India is located at the confluence of the tectonic plates of the Himalayan Mountain and meeting point of the Malayan Peninsula, there are the peripheries of the Himalayas which has constituted the Himalaya as a region over the course of time, according to A.C. Sinha.[4]

The western Himalayas has a close affinity with the Middle- East cultures, while the southern Himalayas has a close cultural affinity with the Indo-Gangetic culture of India and the eastern Himalayas has an interesting mix of the mystical world of Tibetan Buddhist culture with strong connotations of the indigenous cultures.

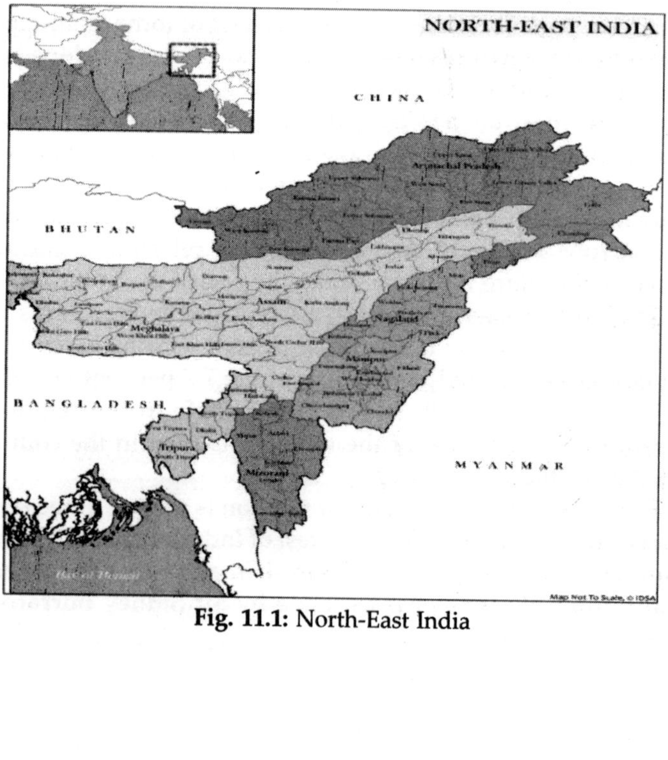

Fig. 11.1: North-East India

In the west, Mr. Sinha has identified the 'Muslim-Persian-Pamir-Kashmir Himalayas to be an extension of the cultural core that is still found in Iran of Kabul valley. According to him, the western Himalayas has a strong cultural affiliation with the Islamic Middle East countries in their racial, linguistic trait, tribal band organisations, material culture, religion and civilisation as well as their horticulture and market gardening dry economy. While for the Indian Himalayan slopes, the cultural core lies in the Gangetic plain and the Vindhya ranges as can be seen in the racial, linguistic economic, socio-cultural and religious view point.

The eastern Himalayas in which the North-East India is in the interesting confluence of the northern Himalayan slope, which is located from Leh to Tawang is an extension of the core Tibetan system and the mystic world of the indigenous cultures with their own distinct cultures of the different ethnicity that inhabits them.

Moreover, the North-Eastern region has an influence of the countries of South and South -East Asia with which she shares her political borders, such as Bangladesh from the South Asian countries with the North-Eastern States of Assam, Meghalaya, Tripura and Mizoram; while the States of Assam and Mizoram in the East share 16 per cent of the total border area while the South-East Asian countries of Myanmar shares her border with the North-Eastern States of Manipur, Mizoram and Nagaland in the east. There is also the other political boundary that shares the international border with Bhutan in the west with the North-Eastern States of Assam, Sikkim and Arunachal Pradesh boundary.

The close physical proximity along with the cultural and ethnic ties has made the North-East region susceptible for cross border migrations from India's neighbouring countries, and indirectly making the sovereignty of the country vulnerable.

II. Migrations in North-East India

The North-East India being a land locked region has always been susceptible for migrations from time immemorial, for more reasons than one. It was part of the Silk route, the famous trading route of ancient period. In ancient times, migration usually takes place in small groups, such as tribes or clans, whereas today, it is generally by individuals or families. However, migrations have received negative connotations today as people migrate when facing insecurity in their present location be it economically or politically. That is why, migration has influenced the political dynamics of the North-East region in particular and the country as a whole.

Migration basically involves more or less permanent movement of individuals or groups across symbolic or political boundaries into new residential areas and communities. In the contemporary period, migration has occurred at a mass scale, which has been voluntary as well as involuntary. The voluntary migration occurs due to the 'pull' factors of the destinations such as better employment avenues, political or religious freedom, etc., while involuntary migrations occur due to the 'push' factors that compel the individuals or groups to move to another place on account of economic, political or religious reasons.

In the North-East region, migrations occur due to both the 'pull' and the 'push' factors from the two neighbouring countries of Myanmar in the east and Bangladesh in the west. Both the neighbouring countries of Myanmar and Bangladesh face religious persecutions, against Hindus for Bangladesh and against Christians in Myanmar as a result, there is an exodus of population into India's North-East.

Many of these migrations have occurred over a period of time since India's independence and are illegal in nature. This is because of the fact that many of the people, who flee to India without any legal permits or documents, enter the Indian border. The check points at the border area are ambiguous and not clearly demarcated as the borders were drawn without taking cognizance of the political reality.

The word 'refugees' is a colloquial term used for immigrants who enter Indian borders either to seek asylum due to the political or religious persecutions in their home country or migrate and take residence, without any significance of the real assumptions of what the word 'refugee' mean. According to the Indian laws, all refugees are treated at par as an alien or a foreigner, since India is not a signatory to the 1951 UN Convention to the Status of Refugee.[5]

According to International Law, a refugee is a person who has been forced to leave their home and seek refuge elsewhere "owing to a well-founded fear of being persecuted for reasons of race, religion, nationality, membership of a particular social group, or political opinion, outside the country of his nationality, and is unable to return, owing to such fear is unwilling to avail himself of the protection of that country"[6].

India, on its part, regulates trade and the movement of people through its policy on foreigners which is mediated through its legal institutions and administrative structures. In contra-distinction to the States's policy of regulating the borders, in the South Asian subcontinent, borders are porous and at best, minimally regulated[7]. The fact that Mizoram (as also Manipur and Arunachal Pradesh) houses a large number of Burmese nationals, who then disappear in the society, is telling as to the extent to which borders may be circumvented by people.

The North-Eastern States in which the issue of migrations has had serious implications for security concerns in contemporary India are in the States of Mizoram and Tripura where the increasing migrant's populations have led to a strong wave of 'nativism' in the domestic politics.

III. Migrations from Bangladesh in Tripura

The State of Tripura in the North-East which has a total land area of 10,466 square miles, has more than 85 per cent of her border has an international border with Bangladesh in the east as well as in the west. (See Fig. 11.2). It is no wonder that there have been more migrants from Bangladesh than the rest of the country. In fact, the number of migrants is much more than the native populations as the Census reveals. In the Census of 1931, the native Tripuris were said to be 95 per cent of the total population, who have said to be reduced to a mere 31 per cent in the 1991. This demographic seachange has been caused by migration of hundreds of thousand of Bangladeshis.

The immigrants now constitute over sixty-eight percent of State population and their mothertongue Bengali is the official State language against KOK-BARAK, which enjoys the status of second language. The indigenous population is composed of 19 tribes that are collectively called Boroks. The common language that the natives use is called Kok Borok. The 19 tribes are as follows:

Fig. 11.2: State of Tripura

1. Bhil
2. Bhutia
3. Chaimal
4. Chakma
5. Garo
6. Halam

7. Jamatia
8. Khasi
9. Any Kuki including:
    (i) Biate, Biete
    (ii) Changsan
    (iii) Chongloi
    (iv) Darlong
    (v) Doungel
    (vi) Gamalhou
    (vii) Gangte
    (viii) Guite
    (ix) Hanneng
    (x) Haokip, Haupit
    (xi) Haolai
    (xii) Hengna
    (xiii) Hongsung
    (xiv) Harangkhwal, Rangkhol
    (xv) Jongbe
    (xvi) Khawchung
    (xvii) Khawathlang, Khothalong
    (xviii) Khelma
    (xix) Kholhou
    (xx) Kipgen
    (xxi) Kuki
    (xxii) Lengthang
    (xxiii) Lhangum
    (xxiv) Lhoujem
    (xxv) Lhouvun
    (xxvi) Lupheng
    (xxvii) Mangjel
    (xxviii) Misao
    (xxix) Negrito
    (xxx) Riang
    (xxxi) Sairhem
    (xxxii) Selnam
    (xxxiii) Singson
    (xxxiv) Sithou
    (xxxv) Sukte
    (xxxvi) Thado
    (xxxvii) Thangngeu

(xxxviii) Uibuh
(xxxix) Vaiphei
10. Lepcha
11. Lushai
12. Nag
13. Munda
14. Oraon
15. Naotia
16. Reang
17. Santhal
18. Tripuri, Trupiri, Treppera,
19. Uchai[8]

The demographic imbalance has occurred over a period of time due to the mass exodus of population from the Hindu communities following major political events which have occurred in the Indian subcontinent. These major political events have historical significance not only in India but in the Indian subcontinent as a whole as they have had its impact in the present day neighbouring countries of Pakistan and Bangladesh.

These political events in history can be traced from the time of Post Independence Period in 1947, Partition of East Pakistan from West Pakistan to the recent communal riots in Ayodhya after the Babri Masjid demolition in 1992. The Indian Government ignored the demographic complexity while rehabilitating the unrestricted flow of non-tribal Bengali refugees in this smallest State of north-east. Transformed from a predominantly tribal State to a non-tribal majority state the population of the tribes was reduced from 64 per cent in 1864 to 52 per cent in 1901, 37 per cent in 1951 and 29 per cent in 1971[9]. By the end of twentieth century their population was reduced to 28 per cent[10].

(a) Post Independence Period in 1947

The first phase of migration could be traced back to the early twentieth century when a sizeable number of non-tribal Hindu Bengali peasantry had migrated at the instance of its ruler from East Bengal with a view to augment the revenue offered in lieu of settling at the cultivable land in the valley at low rent. The king also employed the educated Bengalese in State administration and over the years and they also accepted Tripura as their homeland. However, the natives always regarded them as aliens although the relation between the two was relatively stable till the former was in majority.

The current ethnic set-up in Tripura is a consequence of the Partition of India, when large groups of Bengali Hindus left the area that became East Pakistan (today Bangladesh). The previous majority population, the native population of Tripura became a minority and socio-economically disadvantaged in comparison to the new majority which comprised of the Bangladeshi Bengali populations.

It did not take long for the trouble to start. In 1940s when the anti-Hindu riots took place in East Bengal, the scared and hapless Hindu Bengalese were forced to cross over to Tripura for a safer haven. Later when the partition took place in the subcontinent in 1947, history witnessed perhaps the largest movement of evicted people in modern history, resulting in a heavy influx of people from the erstwhile East Pakistan to seek refuge into Tripura, especially from Chakla Roshanabad area which became a part of East Pakistan.

The new central government went forward to help in the rehabilitation of the political refugees from East Pakistan in places such as Tripura as well. The refugees brought with them new methods of settled agriculture, and cultural interaction between tribal and non-tribal peoples paved the way for new social developments. At the same time, the tribal population was converted to a minority in its own land, and the demographic change triggered social divisions that racked the State for years to come.

The heavy influx of the political refugees took a toll on the economy of Tripura as the surplus turn into deficit, communication links were disrupted and a stable population became highly unstable and unmanageable

The Partition thus had a dramatic effect on both the economy and demography of the State. The large-scale immigration not only put a tremendous burden on the resources of the State, but also led to an upheaval in the social composition of the State's population.

(b) Partition of East Pakistan

The population of Tripura saw a dramatic shift as the natives were getting marginalized when Pakistan was partitioned into two leading to the birth of the new nation of Bangladesh, in 1971.[11]

In 1971, the population of Tripura was only 16 lakhs. However after the liberation of Bangladesh from Pakistan, saw a large number of the Hindu Bengali people move into Tripura. The population of Tripura more than doubled at the time.

The Indian Government ignored the demographic complexity while rehabilitating the unrestricted flow of non-tribal Bengali refugees in this smallest State of north-east. Many of the people stayed in Tripura for nearly one year as *sharanarthi* (refugee) in the refugee camps. After Bangladesh was liberated, most of them returned to their homes although a substantial number of people stayed back in Tripura and merged with the local residents.

Tripura, which was a predominantly tribal State changed to a non-tribal majority State as the population of the tribes was reduced from 64 per cent in 1864 to 52 per cent in 1901, 37 per cent in 1951 and 29 per cent in 1971. By the end of twentieth century their population was reduced to 28 per cent. The population of Tripura in general and that of Agartala in particular has abruptly increased due to this war. The growth rates are quite high for the period of 1971-1981. It was unprecedented because of the state of influx and is clearly not a natural rate of growth (See Table 11.1).

Table 11.1: Migration and Natural Growth Rate (NGR)

	1971-81		*1981-91*	
	Migration	*NGR*	*Migration*	*NGR*
Tripura	12.44	19.48	16.75	17.55
India	4.66	21.02	2.48	20.40

Source: Various census reports.[12]

In Table 11.1 above shows that in regard to natural rate of growth, Tripura and India are close to each other. Rather Tripura's figures are less than the all-India averages. The growth due to migration is very high, almost three times higher in 1971 – 81 and six times higher in 1981-91 in Tripura compared to India.

The tragedy of partition has disturbed the demographic composition in Tripura and led to the steady decline of the native's population, which has a cascading effect on the economy as well as in the society. In fact, the socio-economic turbulence has witnessed differentiations to be based on ethnicity, which has spilled into the political field to become a battle ground of ethnic assertions.[13]

(c) Communal Riots following the 1992 Babri Masjid Demolition in Ayodhya

The communal riots following the 1992 demolition of the Babri Masjid in Ayodhya, in Uttar Pradesh, India found its resonance, which echoed in the neighbouring country of Bangladesh. The demolition created a fear psychosis among members of the minority Hindu community in Bangladesh as they felt threatened and were persecuted on behalf of the Muslims in India due to the feeling of the fraternity that they share on the grounds of their religion. The Hindu minority felt that they had no option but to leave their country Bangladesh and seek refuge in India such as the neighbouring States of Tripura, which was just across the borders, literally.

Although, the figures of the Bangladeshi population who had taken refuge in Tripura has not been documented but the statistical figures in the sudden increase of population in Tripura can be concluded that it is not due to the natural high growth rate of the population but rather due to the increase in immigration population.

IV. Migrations from Myanmar in Mizoram

Mizoram borders the Chin State of Burma and has been the major recipient of migration of people from Chin State as Myanmar is also another neighbouring country that shares not only its political borders but also the ethnic and social relations with the North-East region of India.

However, Myanmar is boiled with political turmoil of imposing military junta over democratic aspirations and suppressing them. The suppressions of the democratic freedom of the political aspirations spill over the restrictions on freedom of religious beliefs. The dictate of the military junta over the ethnic minorities and their suppression on their religious beliefs as well as their political aspirations has led to a fear of persecution among the ethnic minorities due to which they flee for a safer haven.

That is why there exists a large number of Burmese refugee populations in India. They are mainly concentrated in the North-Eastern States of Mizoram, Manipur, Nagaland and Arunachal Pradesh and Delhi.

Besides the North-Eastern States which host refugees from Myanmar, the capital city Delhi also hosts a sizeable population of Burmese refugees. There are 1452 Burmese refugees in Delhi of which 805 are recognized by United Nations High Commissioner for Refugees (UNHCR) office while the remaining 647 are asylum seekers from Burma who have not been recognized as refugees by the office of UNHCR.

Mizoram being not only a neighbouring State but also the Mizo people having close ethnic ties with some of the ethnic minorities such as the Chin ethnic groups, who find it more convenient to cross the international border through the Champhai border and seek refuge here. It has been reported that there are more than 50,000 Chin refugees in Mizoram, although the Mizoram State Government recorded only 9,363. Besides, Mizoram there is also large number of Chin refugees in Manipur. Besides, the Chin refugees, there are around 6,000 of Naga refugee from Myanmar in the State.

(a) Ethnic Affinity among the Mizos and the Chins

The main reason why the Chins ethnic groups find it an access to seek refuge in Mizoram is because of the fact that the Mizos and the Burmese, especially the Chin belongs to the same ethnic group, the Chin-Mizo-Kuki tribe. The relationships between the two have existed since time immemorial. Both the groups have accommodated each other in times of difficulties.

During the period of political agitation for a statehood in Mizoram, many of the stalwarts who were on the forefront of the struggle movement fled to Burma. It was the fruits of the political agitation that it became the 23rd State of the Indian Union in February 1987. Prior to that it was administered as one of the districts of Assam under British India which continued till 1972 when it became a Union Territory.

The State of Mizoram is a mountainous region which is

sandwiched between Myanmar in the east and south and Bangladesh in the west, occupies an area of great strategic importance in the north-eastern corner of India. It has a total of 630 miles boundary with Myanmar and Bangladesh.[14]

The people of Mizoram share a close affinity with the people of Myanmar especially among the Chin ethnic groups.It was the Chin who gave shelter to them. In the report written by the Mizo Zirlai Pawl (MZP), has stated that "*The Mizo speaking or Lusei/Lushai happens to be those of Mizo origin who migrated to Myanmar in the hope of improving their means of livelihood in a country which was at the wake of independence. These people returned back to Mizoram in the later years*"[15]; which in a way reaffirms the strong kinship that the people of Mizos and Chins share with each other.

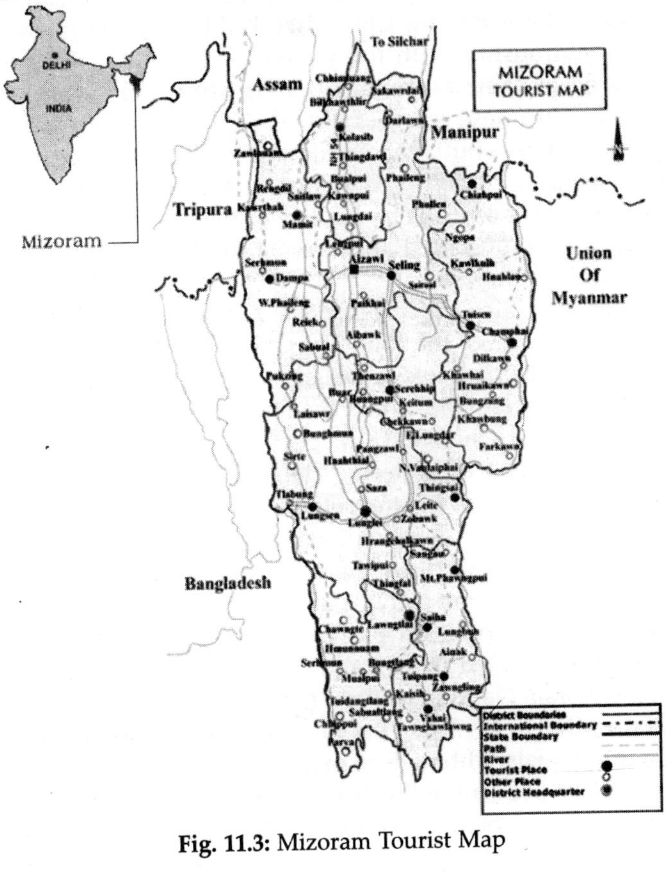

Fig. 11.3: Mizoram Tourist Map

Besides, that the Chins has also reiterated the same sentiment that "The Mizos not only came and stayed in Chinland but they came along with the names of their village and they stayed in the Chinland giving Mizo names to the area where they put up."[16] This is substantiated by the fact that presently in Chinland there are villages named Tahan, Haimawl, etc. Both the Mizos and Chins have exhibited kinly attitude towards each other.

(b) *Political Accommodation of Ethnic Affinity of the Chins in Mizoram*

The brotherly affinity of the Mizos and the Chins could not be sustained for very long since the relationship between the Mizos and the Chin has fallen apart over the years. The Mizo claim that since they belonged to the Chin-Mizo-Kuki tribe, they co-exist in cordial relationship with the people of the State. They were considered as their kinsmen till 1995 after which they were regarded as Burmese refugees. Prior to 1995, the Chins were not treated as refugees but as an immigrant for they could naturalize themselves as a citizen of the State in Mizoram, without any differences in the attitude and policy of the government, as they could acquire ration card and even enrolled themselves in the electoral rolls of the State.

Rough estimates suggest that there are about 1,000,000 Chin nationals living across the State. The Chins migrate for a variety of reasons, which has its roots in the larger context of militarization of all ethnic States after 1988. While, the Chins and the Mizos migrated to Mizoram and Chin State respectively, the recent wave of migration, especially those fleeing Chin State has been in the context of heavy militarization and the deteriorating economic conditions.

However, the Burmese nationals who had acquired voting rights in the State, majority of them, around 95 per cent belongs to the Mizo National Front (MNF) party. The MNF party was among the most popular political party even among the other ethnic groups who migrated to Mizoram. The MNF (Nationalist) later known as Zoram Nationalist Party (ZNP), a party which emerged out of the MNF in 1997, had the support of good number of these Burmese nationals. Although, at present, the scenario has changed as less than 95 per cent of the Burmese Nationals who had voting rights in Mizoram belong to either the MNF or ZNP.

C. Drive for Refoulement of the Refugees from Mizoram in 1995

The Indo-Burma border holds immense significance in the region for this continuing migration and the high level of cross border trade. While the trade is encouraged and supported, the migration of Chins is not always welcomed. The Mizo Zirlai Pawl (MZP), which is the students wing and is also known as the Mizo Students' Association or the Young Mizo Association (YMA), is the largest and most powerful and influential organization in the State of Mizoram. They do not have any political affiliation with any political party, yet their influence is such that not a single political party could afford to go against its wishes and then lose its favour as they represent the Mizo civil society irrespective of any political ideology.

In a way the Young Mizo Association (YMA) dictates the political ideology and climate in the State as the State had a strong surge of "nativism" as the number of refugees increased manifold and put a strain on the resources of the tiny State. It is in such a backdrop that YMA had launched a massive campaign of 'Chakma Foreigners Quit Order' in 1995 due to the increasing number of Chakma refugees taking refuge in Mizoram. As a result, of which a large number of the Chakma refugees who are from Chittagong region in Bangladesh have had to leave the State.

The drive for Refoulement is not only a call for 'nativism' in this side of the country as it has strong political implications in this region that affects both South Asia and South-East Asia.

The call for nativism by the YMA had an adverse affect to the fortunes of the political party of Congress as the Chakmas were the strong "vote bank". That is why, they urged them to look at the issue holistically and take measures in driving out all the refugees irrespective of the country that they come from. Taking holistic considerations of all refugees meant that the Burmese refugees would also be affected as the YMA had taken a soft attitude towards them as they consider them as their "own brothers"[17]

However, the soft sentiments against the Burmese immigrant community turn against them due to the political reality of their background. Many of them struggled to reach Indian borders in Mizoram with few economic luxuries and due to which there was a strong attraction of earning fast money, which sometimes was

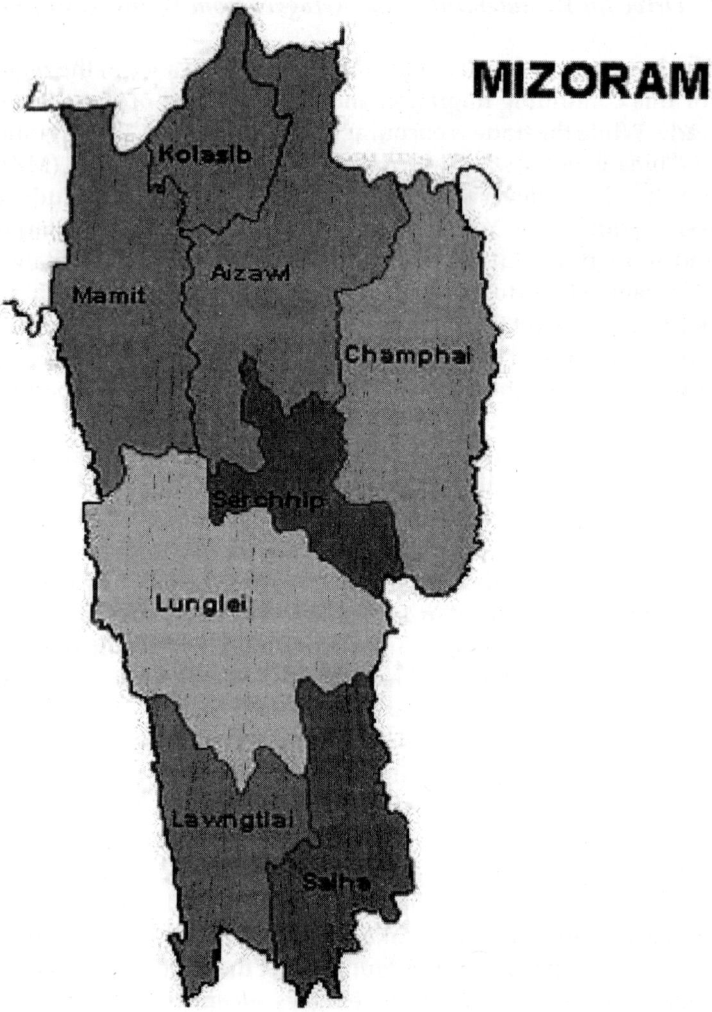

Fig 11.3: Map of the State of Mizoram

through devious means. The devious means include peddling drugs and liquor, besides prostitution. In fact, with the increasing number of immigrant communities in Mizoram, the devious means of livelihood became more rampant that it enraged the morality of the local community in Mizoram and the Burmese community had to face the brunt of it. A strong sentiment of dislike started developing against the Burmese migrant community[18] which was based on many allegations against them that ranges from plausible reasons due to the increased pressure on the local resources to the implausible, where they are made as the proverbial scapegoat for all their misfortunes.

One of them is that they have been the cause for the loss of forests and their products as the Chins from Burma gather them from the forest and sell them in order to earn their livelihood. Also being an immigrant community they cut into the employment of the local people and many of them have become unemployed. A host of other factors are also responsible. Besides the drugs and liquor trade, the sheer number of people migrating and the allegations that the Chins are carriers of diseases such as HIV/ AIDS, etc.

Moreover, the fact that the Burmese community likes to retain their ethnic identity of Chins and not get assimilated into the Mizo society has opened a Pandora's box. The Mizo have segregated themselves in social functions even attending the funerals of the Chin people. While the Mizo's has clarified that this is because the Chins have established their own churches and, therefore, the socialization has not been on the same tangent.

The Chins said that as they are from a migrant community they could not maintain the same standard with that of the local Mizo community, when it came to their dress and etiquette. Moreover, having established their own Chin churches has given them the freedom of singing and praying in their own dialect, which they treasure a lot and also retaining their own culture and language.

Besides, the socio-cultural factors that irks the Mizo community the most about the Burmese community is the remittance that they send to their home country in Myanmar shows their unwillingness to accept Mizoram as their home and adopt the Mizo cultures.

It is in view of these problems that the Chin ethnic communities were also felt to be treated as any other foreigners like the Chakmas and were send for Refoulement i.e., the refugees is forcibly being sent back to their home country.

It strategically makes a point to the Congress party as this disturbs the "vote bank" of the political party of the Mizo National Front (MNF), the arch rival of the Congress. It is in the light of such developments that some Mizo families refuse to rent houses to the Burmese community as it invokes trouble from the local authorities. That is the reason why many of the Burmese families come to Delhi to be recognized as refugees under the protection of UNHCR.

However, the YMA seeks to make amends. The President of YMA, Mr. P. C. Laltlansanga, has empathized their situation, "due to social causes and bad governance". He said that "they are more our brothers and the international boundary should not hinder our relationship."[19] That is why they seek to bring a change in the policy. Accordingly the government of Mizoram issued permits to Burmese nationals that will allow them to stay for a maximum of one year after which they can leave the State and make a re-entry.

IV. Impact of Migration on North-East India's Security

The implications of migration in the North-East have strategic importance for the North-East as well as the country as a whole due to the consequences on the security of the South and South East Asian region. South Asia has perpetually faced numerous, intractable threats and challenges to nation-states, particularly those, emanating from the unresolved territorial and boundary disputes due to the colonial legacy.

Besides that the South Asian states such as India and Bangladesh have found themselves to be hemmed in between the Golden Triangle, which is the drug-producing sub-region in the highlands of South-East Asia that overlap Myanmar, Thailand and Laos and the Golden Crescent, that is the narcotics-producing sub-region constituting Afghanistan, Pakistan and Iran, and the illegal arms trade from Bangladesh. The close proximity of North-East to the Golden Triangle, which is one of Asia's two main illicit opium-producing areas, makes drug smuggling as an easy route to finance their illegal arms trade and sustaining the militancy movement.

Moreover, migration from the two neighbouring countries of Myanmar and Bangladesh has had an interesting dynamic with democracy as the military dictate clouds the horizon of their politics and any voices of dissent are often snubbed by the states. That is why an armed struggle against the state has mushroomed and breeds insurgencies among the people across the geo-political borders. The militancy finds an easy nexus with the insurgencies that operate in the North-East as they indulge in illegal arms trading from across the border for fuelling the arms struggle against the state.

In addition, the unchecked migration of immigrants from Bangladesh and Myanmar is one of the strategic concerns to India's North-East. In the case of Mizoram where some of the refugees get trapped in the tentacle of drug trafficking. Meanwhile many of the local people are forced to grow opium as a cash crop in order to avoid heavy penalties when faced with a situation of being defaulters, or of being unable to pay the high taxes imposed by the military junta. Besides this, the easy nexus with the Golden Triangle has made drug smuggling rampant in South-East Asia that has had a disastrous effect among the youths of North-East India, and also the illegal arms trade from Bangladesh has fueled the armed struggle among the insurgencies in north-east India alive.

(a) Drug Trafficking

The North-East region is close to the golden triangle, which is one of Asia's two main illicit opium-producing areas, that overlaps the mountains of four countries of South-East Asia: Burma, Vietnam, Laos, and Thailand in an area of around 367,000 square miles (950,000 km^2).

The heroin, which is available in the North-Eastern States of India, is locally called as "No. 4" and is brought in through the borders of Manipur, Mizoram and Nagaland. Heroin trade in this region is meant to meet the demand of the local population. And these are also being transported to foreign destinations from India. At the same time, it has been marked by the International Law Enforcement officials to gain more attention due to its geostrategic location.

According to the Annual Report made by the Narcotics Control Bureau, 2001-2002, the Indian States of Arunachal Pradesh, Nagaland, Manipur and Mizoram have been vulnerable to the trafficking of heroin from Myanmar[20]. As a result of the proximity to the Golden Triangle these States have been vulnerable to trafficking of high purity heroin flowing in small quantities. The route for trafficking from Myanmar into the North-Eastern States of India is either through Moreh and Churchandpur in Manipur, Mokochung in Nagaland and Champai in Mizoram. The report further states that in this area trafficking occurs in smaller quantities and is, therefore, difficult to detect. Besides, the existence of traditional cross border ethnic links, lack of restriction of movement, inhospitable terrain and the problem of insurgency for the assertion for political freedom has complicated the situation.

The use of heroin has been noted in States of Manipur, Nagaland and Mizoram from the late nineteen seventies. It is in this area that injecting mode of use became prevalent at first in India and as a result has spread HIV among the drug users, which has become a major concern as well as a menace to the society. In addition to drug use, the presence of frequent political tension, the absence of adequate steps towards development of the region and the sense of social, economic and political isolation faced by the local people only complicates the drug use and trade situation.

In the national sample the current percentage of users who reported injecting mode of intake is 9 per cent and 14 per cent reported life time use. In the North-Eastern States for both life time use and current consumption in Mizoram it is 76 per cent; for Manipur 7.5 per cent and Nagaland 51 per cent. With regard to sharing of needles, at the national level life time sharing of needles was reported by 8 per cent and 4 per cent reported sharing needles currently. In the North-Eastern States of Manipur, Mizoram and Nagaland the percentage of drug use is high (43-66%).[21]

(b) Illegal Arms Trade

Bangladesh is one of the countries which acts as the cradle of illegal arms trade in the region. Since the liberation of Bangladesh in 1971, many of the fire arms used in the conflict were never fully accounted for and have remained in circulation. The illegal arms market started in Bangladesh after 1975 under the reign of President Ziaul Haque. Arms were smuggled from Pakistan and China.

It has been observed through different sources, that it is from Bangladesh that the arms such as AK-47, US pistol, M-16, 9MM Pistol, Mouzer pistol, US Taraus, Italy's Pertrobarota, Germany's Ruby, US Revolver, Chinese Rifle Kaslashnikov, Indian pistol,

Indian revolver, LMG, SMG, pipe gun, 22 bore pistol and many other fire arms illegally traded. The smugglers are selling these arms to the insurgent groups who have no qualms in using them in their political quest. These lethal arms have been found in the hands of the North-East insurgents.

According to Major General Syed Muhammad Ibrahim (Retd), till 2006, as many as 128 crime syndicates in Bangladesh were using 400,000 illegal Small Arms Light Weapons. In fact, gun-related violence has facilitated the spread of organised crime, undermined fragile democratic politics and fuelled sectarian violence in Bangladesh.[22]

The National Socialist Council of Nagaland (NSCN, IM and K groups) had introduced the United Liberation Front of Assam (ULFA) to the Kachins ethnic groups of Myanmar. It was widely reported in 1986 that Paresh Baruah, the military commander of ULFA, had travelled through north-west Myanmar and paid the Kachins a substantial sum of money to begin training and arrange for the supply of weapons from the arms bazaars in Thailand and smuggling networks operating on the Myanmar-China route.

The problem gets compounded also due to the fact that the free movement regime between India and Myanmar facilitates cross-border smuggling of small arms. In fact, Ruili, a town in the Yunan Province on the Myanmar-China border, was a nerve centre for the illegal trade of small arms into India. The arms came into Mizoram, Manipur and Nagaland *via* the land route and through the sea route *via* Chittagong. This trade became apparent following Bangladesh's biggest ever arms haul, on a jetty in the Karnaphuli river, Chittagong, in April 2004. The haul netted 1,790 rifles (including Uzi submachine guns and assault rifles of the AK series), 150 rocket launchers, 840 rockets, 2,700 grenades and more than a million rounds of ammunition.[23]

Moreover, insurgency in the Chittagong Hill Tracts over the past few decades has further added to the demand for small arms. The easy opportunity for money-laundering has led to the emergence of Bangladesh as the main transit point for at least five major militant groups that are active in North-Eastern India, especially the United Liberation Front of Assam (ULFA). Emerging as a convenient transit route for the flow of illegal weapons from South-East Asia, the Sylhet and Cox's Bazaar areas are being used to hoard and transfer arms procured by the ULFA from Thailand

and Myanmar. Moreover, the munificence of the Inter-Services Intelligence (ISI) has enabled ULFA to buy arms in Cambodia and pay for them in hard currency routed through Nepal.[24]

According to intelligence sources, there are around 400 arms smugglers, with 88 in Dhaka, 34 in Chittagong, 87 in Khulna, 70 in Rajshahi, 35 in Sylhet, 58 each in Barisal and Rangamati. In fact, illegal arms are being produced at factories inside the country in the remote hills such as Moheskhali and deep forests of Khagrachhari. These factories, which produce guns are in great demand among the local terrorists illegally as during the day time the factory functions as a workshop or as a shop of blacksmith. There are iron-blade, iron cutting machine and gun handle making machineries in the factories.

Conclusions

In conclusion, the significant point in the discussion and discourse of nature of migration has become one of the politically vibrant issues of concern. This had led to a contemporary security concerns that have its impact on the traditional concept of security. One of the main reasons being that North-East India may seem peripheral to the political centre of the Indian State which is dominated by the Central Government at the centre. And their strategic concerns, geographically are to the contiguous landmass that enjoins with the South-East Asian countries and is landlocked. Therefore, the security concerns overlapped into Indian sovereignty as migrations occur across the States. Addition to this, sometimes aided by the State as in the case of Bangladesh or sometimes due to the close ethnic ties, in the case of Myanmar.

It is in this context that this strategic concerns of South and South-East Asia that make the North-East region a melting pot of the dissent and disorder that has let to anarchical disorder. These have challenged the traditional concept of security and has evolved from a non-conventional 'security issue'. Such as migrations in North-East India from the South and South-East Asian countries as well like Myanmar and Bangladesh.

REFERENCES

1. Water Resources of Bangladesh Accessed 2011-06-12.
2. *Census of India 2001,* http://www.pon.nic.in/open/depts/ecostat/census/homepage.htm accessed on 2011-06-12.
3. Burard, Sidney G., Bannerman W.B., Mookerjee Ashutosh, *The Shaping of Indian Science,* Indian Science Congress Association Presidential Address, Vol 1: 1914-1947, Universities Press, 2003.
4. Sinha, A.C. 2005: 'Colonial Anthropology *versus* Indological Sociology: Elwin and Ghurye on Tribal Policy in India' in *Between Ethnography and Fiction: Verrior Elwin and Tribal Question in India,* Orient Longman, Hyderabad.
5. *Ibid.*
6. Article 1A, United Nations Convention relating to the Status of Refugees of 1951.
7. Fencing of the borders of India in both the Western as well as the Eastern side is continuously debated and is also in place in the Indo-Bangladesh and Indo-Pakistan border areas. Other area, such as the one on the North-Eastern side is not so easily fenced.
8. The People and their Culture in www.tripura.nic.in/ttaadc/people.htm accessed on 2011-06-06.
9. Bareh, H.M, *Encyclopedia of North-East India,* Volume VIII, Gyan Books Publisher, 2007.
10. Ali, Salim, *Migrations and Ethnic Violence in Tripura,* Faultlines, Volume 20, January 2011.
11. Upadhyaya, R., *Tripura Bleeds—In the Crossfire of Mainstream Political Parties and Virulent Ethnic Conflict,* South Asian Analysis Group,www.southasiananalysis.org. Accessed on 2011-07.07.
12. www. Censusindia.gov.in accessed on 2011.05-05.
13. Vaiphei, Lianboi, *Politics in Northeast India* for Tripura University, Vikas Publications, New Delhi, 2011.
14. Bissinger, Jared, *The Maritime Boundary Dispute between Bangladesh and Myanmar: Motivations, Potential Solutions, and Implications,* in *Asia Policy No. 10 (July 2010), 103-42.*
15. Assessment Report on Burmese Refugees living in Mizoram and Delhi, www.chro.ca accessed on 2011.06.06.
16. *Ibid.*
17. *Ibid.*
18. Annexure–II in *A Report by Government of Mizoram on the Involvement of Burmese Nationals in Criminal Cases* www.chro.ca.
19. Mizimma News, *Mizo Students Empathize with Burmese Migrants,* 19 October, 2006.
20. Charles, Molly, "Different Sources for Heroin" in Drug Trade Dynamics in India fo a Project Undertaken for the Max Planck

Institute of International Criminal Law, Germany and RAND, USA, Accessed on 2011, 8, 8.

21. Kanwal, Gurmeet and Chansoria, Monik, *Small Arms Proliferation in South Asia: A Major Challenge for National Security*, Centre for Land Warfare Studies (CLAWS), New Delhi.
22. *Ibid.*
23. *Ibid.*
24. *The Telegraph*, "Concern in Tripura over Arms Trades", Aug. 9, 2005, Calcutta, India.

12

Trafficking of Women into Forced Prostitution in India

Amrita Banerjee

Introduction

Millions of women venture in a hope of new pastures and better livelihood from the village to the city and abroad, and the nature, magnitude, causes, and consequences of these women are variant. Sometimes they are driven by poverty or economic distress, social exclusion or civil unrest (ethnic strife), ill treatment by parents and ignorance. Eventually, their strong desire and goal is to survive and earn money to support themselves and their families. But in reality, there are some who often end up catastrophically by being trafficked to brothel and forced to work in sex industry. Women make up 50 per cent of the Population of the world and despite most often have been going through different kinds of pain and sufferings. Besides this, they are also been sold into slavery and held captive against their will which is inhuman in nature. Consecutively, these have led to various other kinds of exploitation of women which is physical, economical, political and social. For example, the recent trend is women are sold into the 'global sex trade' and exploited as sex slave for the purpose of economic growth by encouraging prostitution, sex tourism and other commercial sexual services.

The study focuses on the trafficking of women into forced prostitution which is the most noteworthy human rights violation and also it has now been exacerbated by the process of globalization, which legalizes some of the norms as trade and commerce.

The Position of Women in a Society

In the existing social system a girl child is still yet perceived to be a burden of the family as daughters require extreme financial investments with no material returns. This form of perceived inequality that prevails everywhere is gender based which results in the subordination of women to male authority, binding them to their reproductive and domestic function—isolated and undervalued.

Throughout the centuries women were considered as the basic playing machines for the development of future generations only. They are deprived of their natural, social, political and economic rights because they were being dominated by the male power in the society. Female oppression originates from the family itself and it is prevalent in all fields of life. Patriarchy rule was there in the society and is still now prevalent inside the society, i.e., the rule by the father and, therefore, the subordination of the mother. A society that operates on the basis of patriarchy rule cannot be called a just society as women and men should not be judged by their gender, but as an individual and as a person. The biological factor that is most frequently linked to women social position is their capacity to bear children, and child bearing without doubt is a unique to the female sex, but the domestic responsibilities could be undertaken by the husband, or they could be shared equally between husband and wife. Marriage is an established institution of the civilized society. Generally, it is said that marriage defines a women's place, whereas it has got very little or no effect on man's status and as there were no system of marriage, the family life was not practised. But as the family life was developed the complications and the dominations started to exist, the patriarchy rule evolved and the subordination started taking place by the male class over the female.

In the present changing world still the women are generally bearing a greater workload in the family, taking the lion's share of the responsibility for rearing children and women can burn up to 85 per cent of their daily calorie intake just fetching water. They are excluded from crucial economic and political activity and women around the world are still routinely denied rights granted to men. Yet some 75 per cent of the world's women cannot get bank loans because they have unpaid or insecured jobs and are not entitled to property ownership.

The evolution of patriarchy curtailed the liberty and freedom of women in society and come directly under the rule of male dominated society. But every individual and human being has got the right to live their life in their own way according to their wish, then why is this curtailment of freedom happening with women? The deprivation of the women' occurs due to their own fault as they remain silent and don't raise the protest against the male culprit. So still now in the welfare state the position of women is full of paradoxes and contradictions.

What is Trafficking?

Trafficking is one of the oldest lucrative businesses in the world and one of the fastest growing forms of criminal activity, next only to drugs and weapons trade, generating unaccountable profits annually. The UN Protocol of 2000 to prevent, suppress and punish trafficking in persons defines trafficking as: "... the recruitment, transportation, transfer, harbouring or receipt of persons by means of the threat or use of force or other forms of coercion, of abduction, of fraud, of deception, of the abuse of power or of a position of vulnerability or of the giving or receiving of payments or benefits to achieve the consent of a person having control over another person, for the purpose of exploitation. Exploitation shall include, at a minimum, the exploitation of the prostitution of others or other forms of sexual exploitation, forced labour or service, slavery or practices similar to slavery, servitude or the removal of organs".[1]

According to the mentioned definition, the diverse means and ways of trafficking and being trafficked boil down to the involvement of anti-social and criminal elements into the trade of prostitution. These elements are termed as 'the trafficker'. The nature of the traffickers are not well identified or who can be the one. Generally, the traffickers are the tradesman who considers women purely as profitable goods or commodities. The traffickers buy the women, sell them, and move them about within the same country or from one country to another (International trade market).[2] 'Traffickers including family members can be part of an organized criminal network and beneficiaries of the business. They are waiting like hawks for the girl child to grow old enough to be sold for this trade which we can term as 'forced prostitution'.

There are several factors that promote trafficking: One of the eminent factor that starts the trafficking process is poverty, second factor is low-status of women, third factor is lack of literacy and awareness amongst girls, and fourth factor is lack of employment etc. The traffickers identify the women who are in vulnerable situations like, lost in the city or who seem depressed, etc., thereafter the traffickers approach the girls and lure them with various false promises like promise of jobs and money, marriage, adoption, etc. Sometimes the traffickers even drugged their victims and use their force to get hold of the girls for trafficking purpose. The victims who are forced into the trade of prostitution after being trafficked are exposed to health risks, especially Sexually Transmitted Diseases (STD's) and those who develop these kinds of diseases cannot get out of this trade rather stays into the trade in order to support themselves.

According to the market valuation the whole process of the trafficking phenomenon takes place because of two main factors: (1) Demand, and (2) Supply.

Demand factor is due to increasing tourism and industrialization, rural-urban migration, expanding demand for commercial sex workers promoted by organized criminal networks, a demand for exploitation for cheap labour and the male dominated value system, and the clientele are an important aspect of the demand for trafficking. On the other hand the supply factors primary reason is poverty, with that the traditional family system and values, gender disparity, etc.

Exploitation and Export of Women

Much of 'women pain' is the result of different forms of sexual exploitation, and prostitution is particularly iniquitous example of such exploitation. Men take the opportunity of women who are simple and emotional and grasp them into the field of prostitution. There are different ways of alluring and wooing women and then through the process of trafficking getting them into the flesh trade. Trafficking of women is on the rise, although the accurate figures are hard to come by for example between 1 to 2 million people are trafficked worldwide, including 1,50,000 from South Asia and 2,25,000 from South-East Asia, and over 2.3 million girls and women are believed to be working in the sex industry against their will within the country at any given time and more than 2,00,000 persons are believed to be trafficked into for this purpose, within or through the country annually. Women from the rural areas migrate to town or cities through export processing in search for lucrative job opportunities. Like news was flashed on 14th June 1997 stating that 2,00,000 Nepali women sold into prostitution in India every year, aged between 10-14. The very mention of Mumbai, conjures up images of good jobs, success, money and glamour. The desperate people of the villages are more than willing to try their luck, thus becoming the perfect target for traffickers.[3] Poorer South Asian and South-East Asian countries export the women workers, while the richer countries import these women like commercial commodities, so they are mostly from the developing countries where poverty factor and socio-economic deprivation takes a heavy toll among families and children. Also the low social value of the girl is sometimes reflected in extreme forms in the trafficking of women. Sometimes the women are also sold by their parents for profit into the trade of prostitution to pimps who in their turn sell them to the brothels. These pimps collect or get hold of the girls from the remote and slum areas promising them employment in cities or marriage. The pimp sometimes operate under the protection of the local politicians, village headman or even the police and then the women are taken by the pimps to cities or to the countries like Middle-East, Singapore, Pakistan, etc., through the chain of international gangs, and this whole processing or method is known to be the nexus trafficking and networking of women worldwide. It should be mentioned here that the pimps who generally collect the girls are not the real owner of this trafficking network, rather they are the procurers who are employed for this purpose, the real owners of this business are the businessmen, gangsters of the underworld, politicians and also the bureaucrats and as the police officers, government officials, politicians, bureaucrats and other officials facilitate and profit from this business for a price. They ignore the abuses that occur in their jurisdiction, protect the traffickers, brothel owners, pimps, clients and buyers from arrest. On 19th April, 2007, one of the MP from Gujarat was arrested at the international airport at New Delhi, after he allegedly tried to take a woman and a teenage boy to Canada on the diplomatic passport of his wife and son.[4] The offence of trafficking is not recognized until proved by the victim's rescue, which is very rare in number as most of the people would prefer to avoid as it has got risk and for which still now this business is working full fledged.

Women Trafficking in India

In cross border trafficking, India is a sending, receiving and transit nation. Receiving women from Bangladesh and Nepal and sending women them to Middle East countries and other parts of the world. In India, Karnataka, Andhra Pradesh, Maharashtra, and Tamil Nadu are considered "high supply zones" for women in prostitution. Bijapur, Belgaum and Kolhapur are common districts from which women migrate to the big cities, as part of an organised trafficking network.[5] Districts bordering Maharashtra and Karnataka, known as the "*devadasi* belt," have trafficking structures operating at various levels. The women here are in prostitution either because their husbands deserted them, or they are trafficked through coercion and deception. Many are *devadasi* dedicated into prostitution for the goddess Yellamma and it is found that in one Karnataka brothel, all 15 girls are *devadasi*.[6]

In Bombay, children as young as 9 are bought for up to rupees 60,000, or US$2,000, at auctions where Arabs bid against Indian men who believe sleeping with a virgin cures gonorrhoea and syphilis.[7] Approximately 50,000, or half of the women in prostitution in Bombay, are trafficked from Nepal.[8] The brothels of India hold between 100,000 and 160,000 Nepalese women and girls, 35 per cent were taken on the false pretext of marriage or a good job.[9]

Calcutta is one of the important transit points for the traffickers for Bombay and to Pakistan. Around 99 per cent women are trafficked out of Bangladesh through land routes along the border areas of Bangladesh and India, such as Jessore, Satkhira, and Rajshahi.[10] In Bombay, one brothel has only Nepalese women, whom men buy because of their golden skin and docile personalities.[11] 2.5 per cent of prostitutes in India are Nepalese, and 2.7 per cent are Bangladeshi.[12] Some Indian men believe that it is good luck to have sex with scalp-eczema afflicted prostitutes who are sold by their parents to brothels for a premium.[13] Every year between 5,000 and 7,000 Nepalese girls are trafficked into the red light districts in Indian cities. These girls are sold by poor parents, tricked into fraudulent marriages, or promised employment in towns only to find themselves in brothels. They're locked up for days, starved, beaten, and burned with cigarettes until they learn how to service up to clients. Some girls go through 'training' before being initiated into prostitution, which can include constant exposure to pornographic films, tutorials in how to 'please' customers.[14]

Trafficking in women and girls is easy along the 1,740 mile-long open border between India and Nepal. Trafficking in Nepalese women and girls is less risky than smuggling narcotics and electronic equipment into India. Traffickers ferry large groups of girls at a time without the hassle of paperwork or threats of police checks. The procurer-pimp-police network makes the process even smoother. Bought for as little as Nepalese rupees 1,000, girls have been known to fetch up to Rs 30,000 in later transactions. Police are paid by brothel owners to ignore the situation. Girls may not leave the brothels until they have repaid their debt, at which time they are sick, with HIV and/or tuberculosis, and often have children of their own.[15] The areas used by traffickers to procure women and girls are the isolated districts of Sindhupalchow, Makwanpur, Dhading and Khavre in Nepal where the population is largely illiterate.[16]

Preventing Trafficking

Trafficking both for commercial sexual exploitation and for non-sexual exploitation is a complex process as it is known as an organized criminal activity and which is known to be an extreme form of human rights violation, and as a matter of fact illegal migration cannot be stopped, it can only be checked and for it an immediate need to designate and empower a national law enforcement entity that will carry out investigations and law enforcement operations against rampant trafficking crimes with nationwide jurisdiction are required, but nothing has been done enough to deal with the problem. For instance Article 23 of the Constitution of India, Article 20 of the Constitution of Nepal and Article 18 and 34 of the Constitution of Bangladesh contain provisions prohibiting trafficking and forced labour. But still there is a lack of laws establishing federal jurisdiction over inter-state crimes. 'The legal frameworks that typically come to mind in the context of human trafficking are criminal law against trafficking (however defined), or against related criminal activities such as kidnapping, wrongful confinement, slavery or forced labour, and rape or sexual assault. Anti-trafficking laws have been associated historically with efforts to combat prostitution and, therefore, many anti-trafficking laws focus primarily or exclusively on trafficking for prostitution'.[17]

In general there is an unwillingness among the government figures to recognize trafficking of women into forced prostitution as a problem because if they would have shown a little bit of consciousness then the whole process of the business have not been running successfully. 'Experts in the field say that one of the most difficult realities in the trafficking issue is the propensity of governments worldwide to treat trafficked persons as criminals or as unwanted undocumented workers rather than as people with human rights that are being violated'.[18]

Strategies of Prevention

The countries in which the women are forced into prostitution through trafficking like India, Bangladesh, Nepal, Bhutan, Pakistan, Thailand, Malaysia, etc., their police and department of justice play a vital role in carrying out the business successfully. These countries permit prostitution and the existence of brothels etc., because the police officers and other government officials facilitate and profit from the trade for a price, they just ignore the abuses that occurs in their jurisdictions, rather they protect the traffickers, brothel owners, pimps, clients and buyers from arrest, and if sometimes they raid on brothels then instead of arresting the main culprit they generally arrest the women and girls who are the victim of prostitution.

"The UN's Protocol contains a number of provisions aimed at preventing trafficking. State parties are required to establish policies, programmes and other measures aimed at preventing trafficking and protecting trafficked persons from revictimization. The existence of vulnerable situations of inequality and injustice coupled with the exploitation of the victim's circumstances by the traffickers and others cause untold harm to the trafficked victim who faces a multiplicity of rights violations. Therefore, policies, programmes and strategies that address prevention have to be unique with a focus on and an orientation towards all these issues. Accordingly the prevention of trafficking needs to be addressed not only in relation to the source areas but also in the demand areas the transit points and the trafficking routes. Strategies in all these areas have to be oriented towards the specific characteristics of the situation and the target groups.

- The best method of prevention is its integration it with prosecution and protection. Prosecution includes several tasks like the identification of the traffickers bringing them to the book, confiscating their illegal assets. Protection of the trafficked victim includes all steps towards the redressal of their grievances thus helping the victim survive, rehabilitate and establish herself/himself. Thus prosecution and protection contribute to prevention.
- The strategies should address the issues of livelihood options and opportunities by focusing on efforts to eradicate poverty, illiteracy, etc. There should be special packages for women and children in those communities where entry into CSE may be perceived as the only available option. Education and other services should be oriented towards capacity building and the consequent empowerment of vulnerable groups.
- Gender discrimination and patriarchal mindset are important constituents and catalysts of the vulnerability of women and girl children. This manifests itself in several serious violations of women's rights such as high incidence of female foeticide and infanticide and the discrimination against women in healthcare, education and employment. Since these are vulnerability factors that trigger trafficking prevention strategies need to be oriented accordingly.
- Natural calamities and manmade disturbances do exacerbate the vulnerability situation. Therefore, relief and aftercare programmes need to have specific components focused on the rights of women and children.
- At the micro level the prevention of trafficking in the source areas requires a working partnership between the police and NGOs. Public awareness campaigns and

community participation are key to prevention programmes. Prevention is best achieved by community policing.

- Political will is an essential requirement to combat trafficking.
- Creating legal awareness is one of the most important functions of any social action programme because without legal awareness it is not possible to promote any real social activism. Legal awareness empowers people by making them aware of their rights, and can work towards strengthening them to develop zero tolerance towards abuse and exploitation.
- Immigration officials at the borders need to be sensitized so that they can network with the police as well as with NGOs working on preventing trafficking.
- Help lines and help booths are very important for providing timely help to any person in distress. The Ministry of Social Justice and Empowerment is considering collaboration between government agencies and NGOs for setting up help lines and help booths that can provide timely assistance to child victims. It will be appropriate if the Child help lines are set up all over India, NGOs working on child rights, missing person bureaus and police help lines are linked together as a formidable tool against trafficking.[19]

International Response

A growing number of governmental bodies and international organizations have adopted conventions and action plans to direct their responses to trafficking as it is a crime against humanity. It is known to be a global problem so an increase and improve international law enforcement cooperation is required in order to help combat this crime. Some of the international responses are as follows:

- The South Asian Association for Regional Cooperation (SAARC) Convention on trafficking of women and children 2002.
- 'The organization for security and cooperation in Europe

(OSCE), Action plan to combat trafficking in Human Beings 2003'.[20]
- 'The Convention on the Elimination of All Forms of Discrimination Against Women (CEDAW) 1979'.[21]
- 'The United Nations Protocol to Prevent, Suppress and Punish Trafficking in Persons, Especially Women and Children, Supplementing the United Nations Convention against Transnational Organized Crime 2000'.[22]
- 'The Council of Europe Convention on Action against Trafficking in Human Beings 2005'.[23]

Actions Undertaken by Government of India

The Government of India is currently considering amendments to its law on trafficking and prostitution. The Immoral Traffic (Prevention) Amendment (ITPA) Bill 2006 proposes significant changes in a number of areas including decriminalizing prostituted women and penalizing buyers of prostituted women. Groups including Apne Aap Women Worldwide, a survivor-led organization that began in 1998 as a community-based initiative of women in prostitution in the red light area of Mumbai, have been advocating for the proposed changes.[24] However, they face growing opposition to the provision that would penalize the buyers, which is set forth in Section 5C of the Bill. One of the arguments made in opposition to the Bill is the belief that regulation of prostitution—and hence its legalization—would guarantee the use of condoms to prevent the spread of HIV/AIDS, which is prevalent in the sex industry. While the use of condoms has a beneficial effect in halting the spread of sexually transmitted diseases and HIV/AIDS, the condom provision approach to prostitution fails to take into account that prostituted women.[25] Regulation of the sex industry has not shown any appreciable improvements in being able to negotiate use of condoms. In fact what happens in countries where prostitution has been legalized is that the illegal sex industry has blossomed in parallel and trafficking of women increases to meet the demand for prostitution.[26]

It would be more effective to address the HIV/AIDS crisis, as well as the life crises of girls and women by reducing rather than promoting the commercial sex industry, which plays a tremendous role in the spread of HIV/AIDS. Curbing the demand for prostituted women and holding commercial sex buyers accountable, as provided for in Section 5C of the ITPA Bill, is a critical step in this process. At the same time, there should be provision of sustainable programmes to provide prostituted women and girls with real alternatives to prostitution.[27] This is in line with Article 14 of India's Constitution, which guarantees equality before the law and equal protection of the law, as well as the provisions of the Convention for the Suppression of the Traffic in Persons and of the Exploitation of the Prostitution of Others (the 1949 Convention) to which India is a party. Under Article 16 of the 1949 Convention, state parties agree to "take or to encourage, through public and private educational, health, social, economical and other related services, measures for the prevention of prostitution and for the rehabilitation and social adjustment of the victims of prostitution."[28]

Government and NGO reports estimate that there are from hundreds of thousands to millions of women and girls prostituted in India, many of whom are victims of sex trafficking. The majority of women prostituted and trafficked within India are from "lower" (scheduled) castes and many are girls, some brought into the sex industry as young as 13 years old. The United Nations Committee on the Elimination of Racial Discrimination in March 2007 raised concerns with India about the sexual exploitation of *Dalit* ("lower" castes) and tribal women trafficked into prostitution. India's Parliamentary Standing Committee on Human Resource and Development when discussing the ITPA Bill 2006 in November 2006 itself drew attention to "the prevalence of caste and religion based prostitution", noting that "traffickers were clandestinely using this route to traffic the girls into prostitution." This exploitation of women and girls continues despite Article 15 of the Indian Constitution, which prohibits discrimination on grounds of religion, race, caste, sex or place of birth.[29]

Role of NGOs

NGOs provide a wide range of services and are highly active in advocating limiting trafficking and resolving some of the bottlenecks in the current programming. The NGOs tend to be specialized in addressing trafficking, their activities include awareness raising through mass information campaigns, rallies, street theatres, seminars, education, etc. Other programmes focus on rescue and repatriation of trafficked persons, followed by reintegration. The story of Anita, a young girl who grew up in Bihar, is important to mention here because through one of the supportive NGO only she was rescued and now she is doing well and her story of survival was so stirring that she even had the opportunity to meet the P.M.[30] At present NGOs function separately, there needs to be co-ordination among the NGOs within States, across States and across borders. The NGOs are playing an important role in the rescue, reintegration and rehabilitation of victims of trafficking. Women trafficking especially transborder trafficking into forced prostitution can be effectively addressed only if a proper institutionalized network is established by involving governmental agencies and NGOs.

Conclusion

As trafficking is known to be the most profit making business all over the world, every society large or small, rich or poor has lived with the problem and women of the society are paying the price of being an ignorant and selfish nature of male chauvinism. The Government never considered looking at women trafficking as a major problem area of the future, they always turn a soft blind eye towards trafficking which is one of the worst violations of human rights, and which certainly is not possible without their convenience, and the laws will always remain ineffective unless they are enforced properly by the government agencies. This gap in the information should be addressed along with studying the factors which changes accordingly with the change of time and which generally drive towards trafficking phenomenon.

REFERENCES

1. "Trafficking in women and children in India", study was conducted by the research team of the Institute of Social Sciences, Orient Longman Private Limited, 2005 (Chapter 1, p. 2).
2. *The World of Prostitutes,* Vol. 2, S.K. Ghosh, A.P.H. Publishing Corporation New Delhi, 1996 (Appendix 45, p. 1024).
3. *Asian Age,* 14th June, 1997, "40,000 Nepali girls sold as prostitutes in India".

4. *The Times of India*, 19th April, 2007 (New Delhi) "Passport fraud lands BJP, MP in police net".
5. Central Welfare Board, Meena Menon, *The Unknown Faces*.
6. Meena Menon, *The Unknown Faces*.
7. Robert I. Freidman, "India's Shame: Sexual Slavery and Political Corruption Are Leading to An AIDS Catastrophe," *The Nation*, 8 April 1996.
8. *Ibid*.
9. Radhika Coomaraswamy, UN Special Report on Violence against Women, Gustavo Capdevila, *IPS*, 2 April 1997.
10. *Trafficking in Women and Children: The Cases of Bangladesh*, pp. 18 and 19, UBINIG, 1995.
11. Robert I. Freidman, "India's Shame: Sexual Slavery and Political Corruption are Leading to an AIDS Catastrophe," *The Nation*, 8 April, 1996.
12. "*Devadasi* System Continues to Legitimise Prostitution: The *Devadasi* Tradition and Prostitution," *TOI*, 4 December, 1997.
13. Robert I. Freidman, "India's Shame: Sexual Slavery and Political Corruption are Leading to an AIDS Catastrophe," *The Nation*, 8 April, 1996.
14. Soma Wadhwa, "For sale childhood," *Outlook*, 1998.
15. *Ibid*.
16. *Ibid*.
17. Combating trafficking of women and children in South Asia—Regional synthesis paper for Bangladesh, India and Nepal. (April 2003). Book was prepared by staff and consultants of the Asian Development Bank.
18. thirdworldorphans.org/gpage31.html.
19. http://www.azadindia.org/social-issues/WomenTrafficking-in-India.html.
20. Decision No:557, July 2003, http://www.osce.org/press rel/2003/pdf documents07-3447_pcl.pdf.
21. http://www.un.org/womenwatch/daw/cedaw/text/econvention.htm.
22. www.ohchr.org/english/law/protocoltr_affic.htm.
23. http://www.coe.int/T/e/humanrights/trafficking/.
24. India: The Demand for Sex Trafficking: Holding Commercial sex Buyers Responsible http://saynotoviolence.org/join-say-no/india-demand-sex-trafficking-holding-commercial-sex-buyers-accountable.
25. *Ibid*.
26. *Ibid*.
27. *Ibid*.
28. *Ibid*.

29. *Ibid.*
30. David. C. Mulford (2006) 'Fighting Human Trafficking: India offers example of combating global evil', *The Times of India,* 6th June.

Index